P9-DUD-140

Scenario Planning

Managing for the Future

Gill Ringland

JOHN WILEY & SONS

Chichester • New York • Weinheim • Brisbane • Singapore • Toronto

Copyright © 1998 John Wiley & Sons Ltd,
Baffins Lane, Chichester,
West Sussex PO19 1UD, England

National   01243 779777
International (+44) 1243 779777
e-mail (for orders and customer service enquiries):
cs-books@wiley.co.uk
Visit our Home Page on http://www.wiley.co.uk
  or http://www.wiley.com

All Rights Reserved. No part of this publication may be reproduced, stored in a
retrieval system, or transmitted, in any form or by any means, electronic, mechanical,
photocopying, recording, scanning or otherwise, except under the terms of the
Copyright, Designs and Patents Act 1988 or under the terms of a licence issued by the
Copyright Licensing Agency, 90 Tottenham Court Road, London, UK W1P 9HE,
without the permission in writing of the publisher.

Other Wiley Editorial Offices

John Wiley & Sons, Inc., 605 Third Avenue,
New York, NY 10158-0012, USA

WILEY-VCH Verlagsgesellschaft mbH, Pappelallee 3,
D-69469 Weinheim, Germany

Jacaranda Wiley Ltd, 33 Park Road, Milton,
Queensland 4064, Australia

John Wiley & Sons (Asia) Pte Ltd, 2 Clementi Loop #02-01,
Jin Xing Distripark, Singapore 129809

John Wiley & Sons (Canada) Ltd, 22 Worcester Road,
Rexdale, Ontario M9W 1L1, Canada

Library of Congress Cataloging-in-Publication Data

Ringland, Gill
  Scenario planning : managing for the future / Gill Ringland.
        p.   cm.
  ISBN 0-471-97790-X
  1. Strategic planning.   2. Decision making.   3. Communication in management.
  4. Business planning.   I. Title.
  HD30.28.R56   1998
  658.4'012—dc21   97-31194
                                                CIP

British Library Cataloguing in Publication Data

A catalogue record for this book is available from the British Library

ISBN 0-471-97790-X

Typeset in 10/12pt Garamond from the author's disks by Rede Design
Printed and bound in Great Britain by Bookcraft (Bath) Ltd, Midsomer Norton, Somerset

Contents

Contents

Acknowledgements

This book has been fun to write, not least because of the people who have contributed to it.

Laura Mazur has worked with me throughout its gestation, from debriefing on the ICL experience, and working with The Conference Board Europe, through drafting the bulk of the book, to working with the providers of case studies, to proof reading and critiquing. In addition, she cheered me up when the shape of the subject matter seemed to move - and get bigger - every time we looked.

Gordon Ringland's ideas were instrumental in shaping chapter 1. He also bravely offered to read early drafts - and did so. This book in its final form owes much to his wide interests and cogent comments.

Steven Rosell's comments over the Internet helped to clarify and improve the structure of the book.

Bill Ralston has provided great help on the history and present status of scenario thinking in SRI.

A number of people provided case studies: Jan Agri, Stephen Black, Roger Camrass, Philip Hadfield, Sally Jones, Adrian Kamellard, Mark Loveless, John McIvor, Kathy Moyer, Nancy Murphy, John Ormerod, Chris Phoenix, Michael Rogers, Gerhard Schnabel: and members of The Conference Board Europe answered our questions on the use of scenarios.

The team who built the ICL scenarios - Paul Clayton, Jane Dowsett, Laurent Douillet, and Steve Parker, and Sue Schreiber who joined us to help in communicating the scenarios - have all been associated with follow-up projects and with various parts of the book.

Discussion with Oliver Sparrow helped shape and focus the ICL scenarios.

Many people in ICL have been associated with the work on scenarios, in particular Malcom Austin, David Berry, Mark Birchenhoff, Valerie Cliff, John Davison, George Hall, Nigel Hartnell, Matti Keiola, Bob Martin, Sue McLaren-Thomson, Dave McVitie, Linnda Neilson, Tony Oppenheim, Bill O'Riordan, Nigel Tout, Roy Towndrow and Peter Wharton: and Ian Neill contributed Chaper 3, on Strategic Planning in ICL.

A number of people have nobly read the draft and provided their comments: Napier Collyns, Tony Hodgson, Hannele Iso-Rautio, Rolf Jensen, Pam Hurley, Steve Rosell, Oliver Sparrow.

Andrew Insleay has liaised with the printers and chased down permissions, while Diane Taylor has provided calm and helpful steering from John Wiley.

My sincerest thank you to all of the above.

Gill Ringland
ICL
1 High Street
Putney
London SW15 1SW

Foreword

In the Post Second World War era the challenges facing decision makers in both the public and the private sectors mounted in complexity and uncertainty. Not surprisingly, throughout that period they have searched for better tools and methods for peering into the seemingly impenetrable fog of the future. Unlike the lords of an earlier era, the crystal ball and other methods of divination no longer gave them any hope.... For modern decision makers it was more scientific and rigorous approaches to looking ahead that drove their efforts.

The uncertainty of the modern era is the result of the complex interaction of forces of many kinds: technological, social, political, economic and environmental. It is the complexity and incommensurability of these forces that defeated most of these efforts. Substantial intelligence and human ingenuity were applied in building ever more elaborate mathematical forecasting equations, computer models, comprehensive surveys of experts (the Delphi method as it was known) or even just simply finding the "right" expert. That failure was measured less by the lack of accuracy about the future - indeed these methods often got the future "right" - than by the fact that they had little influence on decision making. This is the most appropriate measure of success. Were better decisions the result?

There was at the same time another stream of methodological development that was producing an evolving body of ideas, which has become known as scenario planning. Its roots lie with the US military and Herman Kahn and Pierre Wack, my predecessor as Head of Business Environment at Shell. As a result of the success of this approach its use has taken off dramatically in recent years. Several books, including Kees van der Heijden's "Scenarios, The Art of the Strategic Conversation" have also enabled a wider use of the scenario planning method.

Gill Ringland now adds a very useful and comprehensive guide to the method as it is being used in practice, the practitioners and their successes and failures. The book not only provides a guide to the practitioners but the several very widely different variations of the method. The book concludes with a number of very useful case studies including those of British Airways, United Distillers and even the UK Health Service.

The reader will find here not only the state of the art but the debate among the practitioners among the different techniques and their usefulness. It is not always flattering, including to me, but does provide a very useful contribution to pushing that debate forward leading towards real learning and a continuing improvement in our ability to penetrate the fog of uncertainty.

Peter Schwartz
President, Global Business Network.
July, 1997

Preface

ICL's motto is "Eyes on the Future, Feet on the Ground". By this we mean that we can see that there will be major changes over the next decades, as digital information starts to reshape society: but the new world will use many of the aptitudes and capabilities that have served us well over the last decades.

This book, on scenario planning, is consistent with this. It shares the experience we have had in finding ways of thinking about the future, because we believe that many people and organizations are looking for help - not in knowing the answers - but in planning within uncertainty.

We are also a company that is open and encourages debate: so we hope that the reader will find it useful in exploring the issues around strategic planning in general and scenarios in particular.

Keith Todd
Chief Executive, ICL.
August, 1997

PART I

Introduction

SUMMARY

This introduction answers four questions:
   How can this book help you?
   What is scenario planning?
   How is the book organized?
   Why did I write this book?

HOW CAN THIS BOOK HELP YOU?

You have opened this book because you have heard about scenario planning and want to know what it is and what it can do for you.

If I am a manager who is concerned to improve the chance of my business prospering in turbulent times, can scenario planning help?

Scenario planning helped Electrolux spot new consumer markets.

Scenario planning helped Pacific Gas and Electric prepare for the earthquake in California.

Scenario planning helped Shell anticipate the fall of Communism in Russia and its effect on natural gas prices.

Scenario planning helped Austrian insurance company Erste

Allgemeine Versicherung anticipate the fall of the Berlin Wall and enter new markets in Central Europe.

Scenario planning helped wiring and cable supplier KRONE develop 200 new product ideas.

The purpose of the book is to provide a straightforward account of scenario planning, accessible to people facing business decisions, as well as corporate planners and MBA students.

So it is intended to help:

- people who need to decide if, when and how to use scenarios. These could be line managers with a problem to solve, consultants or corporate planners.

- MBA and similar students, who want to understand what scenario planning is and how it is used.

- people in and around the Information Industry who might not normally buy business books but are fascinated by the changes they see in their industry and in the growth of the Information Society

WHAT IS SCENARIO PLANNING?

What is a scenario?

Think of a scenario as a fairy tale.

Michael Porter defined scenarios in 1985 (Porter, 1985) as:
"an internally consistent view of what the future might turn out to be - not a forecast, but one possible future outcome."

We have defined scenario planning as:
that part of strategic planning which relates to the tools and technologies for managing the uncertainties of the future.

CONTENTS OF THE BOOK

This book is divided into four parts. Part I is "the book". It is divided into a set of chapters intended to be read largely in sequence, or skipped for the expert on the topic covered.

In Part I, the first chapter is a guide to some of the developments of scenarios. It starts by showing how scenarios, like any model of the world, are used to explore reality, with the same problems and opportunities. The way that scenarios have been used is explored through several eras: scenarios in the 1960s were used to raise public debate about issues of the day, such as nuclear war; they were picked up by corporate planners in the 1970s after the oil price shock as a way of "avoiding surprises" but failed to live up to their promise so were used less in the 1980s, an era in which "planning has failed".

Chapter 1 also explains some of the vocabulary: trend and cross-impact, and intuitive logics.

Chapter 2 is about where scenario planning is now. This chapter looks at two aspects of "where are we now", viz. what is the current use of scenarios, and how is this likely to change? The published literature and our survey of The Conference Board Europe members suggest that organizations have mostly used scenario planning to help in anticipating specific threats, such as environmental pressures, political changes, or industry structure changes. In information industries, businesses have also used scenarios to think through strategic options in light of changes in technological capability or in the regulatory environment.

The second half of the chapter looks at other forces for change, and asks the question - are we in a period of change which will be as extensive as the oil price shock? The futurists talk about a paradigm shift. We look at some of the changes in the Information Industry, and ponder some of the societal paradigm changes anticipated in the Information Age.

Chapter 3 outlines strategic planning as performed in ICL to set a context for the discussion of scenario planning in ICL in Chapter 4. It explains that ICL is a company made up of (at the time of writing) nine businesses, with a small headquarters (HQ). It outlines the ICL Strategic Planning process, and the use of

Business Value. We also use profit tools like PIMS (Impact of Market Strategy) to benchmark businesses, and the Market Attractiveness/Capability (MA/C) matrix for portfolio analysis. Some examples are given of how these tools have been used to transform the business in conjunction with scenario thinking.

Chapter 4 compares two scenario building projects in ICL that we completed two years apart. In both cases the intention was to link to strategic planning at HQ. In both cases we found that building the scenarios was a fascinating and mind-stretching project. In both cases communicating the scenarios in a useful form was a significant challenge. The sections on Lessons Learned cover these points.

Chapter 5 discusses using the scenarios - the scenarios built as described in Chapter 4 - in strategic planning. The analysis by SRI International of the potential ways of linking scenarios to strategy is used to provide a framework for four applications. These are: applying the scenarios to Information Markets; a sensitivity analysis/risk assessment of an investment portfolio; linking scenarios to a PIMS and MA/C analysis; and using the scenarios to build a more robust strategy

Chapter 6 focuses on the use of a set of scenarios to create a framework for a shared vision of the future, to promote discussion and build consensus, outside a single business entity. Looking at the similarities between organizations who report success in using scenarios, and the way in which for instance the South African or Canadian governments have used scenarios to create coherence, suggests the importance of communication via storyline and image.

The scenarios produced by Chatham House Forum, the Economist Intelligence Unit, and Glen Peters' "Beyond the Next Wave" (Peters, 1996) explore dilemmas for governments and business as the world evolves.

This chapter provides an example of an event which used scenario thinking in a diverse group to drive out recommendations for actions, in a 24 hour timescale. This pattern has been successfully followed on a number of other occasions.

In Chapter 7 we discuss the learning aspects of some of the

scenario projects and case studies described in the book - these aspects have been emphasized by many of the respondents. The chapter also describes three examples of events, working with scenarios, to increase the capability of the individuals (rather than directly to link to policy or to business planning). These are a Global Business Network Workshop on Electronic Commerce, a Workshop on Marketing in 2005, and a Workshop on the Future of Manufacturing run by the University of Loughborough.

Chapter 8 summarizes the book and reaches a few personal conclusions.

Parts II, III and IV are independent sections intended as reference material.

Part II is a set of independent sections, collecting together examples of methods and examples. The sections describe approaches and methods, and give case studies, for organizations which provide help and/or methodology. The organizations/ methods covered are:
- *Battelle's BASICS*
- *Comprehensive Situation Mapping (CSM)*
- *Computer-Driven Simulations - e.g. STRAT*X*
- *The Copenhagen Institute for Future Studies*
- *The European Commission*
- *The French School*
- *The Futures Group*
- *Global Business Network*
- *NCRI*
- *SRI*

The purpose of these sections is to allow readers to expand their understanding of the terminology introduced in Chapter 1 through examples.

Part III is a set of independent sections which are examples of case studies. The purpose of these is to illustrate the range of approaches and working methods which have been used.
- *British Airways*
- *Cable & Wireless*

- *ECRC - European Centre for Research into Computing*
- *Electrolux*
- *UK's National Health Service*
- *KRONE*
- *Shell*
- *United Distillers*

Part IV is divided into sections which contain examples of scenarios - from ICL and elsewhere. The purpose of including these is to help the reader envisage the types of descriptions which have been produced, and understand what principles to build into scenario descriptions.

The scenarios are:
- *Scenarios Developed by ICL in 1993*
- *Scenarios Developed by ICL in 1995*
- *Scenarios for the Internet*
- *Scenarios for the future of the Telecoms Industry*
- *Shell Scenarios in 1996*
- *The Hemingford Scenarios*
- *GBN scenarios for organizations of the 21st century.*

WHY DID I WRITE THIS BOOK?

This book is the one that I would have liked to have had in 1993. That was when I took on the task of improving ICL's ability to predict the future - and create our future in the process.

Before that, my career had been concerned with software, with services, with running businesses. So I write as a general manager. I am not an expert in scenario planning. There are many experts in scenario planning who have been invaluable as I have learned. Many of these are mentioned in the text, others have helped with the text or given their experience in the form of case studies. This book is intended to pass on some of the lessons I, and others in ICL, have learned from them in the last four years.

Nor am I, I hope, unduly enthusiastic about the use of scenarios. I have found that using scenarios, in a number of environments, helps people to be more at ease with uncertainties and to feel more in control of their destiny. I have also found a number of environments in which scenario thinking has prompted new businesses, or confirmed other analyses. And in ICL we have used the technique to create images of the future as a precursor to recommendations and action planning.

The link to planning and action is important. Decisions have to be made and implemented. This is a book aimed at people who are faced with problems in the real world of today, by looking at how scenario planning may be able to help them find better solutions.

A final word to this Introduction: this book is very much designed to provide a way into scenario planning for a manager who has not come across the idea before in any detail. For the strategic context, or if this book whets your appetite, I would suggest the parallel book "Scenarios, The Art of Strategic Conversation" (van der Heijden, 1996).

CHAPTER ONE
Developments in Scenario Planning

SUMMARY
This chapter traces the history of scenario planning to illuminate the different approaches used today. Some descriptions of methodologies and examples are included in more detail in Part II.

MODELS OF THE WORLD

Models of the world are often used to anticipate "real life". For instance:

- wind tunnels are used to test car shapes for aerodynamic features - does the car become unstable at high speeds, does it have higher or lower drag factors than other shapes?

- fatigue tests for airframes. Either a life size airframe or a scaled down airframe is subjected to stresses and strains in a test rig, where early signs of cracks, fractures or breakages can hopefully be encountered before they are seen in the airframes flying passengers.

- the use of mathematical or computer models to schedule and allocate resources, within sets of constraints. Linear programming techniques are used to solve problems such as forest management, agricultural production, production planning in factories, and the selection of hospital menus.

It is clear from these examples that whether physical modelling is used or whether computer modelling is used, the predictions for real life are only as good as the ability of the model to contain enough of the rules and constraints of real life. So, for instance, a model based on fixed proportions of income being available for discretionary spend, as a way of calculating the market for luxury goods, would cease to be applicable if changes in lifestyle meant that increasing proportions were in fact being spent on food, due to changes in diet. (See for instance readings in Moore and Hodges, 1970.)

Two aspects of a successful model are suggested by these examples:

- the ability to anticipate real world behaviour - which may be unexpected - through exploring the constraints or changes in the external environment, or the relationships between forces.

- the creation of a mental model which allows the user to look for early confirming or disconfirming evidence.

In the case of the airframes, the model could suggest where on the frame, and when (how many flying hours) to look for signs of stress in the airframes which are used for flying passengers. In the case of the market for luxury goods, the model might cause the user to ask in which cultures might this diet change occur.

The question for us is how to get these aspects into strategic planning.

It is difficult. If we compare good strategic planners with the Israeli Intelligence Service, we can look at the example of what happened in the run up to the Yom Kippur War. This example of the difficulties in maintaining a view of alternate possible forms of threat, and hence the ability to react to signals, is given in "Military Misfortunes: The Anatomy of Failure in War" (Cohen and Gooch , 1990). It describes how the Israelis, in spite of a superb intelligence operation, were essentially taken by surprise by the Arab attack during the Yom Kippur War.

So, if we are aware that the future is uncertain, how should we deal with this uncertainty?

One approach could be said to have been taken by Clausewitz, who became interested in the effect of chance and uncertainty on war because the *"juggernaut of war, based on the strength of its entire people"* defined a new era. War had become one of the largest and most complex of endeavours, and in this context he dismisses the simplistic use of mathematical techniques, which he suggests illuminate tactics but not strategy. On the topic of how to act boldly despite the inherent uncertainties of war, he suggests *"an educated guess and then gamble that the guess was correct"*. (For a more detailed analysis, see Herbig's article in Handel's "Clausewitz and Modern Strategy", 1989.)

It could be said that scenario planning is a set of processes for improving the quality of the educated guesses and also for deciding what the implications are, and when to gamble.

In the next sections we trace the development of some of the methods which have been tried to improve the quality of these educated guesses.

THE SECOND WORLD WAR'S EFFECT ON PLANNING

The Second World War mobilized large numbers of academics into government, researchers to new areas, and provided the crucible for a number of breakthroughs. Examples which are widely discussed include atomic and nuclear energy, radar, and the computer. Less discussed is the change which the mobilization of energies made on the subsequent developments in the field of corporate planning.

MOBILIZATION OF ENERGIES IN WORLD WAR TWO

"World War Two had been an extraordinary catalyst for the study of complex systems. Just as the war had mingled social scientists in unprecedented numbers, it had also assembled physicists, mathematicians, logicians, and physiologists to work on problems beyond the range of any individual discipline. These were.... students of the nature of complex systems and developers of ways to manage them more effectively by translating them into mathematical models....

> *These operations researchers helped military leaders .... set up complex radar mechanisms, calculate how the fewest boats could patrol the largest stretch of water.... Then after the war they adopted similar game theory and decision analysis techniques to the business arena."* (From "The Age of the Heretics", by Art Kleiner, 1996).

After the war, the RAND Corporation was set up to research new forms of weapons technology. RAND's Hermann Kahn pioneered the technique of "future-now" thinking, aiming through the use of detailed analysis plus imagination to be able to produce a report as it might be written by people living in the future.

The description "scenario" was given to these stories by the writer Leo Rosten, who suggested the name based on Hollywood terminology. Though the terminology was obsolete he didn't think the more current term "screenplay" sounded dignified enough. Hermann Kahn adopted the term because he liked the emphasis it gave, not so much on forecasting, but on creating a story or myth.

When he founded the Hudson Institute in the mid-1960s, he specialized in stories about the future aimed at helping people break past their mental blocks and consider "unthinkable" futures. He was best known for his idea that the best way to prevent nuclear war was to think through in detail what would happen if the war did occur, and publicize the results.

Meanwhile, on the West Coast, Stanford University had set up it own think-tank in 1947, called Stanford Research Institute (SRI), to offer long-range planning for business incorporating operations research, economics and political strategy alongside hard science and military consulting.

The late 1960s saw a shift in the work done by organizations like SRI for a number of reasons, including a movement in military spending towards the Vietnam War, and increased interest in finding ways to look further into the future to help plan for changes in society, an interest underpinned by the upheavals resulting from the war.

Similarly, the Hudson Institute started to seek corporate sponsors, which exposed companies like Shell, Corning, IBM and

General Motors to this style of thinking. At this stage it was largely one man's imagination driving the thinking, as captured for instance in Kahn's "The Year 2000" (Kahn and Weiner, 1967). Ted Newland of Shell, which was one of the corporate sponsors, started to introduce thinking about the future into Shell.

Figure 1.1, based on a chart by Art Kleiner, shows some of the connections between the evolution of organizations involved in scenario planning during the early years.

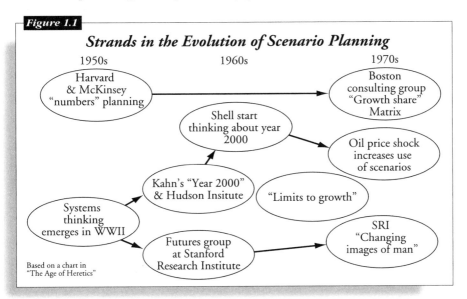

Figure 1.1

Strands in the Evolution of Scenario Planning

1950s   1960s   1970s

Harvard & McKinsey "numbers" planning

Boston consulting group "Growth share" Matrix

Shell start thinking about year 2000

Oil price shock increases use of scenarios

Kahn's "Year 2000" & Hudson Insitute

"Limits to growth"

Systems thinking emerges in WWII

SRI "Changing images of man"

Futures group at Stanford Research Institute

Based on a chart in "The Age of Heretics"

SCENARIOS IN THE 1960S: PUBLIC DEBATE

In the 1960s, the world was fascinated by the apparent triumphs of science. So, for instance, twenty-seven top TRW scientists in 1966 were asked the question: *"What will the world want and need in the next twenty years?"* Schnaars (Schnaars, 1989) reports on the wide publicity and discussion arising from these predictions of undersea motels, factories and recreation centres powered by nuclear power, commercial passenger rockets to the moon by 1980, that by 1977 low-cost 3D colour TV would reduce business travel, and that by 1973 there would be large-scale educational teaching machine systems.

Of the 335 predictions released, nearly every prediction was wrong. The scientists ignored the economic aspects of markets: their mental model included state-driven mega-projects, which by the late 1960s had started to decline, after the moon-shot had succeeded

In early 1968 the SRI "futures group" began to use a variety of methods, from straight-line numeric forecasts to literature searches on utopias and dystopias from science fiction to create plausible scenarios for the US to the year 2000. The customer was the Office of Education, who wanted to envisage what sort of society it was educating children for, to see if the system should change.

They pored through forecasts, coded trends into punched cards, and fed them into a mainframe to examine a range of alternative futures. The result is illustrated in Figure 1.2.

Figure 1.2

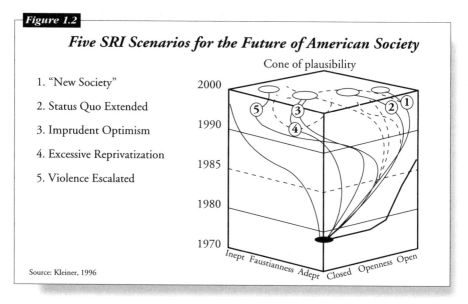

Five SRI Scenarios for the Future of American Society

1. "New Society"
2. Status Quo Extended
3. Imprudent Optimism
4. Excessive Reprivatization
5. Violence Escalated

Source: Kleiner, 1996

The scenarios were based round two questions:

- would society be good at controlling its destiny? or not?

- would society be flexible, open and tolerant or would it be authoritarian, violent and efficient?

The alternates posed by the group do not necessarily correlate with the assumptions we might make today - considering the number of regimes which are violent and authoritarian but notoriously not efficient. However, by considering different combinations of these factors, they created five scenarios, i.e. all the four combinations of the possible answers to the questions, plus the "official future".

The official future - Status Quo Extended - was that the problems of population growth, dissent, ecological destruction, would "take care of themselves". The other scenarios were "Imprudent Optimism" where bureaucracy and a raging recession met head on; "Violence Escalated", with terrorism increasing and schools taken over by street gangs; and "New Society" scenario, in which openness was combined with adeptness to create effectiveness, and which attracted wide attention. It was tied to a US in which consumerism was no longer king, and in which government adopted an ecological ethic.

The SRI researchers believed that the "New Society" provided a more desirable future than any of the other scenarios, but that it realistically could not happen under the existing government and corporate structures. It was inconsistent with the values of the industrial society.

The message reached the sponsors, the US Office of Education, at a time when Richard Nixon's election as President represented the entrenchment of a set of values which made the offered scenario "impossible" - a good example of scenarios needing to echo to their intended audience in order to have an effect.

The work did lead, later, to a major research programme, VALS (Values and Lifestyles), on the American consumer. This described consumers as one of nine categories, and is used extensively as a system for predicting consumer behaviour.

SRI also did subsequent work for the Environmental Protection Agency (EPA). Early members of the group were Willis Harmon, Peter Schwartz, Thomas Mandel, Thomas Thomasen and Richard Carlson. The assignment created 10 to 12 scenarios of the future. Each one was built around a central concept or theme, arrived at by brainstorming. In the early years of scenario development, the process was much more free form and a lot of original thinking occurred, while the connection to decision making was loose. (See the morphological approach in the Box on scenario approaches, p.21.)

Meanwhile Professor Jay Forrester of the Massachusetts Institute of Technology had used the concepts he had developed to describe supply chains and demand (see his "Industrial Dynamics", 1961) to look at the interconnection of population, and supply and demand on the world. The famous Club of Rome model was developed in 1970 using the same feedback loop concepts.

It tracked five key variables - population, food production, industrial production, pollution, and natural resources. However, all the worlds which were simulated with the model seemed to suffer in that growth got out of control. An analysis of the results was published in "Limits to Growth" by Donella (Dana) Meadows, (republished as Meadows et al, 1992). The argument over growth and the use of resources was loud and energetic and continues today. The originators of the work were clear in their aims (which were not always understood by others): they were not predicting the future, they were developing a model which would help people to understand aspects of the nature of growth and help to open up the public debate.

CORPORATE PLANNING AND SCENARIOS: THE EFFECT OF THE OIL SHOCK

Meanwhile, in large corporations, computers were the province of central staffs. They ran the accounting systems and were beginning to be used for planning. The role model in planning during the 1970s was the US corporation, General Electric (GE). As Wilson says (Wilson, 1990), *"In the heyday of strategic planning - from the early 1970s to about 1978 - GE led the way."*

This approach was based on top-down planning by a corporate staff, computer models, forms, charts and graphs, and used technologies like the Boston Consulting Group's growth share matrix to determine investment in businesses within the corporation (see Box, below).

THE BOSTON CONSULTING GROUP (BCG) "GROWTH SHARE MATRIX"

Work at Union Carbide led to a framework for thinking about the relative strengths of the divisions of a company or companies in a conglomerate - the "Growth Share Matrix" (Figure 1.3). This became the most used tool of strategic analysis in the 1970s: it gave a framework for deciding on selecting the parts of the company to invest in.

As Art Kleiner says, *"To use the matrix, you thought of your business as a portfolio of separate product lines. Every one of them fit into one of these compartments. Its placement depended on how much the market was growing .... and on the amount of market share.... Ultimately every product line had one of two destinies, symbolised in the bottom two quadrants.... So the job of a manager was controlled ruthlessness.... The growth/share matrix bequeathed an era of highly intense competitiveness."*

Figure 1.3

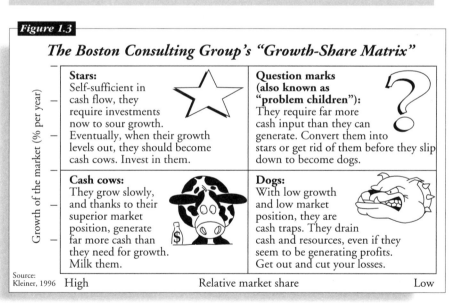

The Boston Consulting Group's "Growth-Share Matrix"

Stars:
Self-sufficient in cash flow, they require investments now to sour growth. Eventually, when their growth levels out, they should become cash cows. Invest in them.

Question marks (also known as "problem children"):
They require far more cash input than they can generate. Convert them into stars or get rid of them before they slip down to become dogs.

Cash cows:
They grow slowly, and thanks to their superior market position, generate far more cash than they need for growth. Milk them.

Dogs:
With low growth and low market position, they are cash traps. They drain cash and resources, even if they seem to be generating profits. Get out and cut your losses.

Growth of the market (% per year)

Relative market share: High — Low

Source: Kleiner, 1996

GE used scenarios as part of their planning process, to think about the environmental factors affecting their businesses. The method involved using Delphi panels to establish and verify critical variables and indicators, while both trend-impact analysis and cross-impact analysis would then help to assess the implications of the interactions among critical variables and indicators. GE pioneered an approach whereby the cross-impact effects among likely developments are dealt with qualitatively, with plus or minus signs, which would then lead to the development of probable scenarios for the environment. Figure 1.4 (Georgantzas and Acar, 1995) outlines this procedure.

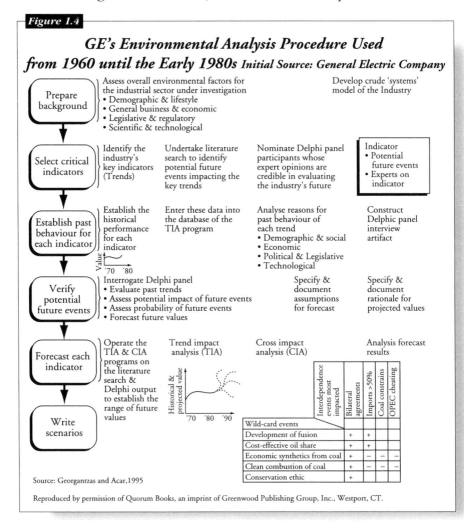

Figure 1.4

GE's Environmental Analysis Procedure Used from 1960 until the Early 1980s Initial Source: General Electric Company

Source: Georgantzas and Acar, 1995

Reproduced by permission of Quorum Books, an imprint of Greenwood Publishing Group, Inc., Westport, CT.

DELPHI

The Delphi technique, named after the ancient Greek oracle, was developed by the RAND Corporation in the 1950s as a method for gathering information about the future. It was based on asking experts in their various fields to estimate individually the probability that certain events will occur in the future. The goal is to get them to converge on future views by comparing their answers with those of the other experts.

Delphi became part of formal planning techniques in the 1970s through the work of Olaf Helmer and Norman Dalkey at RAND (see Amara & Lipinksi, 1983).

Shell (the Royal Dutch/Shell Group) had a basic planning system which was very similar to GE's. As Pierre Wack, the *"undisputed intellectual leader in the area of scenario-based strategic thinking"* in Kees van der Heijden's words, pointed out in his classic articles for the Harvard Business Review (Wack, 1985), for ten years after the Second World War, planning at Shell was very physically-oriented, with the main challenge being to co-ordinate business activities and plan the schedules for setting up new facilities. Numbers began to play a greater role from 1955 to 1965, as planning became more financially-oriented, with research and evaluation done on the economics and the perspective rate of return of projects. By 1965 a new technique called Unified Planning Machinery (UPM) was developed so that Shell could plan for the whole chain of activity, from the oil in the ground through to its sale at petrol stations. The first year was in detail, with the others more broadly-based.

However, Wack pointed out in 1967 that, because of the time scale on which oil companies worked, even six years was too short a time for planning. So a study was set up to look at Shell's position to the year 2000. This showed that the predictable, surprise-free environment would not continue, and that a shift in power from the oil companies to the oil producers in the Middle East for a variety of reasons could create major increases in the oil price. Following on from this, an exercise was carried out from 1969 to 1970 called Horizon Year Planning, in which a dozen of the largest Shell companies around the world, as well as executives in areas such as marketing and production were asked to look forward to 1985.

STEPS IN THE PLANNING APPROACH IN SHELL 1945-1980

1945-55:   Mainly physical planning
1955-65:   Project planning and selectivity
1965-72:   Unified Planning Machinery
1967:   Year-2000 study initiated
1969-70:   Horizon Year planning exercise
1971:   Experimental use of scenarios in central offices, London
1972-73:   Introduction of scenario planning
1975:   Introduction of medium-term cyclical scenarios
1976-77:   Deepening "societal analysis" in planning
1978-79:   Deepening geopolitical and political risk analysis
1979-80:   A fresh look at the very long-term and development of planning capabilities inside the group.

The oil price had been based on seemingly predictable factors of demand and supply since the Second World War. Both were assumed to be predetermined. As Ted Newland said: *"Having developed this scenario, the problem was how to get into Shell's corporate culture the idea that it had a blind side. I still did not have a track record which would let us challenge or confront that culture directly. So we produced a set of absolutely impersonal, mechanical scenarios about the future of oil prices. One of them was the general perception of the corporation, that prices would remain as they were. And one expressed the idea - our feeling, but not presented as such - that oil prices would rise. Even this dispassionate presentation of the idea had a traumatic effect."*

Scenarios after the oil shock

Once the Yom Kippur war broke out in the Middle East, the oil embargo by the producing countries did indeed lead to a sharp increase in the oil price with the inevitable depressing results on the world economy, changes in supply lines, and changes in behaviour and attitudes.

Shell's ability to act quickly has been credited with moving the company into the lead in the oil industry (van der Heijden, 1996).

The effect of this on corporate planning, based on sets of key numbers which had described the business over the past few years, was to look for ways of including the effects of uncertainty.

By the late 1970s scenario planning was adopted by a significant fraction of the Fortune 1000 companies, based on a variety of techniques. Many of these used mutiple scenarios. Roughly three-quarters of the firms had adopted the approach after the oil embargo provided such a deep shock to previously-stable views of the future (Dyson, 1990).

A COMPARISON OF SCENARIO APPROACHES

An extract from Chapter 10, "Futures Scenarios and Their Uses in Corporate Strategy", by Thomas F Mandel, in "The Strategic Management Handbook" (Albert, 1983)

1. *Experts' Scenarios*

    Some companies prefer to externalize their scenario process by asking outside consultants to provide structured information about the future macro-environment. In effect, this means inviting a number of people with their own perceptual maps of the future to provide input into the strategic decision. This sometimes proves awkward to manage, but of course depends on the skills of both the internal scenario staff and the capabilities and views of the outside experts. The key point to remember is that scenarios of this sort implicitly reflect scenario logics deemed likely and plausible by outsiders. Making sure these logics are made explicit will make the resulting scenarios more useful.

2. *Morphological Approaches*

    Some strategic decision makers prefer a larger number of different scenarios to review before making their decision. One process for creating such scenarios is to identify different plausible future "states" for the key driving forces. For example, if the underlying societal forces shaping the macro-environment for strategic issues include the economy, the natural resources base, values and lifestyles, and the effectiveness of the national government, scenario analysts will look at different possible conditions for each of these forces.

Economic growth might be high (E1), moderate (E2), or low to negligible (E3). Critical natural resources might be seen as available and inexpensive (R1), available but expensive (R2) or of restricted availability and expensive (R3). Lifestyles might be traditional (L1), oriented toward survival needs (L2) or changing toward simpler, less consumptive attitudes (L3). And the future effectiveness of the government might be viewed as highly effective (G1), muddling through (G2) or generally ineffective (G3). The scenario analysts then array the different combinations of each of these factors together for future points in time, creating a tree of scenarios that grows outward into more and more branches. Branches that have internal inconsistencies - for example, unavailable and expensive natural resources and high economic growth - are removed. Other scenarios that lead to similar results and implications can also be deleted.

The remainder of the process proceeds as above - fleshing out the scenarios and analysing them for implications. Experience using such an approach is that it tends to consume too many resources and to result in too many scenarios. It does not seem to provide any greater insight than fewer scenarios couched in carefully constructed logics, but it does describe many more specific alternatives.

3. Cross-Impact Approaches
Cross-impact analysis involves identifying a large number of potential events and conditions that appear to influence not only the outcome of the decision but each other as well. These events, trends and conditions typically have probabilities assigned to them, and a computer is used to sort through

different combinations of probabilities and cross-impacts. The advantage of such an approach is that it allows scenario analysts to work through a large number of variables and scenarios, and to be explicit about the interrelationships of particular events and conditions. The logics of scenarios arrived at in such a matter is built into the structure of the cross-impact model and the judgement of the experts who put in data and interpret results.

THE 1980s: "PLANNING HAS FAILED"

However, during the 1980s, the use of scenarios decreased from the peak of interest in the 1970s. The threat of the oil price shock had decreased, corporate staffs were reduced in the recessions of the early 1980s, and perhaps also an over-simplistic use of the technique, with a confusion between forecasts and scenarios, gave scenario planning a bad name.

Ian Wilson in "The State of Strategic Planning: What went wrong? What goes right?" (Wilson, 1990) suggests that the disillusionment was with strategic planning rather than scenarios in particular, that the "failed promise" of massive corporate planning systems in predicting, for instance, the recessions of the early 1980s, led to their being disbanded. He points out that restructuring in a range of industries had by the mid 1980s prompted an interest in strategic thinking, perhaps as an antidote to the routinized planning approach.

Art Kleiner (Kleiner, 1996) suggests that the large losses of corporate bell-wethers - which he ascribes to use of formulae like the BCG matrix - had a dramatic effect. *"The stage was now set for the great managerial event of the late 1970s and early 1980s: the realization by mainstream managers that they did not have the answers. In 1978, Chrysler lost $205 million. General Electric, Kodak, Xerox, General Foods, all saw their market share drop precipitously - if not to Japanese competition, then to smaller firms in the West."*

In this environment, the approach to planning needed to change.

For instance, Michael Porter in his "Competitive Advantage"

went back to basics and proposed that companies consider the forces on their markets as a backdrop to planning. He considered scenarios to be important tools for understanding and so getting ahead of trends, and recommends the building of alternate scenarios as a form of sensitivity analysis. As mentioned in the Introduction, he defined scenarios in 1985 as *"an internally consistent view of what the future might turn out to be - not a forecast, but one possible future outcome."*

This was the environment in which a number of consulting organizations were developing their scenario planning methodologies. For example, Huss & Honton identified three categories in use by 1987:

1. Intuitive Logics, first described by Pierre Wack in (Harvard Business Review) 1985 and used by SRI International and Shell.

2. Trend-impact analysis, used by the Futures Group.

3. Cross-impact analysis, used by Battelle with BASICS (Battelle Scenario Inputs to Corporate Strategies).

The examples in Part II cover these methodologies.

Intuitive logics is the basis of the approach taken by SRI and by the Global Business Network, which under Peter Schwartz has built on both SRI and Shell experience.

Trend Impact analysis is the basis of the example from the Futures Group on the future of the US defence industry.

Cross-impact analysis is the basis of the examples from Batelle (the development of Europe), of the CSM (Comprehensive Situation Mapping) method applied to understanding the contributing factors to a bank profitability; and the work by Michel Godet on the steel industry futures.

During the 1980s, Shell maintained its reputation for using scenario thinking as part of its planning system and two examples of successful anticipation are cited:

- Oil would become a commodity with prices set by the market, not by either the companies or producers. Prices would thus behave like those of commodities like nickel, copper and wheat. Once oil began indeed to act like other commodities, Shell had designed an oil trading system so was once again in pole position compared to its rivals.

- Oil and gas prices could drop. With oil, OPEC's unified facade could crumble, worsened by a slowing demand for oil because of better energy conservation and efficiency. Even more strikingly, the continuation of the Soviet system was not assured, which could have implications for the natural gas market. Shell avoided investing in new oil fields or following the acquisition trail being trodden by its major competitors, who were engaged in an acquisition spree, buying other oil companies at premium prices. Once the dust had settled following the price drop, Shell was able to pick up additional assets at bargain prices.

As Peter Schwartz relates (Schwartz, 1991), *"In 1983, we presented the Royal Dutch/Shell managing directors with two scenarios; one called Incrementalism, and the other called the Greening of Russia. By that time, we knew enough about the Soviet Government to say that if a virtually unknown man named Gorbachev came to power, you'd see massive economic and political restructuring; an opening to the West; arms control; declining tensions in the West; and major shifts in international relationships. It was not that Gorbachev, as an individual, would cause the changes. Rather, his arrival in power would be a symptom of the same underlying causes."*

The Shell planners in the late 1980s began to look for ways to integrate scenario planning more closely into the annual cycle of strategic and business planning within the Group Planning System and also to make it more meaningful to line managers (Schoemaker and van der Heijden, 1992). The system they designed has been refined over the years and was used until recently. It is described in Part III.

THE 1990s: STRATEGY IS CENTRAL

The recent resurgence of interest in scenario planning is part of a new emphasis on sources of value and growth in corporations, after the down sizing and retrenchment of the 1980s.

So, far instance, in "Competing for the Future" (Pralahad and Hamel, 1994), the emphasis is on the strategic context for the corporation.

"Business Week" led with articles on strategy in the September 2, 1996 issue.

The differences between the "new" strategic planning and that in the 1980s has been discussed by Taylor - see chapter 3.

In the next chapter, the current state of scenario planning will show a range of uses and applications beyond the scenario planning equivalent of "massive corporate planning systems".

CONCLUSIONS

This chapter has traced the way that scenario planning has developed since the Second World War. This has set a context for definitions:

- High forecast/low forecast planning, where a plan is reworked with some major driving factors - e.g. market growth, or growth of market share - set to higher than or lower than forecast values. This is a useful and prudent part of strategic planning but is no longer normally thought of as scenario planning.

- Trend-impact analysis, which is concerned with the effects of trends, for instance in markets or populations, over a time period. The work done to isolate the important trends may well be similar to that used in what is more generally called scenario planning, but the basic assumption within scenario planning is that we are looking for the unexpected, i.e. what could upset the trends.

- Cross-impact analysis, which is a technology for analysis of complex systems. It concentrates on the ways in which forces on an organization, external or internal, may interact to produce effects bigger than the sum of the parts, or to magnify the effect of one force because of feedback loops. It has been used successfully where the dominant forces can be identified, and the modelling mechanism can be used to increase management's understanding of the relative importance of various factors.

- What is called the "Pierre Wack" Intuitive Logics school, as practised by SRI and Shell. We will see in the next chapter that most of those organizations surveyed were loosely using this approach. The essence of this is to find ways of changing mindsets so that managers can anticipate futures and prepare for them. The emphasis is on creating a coherent and credible set of stories of the future as a "wind tunnel" for testing business plans or projects, prompting public debate or increasing coherence.

In the next chapter we review the current uses of scenario planning and look for areas where their use may grow in the future.

CHAPTER TWO
Where Are We Now?

SUMMARY

This chapter looks at two aspects of "where are we now?", viz. what is the current use of scenarios, and how is this likely to change? The evidence is that organizations have mostly used scenario planning to help in anticipating specific threats, for instance, from environmental pressures, political changes, or industry structure changes.

The second half of the chapter looks at forces on the world today, and asks the question: are we in a period of change which will be as extensive as the oil price shock? The futurists talk about a paradigm shift. We look at some of the changes in the Information Industry, and ponder some of the societal paradigm changes anticipated in the Information Age.

WHAT THE CASE STUDIES TELL US ABOUT THE USE OF SCENARIO PLANNING

The sources of these case studies are:

- published papers, books, and conference proceedings

- personal contacts with experts through GBN, The Conference Board Europe, and conferences.

The examples in Part II and the case studies summarized below and described in detail in Part III relate to industrial companies or projects. Below is a description intended to bring out the broad themes of the applications.

Use in the Information Industry

The wrenching changes in the Information Industry have led many organization to seek to find patterns or strategies through scenarios.

3M Telecommunications Systems Division has used scenarios, linked to payoff and risk assessment, to implement new strategies following deregulation. International telecommunications group Cable & Wireless creates scenarios at business unit, not group level. The emphasis is on creating scenarios that can form the basis for key strategic and tactical decisions. Scenarios for the telecoms industry are used to explore the inter-relationships between regulatory factors and technical capability, as part of an SRI project (see "Scenarios for Telecoms" in Part IV).

A US-based scenario planning expert and consultant, Doug Randall, has developed four different scenarios for the Internet in order to stimulate business people's thoughts about it and to facilitate strategy building. Computer company Digital Equipment Corporation has developed scenarios for provoking and testing strategic thinking in the face of enormous industrial change. KRONE used scenarios to stimulate new product ideas.

Industry restructuring

Scenario planning is a regularly-used business tool at US-based clothing specialist Levi-Strauss as a way of considering options for decision-making. Issues examined could range from the extreme example of what would happen if cotton no longer existed, to the impact of the deregulation of the cotton industry in the US. In the health sector, several hospital systems in the US have used scenarios to improve the ability of the management team to share a flexible and coherent vision. The UK's National Health Service (NHS) has carried out a scenario exercise - the Hemingford scenarios - to help plan for change in the NHS and as an aid to strategic thinking and learning. In France, scenarios have been used to help plan the way forward for the steel industry. A Finnish forestry company uses scenarios to think about changes in the uses for paper. The use of scenarios to assist strategic planning in the advertising industry has been described in Schoemaker, 1992.

Political and economic changes

In other industries, insurance company Erste Allgemeine Versicherung anticipated the fall of the Berlin Wall and made plans to expand in Central Europe. United Distillers (now United Distillers and Vintners) has carried out a number of scenario development exercises to assess the future of markets such as India, South Africa and Turkey. And in the early 1990s a group of academics, politicians, administrators, trade unionists and business people met to try and create possible scenarios - the Mont Fleur scenarios - for South Africa's future, using as a point of departure the negotiating process then in place between the different political groups. The Copenhagen Institute for Future Studies has carried out a number of exercises examining the future of society, including scenarios for the post-industrial city 2010. In Canada, scenarios have been used in a project involving private sector organizations and government to create a shared view of *"how to organize ourselves and govern ourselves in a world of rapid change and increasing interconnection"*.

Environmental pressures

At consumer products company, Electrolux Group, scenarios for Europe in relation to global warming, use of toxins, and re-use and reprocessing led to a major strategic change in the commercial cleaning business. Triggered by the re-use scenario, the cleaning business became more service-oriented. It became more aware that there was value in its products even beyond the economic use for customers. As a supplier, the business could re-use materials or parts of the product and so sell the customer a service of continuous availability and not a product with a finite lifespan.

At Pacific Gas and Electricity, scenarios dispelled assumptions about the "Official Future" and caused a strategy of working to reduce energy consumption.

BUILDING SCENARIOS AT AUSTRADE

Scenario planning with a small team

The Australian Trade Commission (Austrade) helps Australian businesses to take advantage of export opportunities, as well as assisting with foreign investment into Australia and export-related investment into other countries. Executives tasked with providing strategic advice to the organization were faced with a dearth of information and insights on the future of international trade from the practical perspective required, and chose scenario planning as their methodology for addressing this gap.

Two executives worked on the project on a part-time basis over eighteen months. The executives drew on Austrade's own international network and external consultants to identify and interview a rich selection of experts. The approach taken was to familiarize the two executives with the methodology. The methodology was simplified down to identifying key trends and major uncertainties, then developing scenarios (story line and broad implications). These elements were summarized in electronic presentation format after a series of interviews and round-tables. Presentations were then given to selected internal and external audiences, with modifications made as new issues were raised, and relevant facts uncovered.

Experience to date is that presenting the ideas at a more advanced stage has enabled greater acceptance of the work, rather than rejection due to lack of "ownership". Less time is spent on explaining the methodology, and more on working through the implications of the scenarios. Care has been taken to ensure that new ideas can continually be incorporated.

The work has universally been well received and there is strong demand from staff and externally for presentations. In summary, much has been achieved using scenario planning without large outlays of executive time, staff time or money.

The Shell effect

Shell continues to use scenario planning as an integral tool in the strategy process, and to provide a stream of people who initiate work in other organizations. For instance, British Airways has used the Shell approach to scenario planning to help create a process for developing and testing strategies in the light of future uncertainties. See the case study in Part III for a detailed account.

Chatham House Forum is an initiative of the Royal Institute of International Affairs which has been analysing the main forces of change in society, based on the premise that the next decade will challenge many of the fundamental precepts underlying commerce, government and society, and that these challenges have to be explored and assessed. The driving force behind the Forum is Oliver Sparrow, a Shell alumnus.

A construction company uses the technique for "back of the envelope" examinations of business propositions, and as part of its project portfolio management, influenced by a course at a business school to which Shell staff contributed.

DELPHI FOR FORECASTING

The Delphi method, used to achieve a consensus view among experts, is widely used in connection with technology futures. This is successful because experts have a forward view of technology in the lab, and limitations of current technology, which allows envisaging several years ahead for rollout in product.

In Figure 2.1, technology forecasting is at the "certain" end of the spectrum, and scenarios at the "uncertain" end.

Recent examples of the use of Delphi include the UK's Technology Foresight Programme (DTI, 1996 and Georghiou, 1996), the Technology Forecast carried out in Japan for the period 1990 to 2020 (Japanese National Institute for Science and Technology Policy, 1995), and a forecasting exercise by BP to underpin their research programme (Barker and Smith, 1995).

The "Shaping Actors - Shaping Factors" method in use at the European Commission is a modified form of Delphi (see Part II), and is being applied to a range of economic studies.

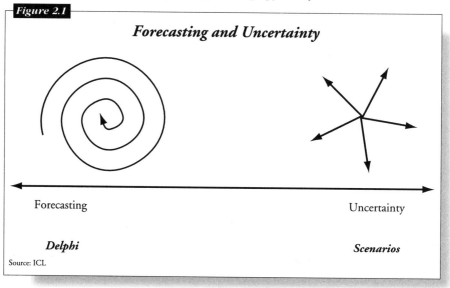

Figure 2.1

Forecasting and Uncertainty

Forecasting   Uncertainty

Delphi   *Scenarios*

Source: ICL

A SURVEY OF CONFERENCE BOARD MEMBERS

The Conference Board Europe is part of The Conference Board, the global business membership and research organization. In 1996 it set up the Futures Council, whose mission is to focus on the long-range issues that will significantly affect the competitive environment in which organizations will operate. The Council was launched with the co-operation of the Copenhagen Institute for Future Studies.

As part of the research for this book, The Conference Board Europe sent out questionnaires about scenario planning to members. It asked companies if they were using scenarios, and if so, why. Replies were received from companies across Europe and across a wide range of industry sectors.

As might be expected, most of the 20 who replied had used scenarios. But for a few organizations, scenario planning "failed". This was mostly because the scenarios themselves had not been integrated into the company's concerns, or the process had not been tied into the company processes.

Across all the respondents, the length of time spent developing scenarios was always within a single year and mostly less than six months. When asked how they developed the scenarios, no replies mentioned a computer model, although all discussed collecting and collating information, consultation and workshops within the organization, and the use of a process. This relates to an important question: how to steer the process if it is not in regular use? Should consultants be used? If so, how to get the feedback into the organization? Most organizations used a mixture of in-house staff and either consultants or academics.

The scenarios had mostly been intended to help with investment management. But only a quarter cited this, after the work, as the main benefit. Other changes cited were in awareness or culture change, e.g. towards new strategies based on environmental trends (as for Electrolux), new political agendas (see Box, Case Study of Erste Allgemeine Versicherung), or creating a new international outlook or framework.

An interesting point made by several respondents was that extensive analysis was not necessarily a prerequisite for the scenarios: it depends what question the organization is trying to answer.

CASE STUDY: ERSTE ALLGEMEINE VERSICHERUNG

Based on an interview by Jane Dowsett with Gerhard Schnabel of Erste Allgemeine Versicherung.

Erste Allgemeine Versicherung first used scenarios in 1988. Scenario planning was introduced on the advice of a consultant who was assisting with corporate planning and recommended the use of scenario planning. There was no sophisticated method. The consultant recommended a simple approach, which was a series of workshops used to stimulate ideas.

Originally there were between 5 and 10 people involved at senior management level, this expanded to around 30 people who were involved in three workshops. It took between 3 and 5 days to develop the scenarios themselves.

The main areas considered were politics, economics, insurance industry structure and changes, technology and demographics.

The objective was to look at the business environment and how other companies might develop.

As a result of the scenario process, the company anticipated the fall of the Berlin Wall and the opening up of Eastern Europe before it happened. This was identified as part of one of the scenarios in 1988. This enabled the company to be ready to move into Eastern Europe and therefore be one of the first companies to set up in Hungary. Companies were also founded in the Czech Republic, Slovakia and Slovenia.

The scenario process allowed management to consider a wider range of external information and the impact on strategy. The scenario planning process is continual with the scenarios revisited every 2-3 years.

The scenario process does not influence the daily running of the business. There is still an issue about how to link the scenarios into business strategy

The company felt that scenario planning had a positive impact on their strategic planning but that they were not using scenarios in the true sense of the word. Although the work groups developed 2 to 3 scenarios, the implications on strategy were only considered for one of the scenarios.

Scenario planning has been used for several years. There is a feeling that there could be in the future a more rigorous approach, and more time could be spent looking at economic data and trends.

THE CASE STUDIES

In Part III, we include eight case studies. They have been chosen to illustrate a range of organizations who have used scenarios, and how they have used them.

British Airways built scenarios to help highlight a number of issues within the company, to provide a forum in which the various divisions which needed to be aligned could discuss the market changes. The case study (Moyer, 1996) is a very detailed account of how British Airways developed and used the scenario building and scenario exploitation staff of the project.

Cable & Wireless wanted to find a way of transferring thinking about the market effects of new technologies - like the Internet - between business units in its federal structure. This was done through a series of workshops with each of the businesses, based round a sequence of:

- brainstorm, maybe build a tentative set of scenarios: follow up with market, technical, competitor research by staffs;

- build scenarios, validate with more research, maybe another workshop;

- decisions and action planning.

Cable & Wireless found that for a federal structure this was the only way to work.

The European Centre for Research into Computing (ECRC) used Godet's tool sets and advice to build scenarios for the future of the IT industry in Europe, in order to focus their research programme. One of the scenarios they developed does describe ICL's chosen route: however, the ECRC itself is now an Internet provider, which the team certainly did not foresee.

A scenario thinking project at Electrolux Group developed three scenarios for Europe in relation to global warming, use of toxins, and re-use and reprocessing.

There were several impacts. One was a major strategic change in the commercial cleaning business. Triggered by the re-use scenario, the division became more service oriented. Electrolux became more aware that there was value in its products even beyond the economic use for the customers. As a supplier, the materials or parts of the product could be re-used. The idea was then to sell the customer a service and not a product.

At Electrolux the scenario process is ongoing, but less effort is now put into data collection and more effort is put into rolling the scenarios out to the businesses. The objective is to pass it on to all the product lines. Currently around 25% of product lines have used the techniques.

The Hemingford scenarios built by the UK's National Health Service in 1994 describe four possible futures for health care.

They are being used to help this large multi-faceted (£35 billion) organization, think strategically - about the nature of the organization, relationships between the parts and their customers, and the way forward.

The scenarios themselves are included in Part IV.

KRONE is the British subsidiary of a £300 million German company. The core business is largely based on copper wiring, so that a lot of the activity is involved with telecommunications infrastructure, or the hardware for telecommunications. For example, the company is a major supplier to BT, making products such as telephone socket boxes.

The company needed to assess things such as the potential impact of optical fibre, and to what extent the use of cable telephones, for example, would affect the business. The company also wanted to look for new product opportunities.

It used PA Consultants to generate four scenarios based on different technologies being adopted. Then, within each scenario, it examined product opportunities using brainstorms and visualizations done by PA designers. Over 200 product ideas resulted, which were then filtered according to viability and the match with KRONE's existing skills.

At Shell, scenarios are used as a basic part of strategy setting. The production of the scenarios every three years has been a major effort, with a team to represent many cultures brought together, and concern taken to communicate the scenarios both internally, in detail, and externally through a well written booklet.

The size, quality and level of the effort of the Shell scenario production has had (at least) two external effects. It has produced a large number of talented people who have carried the way of thinking forward into other arenas - through spinouts, or consultancy. It has also contributed to a feeling that "scenarios are only for big organizations" or "too hard" or "tied to a three year cycle". The evidence found in our poll discussed above is that the successful organizations had adopted a "right for my questions" or "right for my organization" approach: more focused than very global and wide-ranging approach, which Shell has taken in context of their overall business.

There is also a question which needs to be answered: why did the Shell scenarios not help them to anticipate the increased professionalism of interest communities like Greenpeace? and so be out-manoeuvred over the disposal of the Brent Spar Rig, when Shell had a very good case but public opinion swung to Greenpeace? The suggestion is there is a systematic underestimation of the increasing role of informed communities, using information technology and the media to have global influence, in many large organizations, and a difficulty in sorting signal from noise.

At United Distillers (UD), scenario planning started in early 1995. Three scenario exercises have each looked at a wide range of cultural issues in relation to UD's business - the sale of alcoholic beverages.

In the first, scenario building was used to consult with a range of Indian groups on the issue of spirits, where as previously the views of top management only had been canvassed. The results were used to heighten awareness of the issues among the middle level management in India in marketing, external affairs and business development.

Three scenarios were developed for the future of South Africa: and are now central to strategic planning for South Africa.

The next project was to consider the impact on UD's business in the Middle East of changes in Islamic political, economic, social cultural and religious thinking, choosing Turkey as an example because the company faced a particular investment decision.

One of the main benefits of scenario planning that UD has found is that scenarios have helped the people involved in the businesses begin to understand that investment decisions are not just about submitting numbers and justifying budgets, but need to be set in a wider context of what might happen.

In summary, scenarios seem to be helping organizations of a range of sizes - small manufacturing companies through to governments and large multinationals - to anticipate change in a number of dimensions.

The survey responses covered changes:

- in the political arena;

- in environmental factors and/or customer attitudes;

- and in ways of looking for new product opportunities.

This is consistent with the applications reviewed earlier.

Will this pattern change? Or are there new causes of uncertainty hitting us? In the next section we look at what the experts are saying, and at the effects that one of the factors for change, Information Technology, is expected to have on society.

WHAT IS DIFFERENT ABOUT THE WORLD TODAY?

We saw in the first chapter how planning has reacted to changes in the real world, from the Second World War through to the present day, and how the oil price shock caused a surge of interest in scenarios.

Is there any reason to believe we are at the start of another period of dramatic change?

Many commentators believe so. For instance:

- Samuel Huntingdon's seminal work on the changes from a two-centre balance of power in the Cold War to a position in which fractures run on cultural lines, not those of national boundaries and there are seven or eight powers (Huntingdon, 1989).

- Barry Minkin in "Future in Sight" (Minkin, 1995) asserts that *"an epic transformation of our worlds has already begun. By 2005, we will be in the middle of a number of transitions of which the outcomes are highly uncertain. The gap between old and young, rich and poor, north and south, will spark increased conflicts among different cultures. Political and economic restructuring will mean short-term dislocations before we can reap their promised long-term benefits. The emergence of information economies raises fundamental questions about economic activity, growth and wealth."*

- Watts Wacker in "The 500 Year Delta" (Taylor et al, 1997) sees a convergence of a number of changes, with the power of the producers of goods decreasing and that of consumers increasing.

- John Petersen, in his "Road to 2015" (Petersen, 1994) sees that information technology plus new ideas and technologies in science, plus the saturation of the planet will cause a global paradigm shift similar to that seen in the West in the fifteenth and sixteenth centuries.

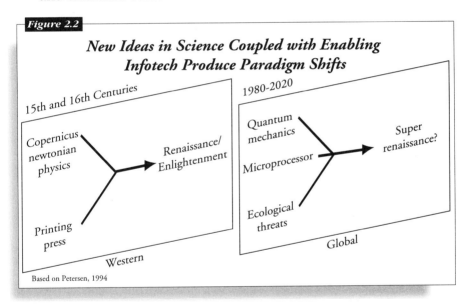

Figure 2.2

New Ideas in Science Coupled with Enabling Infotech Produce Paradigm Shifts

Based on Petersen, 1994

THE ROLE OF INFORMATION TECHNOLOGY

Information technology is a thread which runs through these predictions of change.

Predictions abound for the capability that technology will be able to deliver into this new world. For instance, Nicholas Negroponte says in "Being Digital": *"Early in the next millennium your telephone won't ring indiscriminately; it will receive, sort, and perhaps respond to your incoming calls like a well-trained English butler. Mass media will be redefined by systems for transmitting and receiving personalized information and entertainment. Schools will change to become more like museums and playgrounds for children to assemble ideas and socialize with children from all over the world. The digital planet will look and feel like the head of a pin.*

As we interconnect ourselves, many of the values of the nation-state will give way to those of both larger and smaller electronic communities. We will socialize in digital neighborhoods in which physical space will be irrelevant and time will play a different role. Twenty years from now, when you look out of a window, what you see may be five thousand miles and six time zones away. When you watch an hour of television it may have been delivered to your home in less than a second. Reading about Patagonia can include the sensory experience of going there. A book by William Buckley can be a conversation with him."

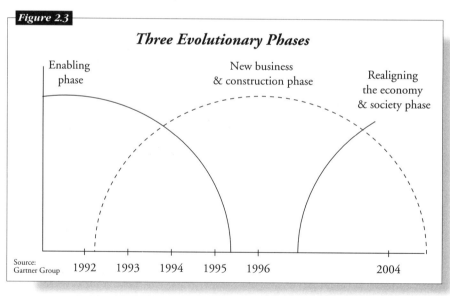

Figure 2.3

Three Evolutionary Phases

But it is harder to think through how this will affect society. A simplified view of how this technological capability may feed through into the Information Industry and the Information Society has been produced by the Gartner Group (Figure 2.3). This figure suggests that an enabling phase of technology is coming to an end and that the information technology in the lab, and emerging into products over the next ten years, is sufficient to spawn the creation of many new businesses. Some of these will help to change society because of the utility of their products.

The adoption phase of technology is well under way, with nearly half the homes in the US and 20% in Europe owning a personal computer, with the rapid increase in satellite and cable communications, with the extensive use of mobile phones, and with the dramatic decrease in communications costs.

Decrease in costs of a product or service lead to new uses becoming practical. For instance, the costs of transatlantic phone calls across the North Atlantic have dropped by orders of magnitude - from tens of pounds, to pennies - over the last thirty years, and the traffic has risen, taking advantage of the new accessibility. The increases in carrying capacity of networking (see Figure 2.4) have formed the enabling platform for the legendary growth of the Internet.

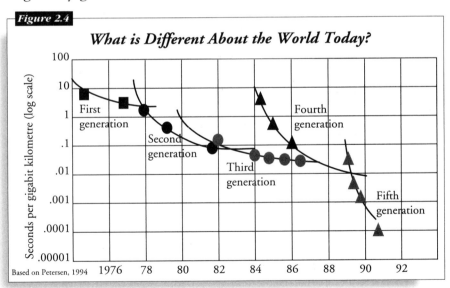

Figure 2.4

What is Different About the World Today?

The second of the Gartner Group phases, that of new business creation, is well under way, with companies such as America On Line, Netscape, and new start-ups in telecoms and the media, growing fast to serve new markets. The existing players - the computer companies, the telecoms companies, the entertainment and education sectors - are scrambling to link and re-form to meet new markets. Scarcely a day goes past without announcement of a new venture or the break-up of a venture only a few months old.

In Figure 2.5, "The Collision of Industries", based on one developed by Harvard University in 1989, the flashes at the boundaries between existing industries are the areas of energy. The new Information Industry is created at the interfaces between the existing computer, consumer electronics, publishing and media, and telecoms companies.

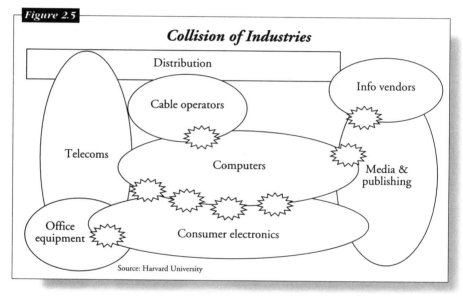

Figure 2.5

Collision of Industries

Distribution

Info vendors

Cable operators

Telecoms

Computers

Media & publishing

Office equipment

Consumer electronics

Source: Harvard University

THE INFORMATION SOCIETY

The growth of new economies based on digital information will not be uniform, nor will the effects which follow.

For instance, it has been estimated that 20% of the publishing sector could be handled electronically with the decade, which would mean the creation of a new industry with a turnover of about 50 billion ECU in Europe alone. The dislocation of jobs in all steps of the publishing chain raises practical problems: the skills needed are different, and the jobs may be in a different place. The potential benefit is that all **can** have greater access to information, but access to the new world will, in all probability be patchy, adding to the gaps that Minkin referred to. The shape of the society which results from these changes is not clear.

Farrell, in his article "The Triple Revolution" (Farrell, 1994) suggested that the digital information revolution takes place on top of revolutions linked to other advances in technology. For instance, very few of the world's workers are needed to produce the food, or the manufactured goods, that we use. He highlights the revolution called "post-materialism", in which the focus of interest moves beyond the acquisition of goods as the prime source of demand, leading to increases in the demand for services.

The moves to the information society and to services economies start to change the patterns of work. Less work is linked to physical labour or operating machines in a production line, more is linked to individual capabilities. Farrell calls this the third revolution, in which the individual is empowered.

Winslow and Bramer in "FutureWork" (Winslow and Bramer, 1994) identify a number of early examples of organizations and applications which are re-aligning to exploit the new world, which they call the Infocosm.

We in ICL have focused on aspects of the world which we call the Information Society, relating to the changes wrought by the use of digital information through "people on-line". We believe that changes will be seen in everyday lives, on a day to day basis. The way people trade, relate to governments, learn, play, and work will all be open to much more choice. People will be able to be much more mobile, or choose to avoid travel. And new communities will form, based on interests rather than geography.

This will have enormous effects on society, and the institutions within society. With the increased power of the individual, companies and governments need to operate differently.

The effects are being seen already in some industries such as financial services. In others it is unexpected, for instance:

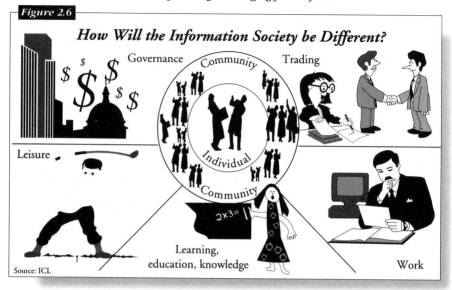

Figure 2.6

How Will the Information Society be Different?

Governance — Community — Trading — Leisure — Individual — Community — Learning, education, knowledge — Work

Source: ICL

- in forestry, pulp mills used to be in the forest, and the customers were a few large publishers buying a few qualities of paper. The changing demand for paper due to the changes in printing technology has turned some forestry companies from being rooted in the forest into companies with pulp mills near good sources of waste paper, and from companies dominated by growing and processing pulp to companies led by a sales force selling many varieties of paper to a multiplicity of customers;

- in construction, the globalization of regulations and the use of IT to transmit working drawings change the quantity and quality of the skill-base needed on the site.

PLANNING FOR THE FUTURE

In this environment, the techniques used for planning business over the past decades are no longer sufficient, and may be misleading. Good planning requires a view of the future. Forecasts based on current trends, or estimates of growth based on history, will be dangerous to organizations if their environment is changing fast.

With these forces at work, the emphasis for planners has moved from forecasting to foresight. As Slaughter (Slaughter, 1996) points out *"Foresight pushes the boundaries of perception in at least four major ways by:*

- *Consequence Assessment: assessing the implications of present actions, decisions, etc.;*

- *Early Warning & Guidance: detecting and avoiding problems before they occur;*

- *Pro-active Strategy Formulation: considering the present implications of possible future events;*

- *Normative Scenarios: envisioning aspects of possible or desired futures."*

This book is about a way of thinking, scenario planning, for encouraging and harnessing foresight.

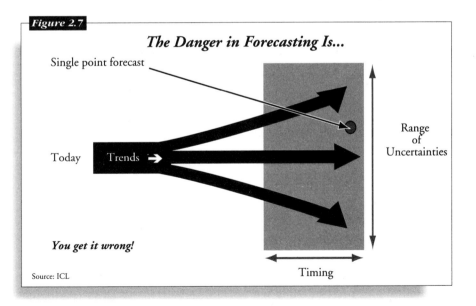

Figure 2.7

The Danger in Forecasting Is...

Single point forecast

Today Trends

Range of Uncertainties

You get it wrong!

Source: ICL

Timing

CONCLUSIONS

Companies that have used scenario thinking claim results including:

- at the insurance company Erste Allgemeine Versicherung, to spot the results of political changes, e.g. the Berlin Wall coming down and so establish themselves early in former Eastern European countries;

- at Electrolux, the consumer goods company, to see the opportunity for new businesses, e.g. a service business based re-using consumer products;

- at wiring and cable supplier KRONE, to develop 200 new product ideas;

- at Pacific Gas and Electricity, to dispel assumptions about the "Official Future" and cause it to work to reduce energy consumption;

- in the UK National Health Service, to provide a way for a very dispersed, large and disparate organization to think through new relationships, internally and to customers.

We found that most scenarios produced by the respondents to our straw poll through The Conference Board Europe took less than six months to build. A number of organizations, for instance Austrade, got significant benefit from projects of less than a man-year. Scenarios were thought of as a management development tool, as a way of creating shared vision as well as better plans, in a number of organizations, and that those who started by concentrating on the scenarios for portfolio management found this to be a valuable spin-off. ICL's experience of this is the subject of later chapters.

The size of organizations using scenarios ranges from KRONE UK, a medium sized organization using outside consultants, to Shell, using internal staff with some outsiders. The key seems to be "geared to the organization" which in some cases means taking a specific topic as focus. For instance in the construction industry, back of the envelope scenarios based on the effect of government regulations may be appropriate for the situation.

Other industries, and some companies in some industries, need to take a systematic long term and global view because of the nature of their business.

The future is always uncertain. But it seems at the moment as though the uncertainties facing us are more likely and more potentially disruptive than at other times. Many people believe that what we are seeing in the 1990s is changing the rules again.

A major source of change in the world today is the adoption of information technology. The changes visible in the last few years, as the financial services industry reinvents itself, are expected to be dwarfed by the changes to come. The Information Society is expected to change the way we work, play, shop, are governed, bank, and the communities we belong to, exceeding those changes provoked by the oil price shock of the 1970s

In this environment, creating models of the future as a way of rehearsing change looks set to increase.

There is, however, an alternative school, which relies on fast reactions - believing a planning cycle is too slow. This view may be derived from a view of scenario planning based on some of the "heavy" planning systems of the past. And companies of the fast reaction school tend to have well-developed processes for spotting events, e.g. good technology watch programmes and fast lines to decision making, for acquisitions, mergers or investment.

But the successful organizations, with any approach, are those which have found ways of looking for early warning signs that current assumptions may become invalid, picking up the significant signals from the noise. The role of staff in this alerting process seems as important today as when Ted Newland described his role in Shell in the early 1970s.

CHAPTER THREE

Strategic Planning in ICL

SUMMARY

This chapter outlines strategic planning as performed in ICL to set a context for the discussion of scenario planning in ICL.

The chapter outlines the ICL Strategic Planning process, and the use of Business Value across the company to create a common language. We also use tools like PIMS (Profit Impact of Market Strategy) to benchmark businesses, and the Market Attractiveness/Capability (MA/C) matrix for portfolio analysis. Some examples are given of how these tools have been used to transform the business in conjunction with scenario thinking.

For more detail on how we implement our strategies, see Neill et al 1998, to be published.

STRATEGIC PLANNING

Scenario planning has to be seen in the context of strategic planning. Volumes have been written about strategic planning over the years, about theories, methods, structures and techniques. It has also come under fierce criticism from some quarters, with theorists like Henry Mintzberg arguing that planning has become too rigid a process, often acting as an end in itself and obscuring actual strategic thinking (Mintzburg, 1994b).

Planning should be about studying the future to make sure the company takes the right action now to be successful in the future.

That involves selecting markets, figuring out what to do to win in its existing or new markets through understanding company strengths, and determining what edge there is over the competition. It should not be overly-complicated. John Kay (Kay, 1993) describes it as understanding what the company's competitive advantage is for the future, which is determined by applying a company's distinctive capabilities to particular market niches. That should help the company decide where to invest its money in terms of products and markets.

A recent article by Bernard Taylor (Taylor, 1997) discusses the history of strategic planning, and looks at its current role. He suggests that some differences in the way strategy is thought about are becoming clear in the "new" environment:

• strategy is around a few major issues, and very distinct from operational plans;

• strategy is part of a continuous dialogue;

• large central planning teams have been replaced by a few senior executives at headquarters;

• businesses within a corporation work to strategic targets agreed with headquarters.

This is the picture to keep in mind when looking at the relationship between strategy and scenarios.

The role of strategic planners

In most companies chief executives and the managers of business units spend much of their time dealing with day-to-day problems and events. Strategic planners thus have an important role to play both in encouraging ideas for strategy formulation and ensuring that the strategic planning process stays on track. There are a number of qualities that make a good strategic planner.

The strategic planner needs to take a view of the broad picture, and also be able to root plans in reality, and to run a process so that business managers get information on the environment and on methods to help them in running the business for the corporation. This needs good interpersonal skills to build credibility both upwards and into the businesses. The balance of these qualities will vary according to the management style of the enterprise - see below for a discussion of the relationship between headquarters and the businesses.

THE ICL STRATEGIC PLANNING PROCESS

In ICL, corporate planning is combined with strategic planning to make sure there is no gap between strategic thinking and the central planning and control activities, including financial control, both for the short and long term

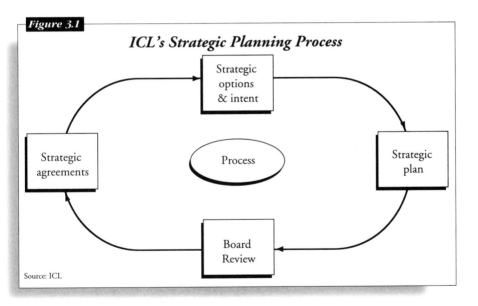

Figure 3.1

ICL's Strategic Planning Process

Source: ICL

The strategic process has evolved considerably over the years. Figure 3.1 shows the annual, cyclical, strategic planning process. The central point is the annual two-day strategy Board Review. Preparation for that meeting will have begun up to six months previously, with input coming from current business forecasts, the existing strategic plan, new strategic ideas from the businesses, and fresh thinking, which is then all woven together. This will be done in parallel with the review process carried on from the previous year's plan.

While numbers are projected for five years, strategic horizons depend on the nature of the business (see below under discussion of Business Value). The Board review sets the budget for the next year and the strategic plan.

To make sure that strategy setting is given a high enough priority by the managers of each business, the process has been facilitated by the use of a questionnaire. It helps the managers think about what their business is good at and why. The questions underpin the strategic plans submitted by each business, increase the emphasis on what, why, and how, to underpin the numbers.

Secondly, close monitoring of what actually happens is maintained through strategic agreements between the centre and the businesses. The agreements are a charter for each business based on a condensed version of the agreed strategy and contain a number of milestones - which may be financial, market driven or capability-based. This process provides for a Board review, not only of the financial performance, on a monthly basis but also the achievements in progressing in the strategic direction.

FRAMEWORK OF QUESTIONS

CUSTOMERS

1. What are your customers' critical success factors, in terms of:

   (i) problems they must solve (i.e. overcome value destruction)

   (ii) ongoing activities they must carry out, to maintain as a minimum, their competitive status quo

   (iii) what they need to achieve to effect competitive advantage (i.e. value creation)

2. Thinking of your customers' critical success factors, how do

your business's systems and/or services offerings add value to your customers' businesses by helping them to achieve their critical success factors? How do you know?

3. *How are your systems and/or services offerings differentiated and distinctive from your competitors? How do you know?*

4. *What are you doing so that you are continuing to differentiate and increase your distinctiveness? What will you need from other ICL businesses and ICL headquarters (HQ) to enable you to do this? What do you need to do with them?*

5. *If your systems and/or services offerings are not distinctive and differentiated from your competitors, how do you know? What is causing this? How do you know? What needs to be done to ensure they do become distinctive and differentiated? What will you need from the other ICL businesses and ICL headquarters to enable you to do this?*

6. *How could the way your systems and/or services offerings are differentiated enable you to increase your prices, relative to your competitors?*

CAPABILITIES

7. *Considering the capabilities required in your chosen markets, which ones, if lost, could result in your losing competitive advantage? How do you know?*

8. *Of those capabilities that are critical to succeeding in your chosen markets which ones do you already have? How do you know? What are you doing to ensure that you retain those critical capabilities you already have?*

9. *What are you doing to develop those critical capabilities that you don't yet have? How will you know when you have achieved them? When will you achieve them?*

10. *What do you need from other ICL businesses and ICL HQ to*

help you develop your critical capabilities? When do you need this assistance and for how long?

11. *What other capabilities do you have access to in other parts of the ICL Group that would add value to your business? How are you utilizing these capabilities?*

12. *Considering the capabilities at which you are distinctive; how could you increase your penetration of existing markets and existing customers; what other existing markets could you enter? How do you know? How could you?*

13. *What future emerging markets could you enter with the capabilities at which you are distinctive? How do you know? How could you?*

14. *Considering the penetration of existing and new markets, what new capabilities might you need to develop? How do you know? What will you need to be doing to develop them? What will you need from other ICL businesses and ICL HQ? When do you need this assistance and for how long?*

15. *Concentrating specifically on leadership/senior management do they have the skills sets necessary to run, challenge and develop your business? If not, how do you intend to acquire them and what will be the implications of so doing?*

16. *Are the skills of your total management team fit for purpose? What redeployment or reduction plans do you have for those without the necessary skill sets? How do you intend to manage these?*

17. *What are the critical success factors for your business, both now and in the next five years. How do your capabilities (existing and planned) help you to achieve your critical success factors?*

18. *In what way are you collaborating with the other ICL*

businesses and ICL HQ to ensure the success of the cross business initiatives of information society, Year 2000, electronic commerce and EMU? What are your shared milestones and by when?

COMPETITORS and MARKETS

19. *Thinking about your competition:*
   (i) who are your current competitors?
   (ii) who will be your competitors in the future?
   (iii) how will these new competitors compete with ICL?

20. *Considering the markets mentioned above:*
   (i) how big are they?
   (ii) what are their growth rates?
   (iii) on what assumptions are your forecasts made?

ORGANIZATION, PROCESSES and INFRASTRUCTURE

21. *What plans do you have to (a) rationalize, (b) reorganize and (c) dispose of your non-core activities? How do you intend to phase your plans? What are the cost implications? What plans do you have for those parts of the business which are not performing? Have you set realistic targets for them and how do you measure them?*

22. *For each of the Breakthrough initiatives what are you planning to achieve and how will you achieve it? What mutual dependencies do you have with other ICL businesses that could impact your ability to achieve the Breakthrough initiatives?*

23. *In providing systems and/or services offerings to your customers, in what way are your information technology (IT), information systems (IS) and business processes lowering the value you provide to your customers? How do you know? In what way are they adding to the value you provide to your customers? How do you know?*

24. *What IT, IS and business processes does your business need? Of those you need which ones are missing and which ones are not*

at the level needed? Of those which are missing or not at the level needed, how are they damaging the capabilities of your business and other ICL businesses? How do you know?

25. What needs to be done to have all the IT, IS and business process capabilities in place? What milestones will you use to monitor your progress?

26. How do you plan to reduce significantly your overheads? What fundamental difference to the structure or cost base of your business do you plan to make?

RISK

27. What are the top three risk areas that could result in value destruction? What contingency plans do you have to overcome those risks?

ONE ICL

28. Thinking through ICL's core values of customer first, one ICL, teamwork, professionalism and society, why are they important to the success and increasing value of your business? What are your reasons? How will the core values help you achieve your strategic plan? How do you know?

29. Considering the ICL corporate strategies, how does your plan add value and support them? How do you know?

30. In achieving your plan, how does being part of ICL continue increasing your business's value? What are your reasons?

BUSINESS VALUE

Business value is the value of a business that can be determined by discounting its future cash flows using an appropriate cost of capital, since future value comes from cash flow, not profit. Traditional accounting measures such as return on capital employed, or earnings per share growth, turn out to be unreliable indicators of a business's value or stock price. Instead, future cash flows discounted at the cost of capital, which reflect risk and time value of money, correlate better with investors' valuations.

The drivers of value are summarized in Figure 3.2. Cash flow comes from having competitive advantage and, in particular, sustainable competitive advantage in so far as that is going to generate cash flows a number of years into the future. The source of sustainable competitive advantage, is the application of distinctive capabilities into specific market niches. John Kay (Kay, 1993) has developed four sources of sustained competitive advantage:

- Architecture: organizational knowledge, network of relationships, interlinked capabilities.

- Reputation: brands, customer trust and perception, market credibility.

- Innovation; new product ideas, new processes, new combinations of known technology, new methods.

- Strategic assets: licences, monopoly, market position in markets that can't support too many competitors.

Figure 3.2

Value Drivers

• Planning horizon	Strategy	– capability
		– customer
		– competitors
		– market
• Revenue growth	Revenue	– forecasting
		– portfolio analysis
• Operating pofit ⎫	Profit	– value chain
• Cash taxes ⎬		– tax management
• Fixed asset expenditure ⎫	Balance sheet	– asset management
• Working capital movement ⎬		
• Cost of capital	Cash	

Source: ICL

These drivers range from revenue, operating profit, to capital considerations, which are different for each business. Figure 3.3 shows the different sorts of values to be found in a portfolio like ICL's.

Figure 3.3

ICL Businesses Impact of Value Drivers

Business	Sales growth	Operating margin	Tax rate	Working capital	Fixed capital	Planning period	Cost of capital
B1	Medium	High	Low	High	Medium	Medium	High
B2	High	Medium	Low	High	High	High	High
B3	High	High	Low	Medium	Low	High	High
B4	Medium	High	Medium	Medium	Medium	High	High
B5	High	High	Low	Medium	Low	High	High
B6	High	High	Low	Medium	Low	High	High
B7	Low	High	Medium	High	High	Low	High
B8	High	Medium	Low	Low	Low	High	High
B9	High	High	Low	Low	Low	Medium	High

Source: ICL

Business Value Creation and Destruction

The business value approach underpins the questions asked in the framework, aimed at helping businesses to create business value

It is also possible to destroy business value with the wrong or dysfunctional internal architecture and processes. Part of the responsibility of headquarters is to provide an environment in which the frequently found destroyers of value are avoided: for instance, by setting effective inter-business trading rules, avoiding internal competition and duplication of capability, and by setting appropriate rewards systems

THE HEADQUARTERS/BUSINESS UNIT RELATIONSHIP

In a complex business there have to be ways for the company's centre to create information flows between itself and the business units as a basis for business direction for the long term, without compromising the initiative and market understanding of those units.

Corporate strategy in a multi-business company is thus the matching of the parent's characteristics with the businesses' characteristics in order to create sustainable competitive advantage. It is not the aggregation of the businesses' strategies.

The Role of Headquarters

The role of the headquarters depends on the planning and control style of the business in which you are operating. This goes back to the research done by Goold and Campbell (1987) which found that there are three types of planning and control companies: strategic planning type, strategic control type and financial control type.

ICL is a strategic control company, which effects the answer to the two basic questions:

- In what businesses should the company invest its resources?

- How should the parent influence and relate to the businesses under its control?

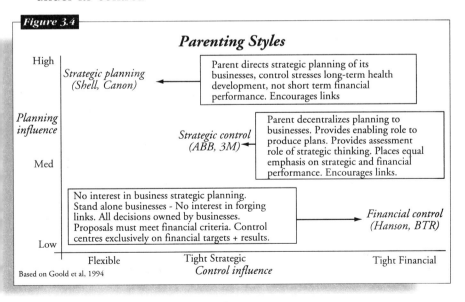

Figure 3.4

Parenting Styles

Based on Goold et al, 1994

At ICL, the parent influences and controls its portfolio of businesses through an umbrella of activities that is to the mutual benefit of all the businesses in the portfolio. The roles of the ICL parent headquarters in relation to the businesses is illustrated in Figure 3.5.

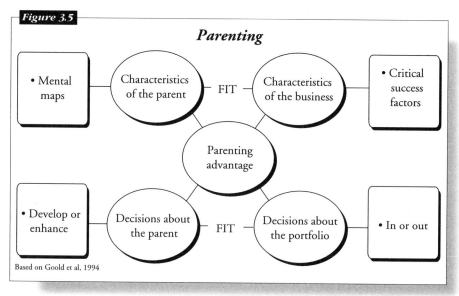

Figure 3.5

Parenting

Based on Goold et al, 1994

Making decisions about the businesses in the portfolio

We use two tools in particular to help make decisions about the fit of businesses in the portfolio. These are the MA/C (Market Attractiveness/Capability) matrix and the PIMS (Profit Impact of Market Strategy) benchmarks.

The MA/C matrix is based on the directional policy matrix, developed independently by Shell and by GE (Kotler et al, 1996). What ICL has done is simplified the approach to a certain extent.

While there are some similarities with the Boston Matrix there are some important differences. This matrix uses market attractiveness and business capabilities as the two main axes, unlike the market growth and relative market share axes used in the Boston matrix. The two axes of market attractiveness and business capabilities are themselves based on a weighted sum of a number of variables. Using these measures, businesses are classified into one of nine cells in a 3 x 3 matrix (Figure 3.6).

Figure 3.6

What the Matrix Suggests About the Portfolio

Capability		Market attractiveness		
		Low	Medium	High
	High	Cash generation	Growth	Leader
	Medium	Phased withdrawal	Proceed with care	Try harder
	Low	Withdrawal	Phased withdrawal	Double or quit

Based on Kotler et al, 1996

The PIMS programme of research on market strategy began in 1972. For a full discussion of the methodology and results, see Buzzell and Gale (1987)*. Since then, more than 450 companies have contributed information on the strategies and financial results of nearly 3,000 strategic business units for periods of between 2 and 12 years. The database covers large and small companies in North America, Europe and elsewhere which range from confectionery to capital goods to financial services.

"While most portfolio planning systems explain business performance in terms of a few key factors, the PIMS approach explores as many possible dimensions of strategy and of the market environment that might influence performance through regression analysis.

There are six statements that appear to have widespread validity across industries and time periods and size of business, as a result of analysis of the database:

*PIMS material reprinted here adapted with the permission of The Free Press, a Division of Simon and Schuster from "The PIMS Principles: Linking Strategy to Performance" by R. D. Buzzell and B. T. Gale. Copyright © 1987 by The Free Press.

1. *In the long run, the most important single factor affecting a business unit's performance is the quality of its products and services, relative to those of competitors.*

2. *Market share and profitability are strongly related.*

3. *High-investment intensity acts as a powerful drag on profitability.*

4. *Many so-called "dog" and "question mark" businesses generate cash, while many "cash cows" are dry.*

5. *Vertical integration is a profitable strategy for some kinds of businesses, but not for others.*

6. *Most of the factors that boost return on investment (ROI) also contribute to long-term value."*

TRANSFORMING THE BUSINESS

ICL has used a number of tools and techniques to transform the company over the past few years. One major shift began in 1993, when we began to move from being a geographically-based group to one based on three global business streams: systems integration, services, and products or technology. This was done in recognition of the fact that the metrics of each type of business were very different. (See the discussion of Vision 2000 in chapter 4.)

We used the PIMS database to benchmark these business streams against paradigms from other industries. For example, systems integration, which is a project-type of business, could be compared to construction, while the features of a US cable company could be used to examine the service level agreement business. The product businesses were beginning to look rather like consumer electronics.

The transformation has continued to the point where ICL now consists of nine businesses, covering systems integration and services. How the portfolio management process works in practice is illustrated by the decision taken about two businesses:

the manufacturing operation called D2D and the Volume Products, personal computer (PC) business.

One of the key elements to consider in terms of parenting advantage is to what extent the parent helps the businesses to achieve their critical success factors. If the answer is that the parent cannot, then it makes sense to get the business a better parent - to provide better value. In the case of both D2D and Volume Products, the three critical success factors were the same: global scale, global brand and low cost production.

Could ICL help those businesses achieve those? It could - but at the risk of not investing in any other part of the portfolio. Also, this would cause strains on a management style evolving to manage the systems integration and the services business streams.

The next question was to assess how these businesses stacked up financially. In the case of Volume Products, it had been a loss-making business and in ninth place in the PC market in terms of size. Analysis with the PIMS database highlighted the fact that the cost-structure of a ninth-place PC company was almost exactly what the PIMS database said it would be. In other words, Volume Products was doing as well as anyone could in that market position. The results showed that unless a PC manufacturer is in the top four, it won't make money.

So it seemed a sensible to move to put volume products with Fujitsu's volume products business because the combination was then getting close to being the fourth largest producer.*

The strength of the PIMS data base is that it contains 28,000 years of business performance data. The limitation is that it is historical benchmark data. So the danger is that decisions taken based on the data become self-fulfilling prophecies which leaves gaps if new competition is changing the rules of the game.

The role of the scenarios in testing the decision to divest both D2D and Volume Products against possible future worlds is discussed in Chapter 5.

---

* After the first 12 months the combined volume products businesses moved into a break even position, as the PIMS model indicated it would.

CHAPTER FOUR

ICL's Experience of Building Scenarios for Strategic Planning

SUMMARY

This chapter compares two scenario building projects that ICL completed two years apart. In both cases the intention was to link to strategic planning; and in both cases difficulties were found in communicating the scenarios in a useful form, and in embedding scenarios into decision-making: the sections on Lessons learned cover these points.

A FIRST SCENARIO PLANNING PROJECT: MOVING UP THE LEARNING CURVE

ICL first began experimenting with scenario planning in 1993. It was part of a comprehensive examination of the forces on the information technology (IT) industry, and a re-examination of ICL's vision of the future.

Vision 2000

Like many other companies in the IT industry, ICL had been growing within an industry with double digit growth most years for more than a decade. (For a short history of ICL, see the Appendix.) But the growth masked major changes in the industry. By 1993, looking back to the ten-year forecasts made in 1986, we could see that what we had correctly foreseen was that the industry was moving towards personal computers and systems integration. What we had not foreseen was the extent to which the industry would restructure and new players dominate niches, and how far margins would decrease as the industry restructured. So we decided that we needed to take a systematic look ahead to see what opportunities and potential dangers were lying in wait for our business.

We set up a project called Vision 2000 as a first step in investigating the possible futures ICL faced, to concentrate on forces in the industry and the ways in which we could meet the challenges of the changing needs of our customers.

We began the project quite informally, involving mainly three people. The author had an HQ responsibility for software and services, Malcolm Austin headed up corporate planning, and Tony Oppenheim was mainly concerned with mergers and acquisitions.

There were three strands to Vision 2000.

One was looking at the outside world, the conventional PEST (politics, economics, society, technical) factors. It was a question of gathering statistics and information, trying to concentrate on what were the megatrends, such as what was happening in the US as opposed to Asia, what is happening to demographics - to get a feeling and a reach for the wider environment.

The second strand was analysing the IT industry, looking for discontinuities in sectors like consumer electronics and telecommunications, examining the competition, and listening to who was saying what about future business directions. Because we sensed that what had been perceived as a monolithic computer business was splitting up, we turned to the PIMS database to look for other industrial parallels for the different components of the IT industry. We used the construction industry as a comparison for our business that dealt with large projects, we looked at utilities for their resemblance to the services business, and consumer electronics for the products/technology-based business. In each case we charted operating profits, the return on investment, investment required and the management profiles.

The third strand was to understand ICL's assets: after exploring several techniques we decided on a SWOT analysis of the ICL assets, business by business. At this level, we were able to separate out ICL corporate assets from those unique to a particular business - for instance, the infrastructure across Europe versus applications software for instore retail systems.

The scenario planning project

At the same time as we were pushing ahead on Vision 2000, we were experimenting with scenario planning to judge how effective an approach it could be in helping the company inform decisions about its direction. Our interest was sparked by Matti Keiola, on secondment to corporate planning for a year from ICL Finland. He brought a number of methodologies and tools which he wanted to pilot. For example, he created a large model of the company by aggregating data from the business units to help analyse the business as a whole. Another technique was business value (see Chapter 3). Both methods are still in use.

He also led a scenario planning exercise, involving the Vision 2000 group.

We met about once a week over ten weeks. The meetings were held in the office and consisted mainly of brainstorming. From those meetings we developed three scenarios, with each one set in the context of a number of basic driving forces: general geo-economic/political conditions, world GDP growth, monetary system/Europe, price stability (especially energy), armed conflicts (defence spending), telecommunications harmonization and what might happen in the integration or otherwise of Europe.

THE THREE SCENARIOS

We called the three scenarios Stagnation, Baseline and Technogrowth.

THREE SCENARIOS FOR THE IT INDUSTRY IN EUROPE, 1993

A. Stagnation
- *Europe stagnates politically and economically, and unemployment rates rather than productivity drives business and government.*
- *World GDP growth approximately 1.5% compound annual growth rate due to tariff walls, unstable exchange rates and drag of Europe.*

- *Europe does not have management that can re-engineer business and exploit IT.*
- *Telecommunications deregulation and satellite/cable coverage provide inadequate inter (European) national framework for business or home use.*
- *Saturation of business use of desktops and servers and increased installed life combine with drag of legacy systems to reduce IT markets significantly. Pressure through mergers and downsizing.*
- *Significant changes in commercial practice (e.g. distribution) driven by business pressures and over-supply of processing power.*
- *Protection by governments in Europe lead to continuation of Siemens as "the last vertically integrated IT supplier".*

B. Baseline
- *European Free Trade Area mostly effective but some tariff barriers with US. Unemployment in Europe and North America not a social problem.*
- *World GDP growth approximately 3% with no major exchange rate fluctuations.*
- *European management is risk averse and focuses on IT for cost reduction.*
- *Telecoms deregulation and satellite/cable coverage allows high bandwidth to businesses but not the home.*
- *Saturation of desktops and servers in business, replacement market.*
- *Changes in commercial practice follow those in US by two years and US companies take major market share of services markets to governments.*
- *Vertically integrated IT companies disappear.*

C. Technogrowth
- *Free trade between blocks, including IT into Japan. Non-working population not a social problem.*
- *World GDP growth is approximately 4% with Europe at 3% lower than North America and Japan.*
- *European management starts to re-engineer business process*

> using IT and European governments make imaginative investments in IT infrastructure.
> - Universal wide bandwidth access to IT in North America and Japan (home and business) but W. Europe still limited access to home.
> - Major growth in mobile workforce expands server/network business as well as personal digital assistant consumer electronic devices.
> - Significant changes in commercial practice due to changes in business process and work style.
> - Vertically integrated IT suppliers disappear.

Trends common to all three scenarios

In creating the scenarios we found that there were trends covering economics, technology and the information industry that were common to all three. These trends formed part of our input to Vision 2000.

Shifts in Economic Power

All the scenarios predicted that GDP growth and growth/capita would be lower in Europe than the other two major blocks (North America, Asia), with the highest GDP growth and growth/capita projected for South East Asia, China, and India. Consequently a shift in the balance of power from Europe to South East Asia, China and India in particular was foreseen.

The population growth in South East Asia, China, India was expected to cause an increase in the buying population and its capacity to spend. This compares with the forecast of no or low population growth in US/Japan/Europe - leaving out the effect of immigration. The increasing cost of caring for the old would be balanced by the decreasing cost of educating the young in US/Japan/Europe in the timescale considered - though the swing in the nature of the expenditure would cause social disruptions.

With more direct effect on the IT industry, the other shift in economic power that we projected was the reduction and change in the role of IT departments. We foresaw that buying points for

IT would move to the Board for large systems integration and facility management (FM), i.e. for large expenditures, to user departments for applications solutions and line of business needs, and to end users for PCs and shrink wrapped software packages.

Technology Push
The single most important factor affecting the industry in 1993 was the continuing applicability of Moore's Law. This law says that the processing power on a chip doubles every 18 months - through competitive forces, adoption of new technology, and new fabrication plants. Moore's law seemed to be likely to hold good for the period to year 2000.

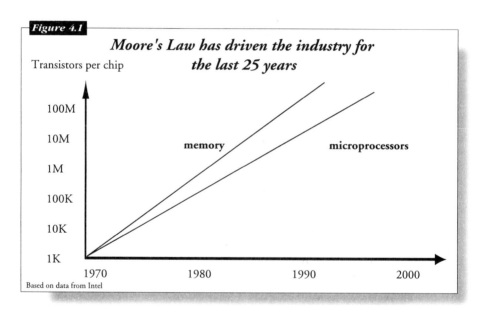

Figure 4.1

Moore's Law has driven the industry for the last 25 years

Transistors per chip

memory   microprocessors

Based on data from Intel

When this is carried through into predictions for systems, we anticipated a major growth in the use of palmtop computers, with prices starting at £100, and added capability like modems, pen input, pushing up the price. By the year 2000 we expected that desktops (for home and business) would start at £300. Added capability like ISDN connection capability, modem cards, multimedia cards and CD-ROMs would push up the average prices. The price expected on current trends in server prices by year 2000 was $2000 tps*. This compared with the 1993 prices for mainframes of $35-50,000 tps, and the price of digital and Hewlett Packard "super-minis" at $10-15,000 tps. We thought that printers would increase in capability and relative price within the system. We expected that networking bandwidth would increase and the price decrease, but that in Europe interactive video bandwidths delivered to the home would not be widespread in the time frame of year 2000.

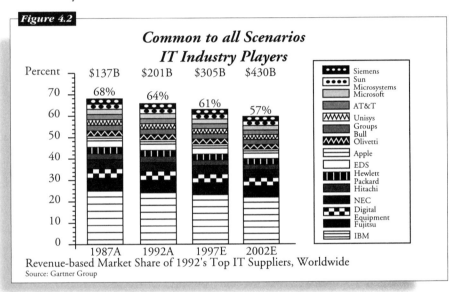

Figure 4.2

Common to all Scenarios
IT Industry Players

Revenue-based Market Share of 1992's Top IT Suppliers, Worldwide
Source: Gartner Group

IT Industry

Based on the view of the Gartner Group (Figure 4.2) we assumed the IT industry would continue to grow. Gartner estimated that by 2002, 57% of the industry sales - then worth $430 billion - would be dominated by the major players, although IBM's share would be less than in 1992. Growth would be accompanied by more fragmentation, with more companies entering the market.

Intel's view in 1992 was that a new computer industry would be formed, with a different value chain from that seen historically. The number of competitors in the various areas of the

* transactions per second.

computer industry such as micro-processors and computer platforms would decrease (Figure 4.3) as large IT companies became less vertically-integrated.

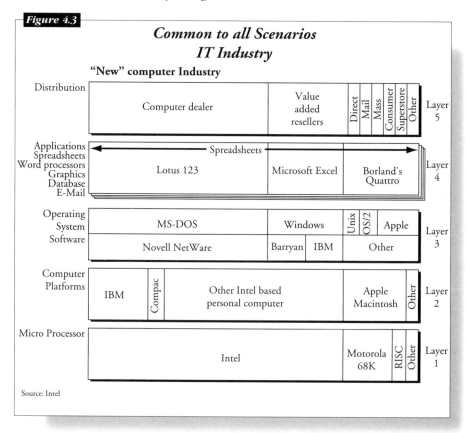

Figure 4.3

Common to all Scenarios
IT Industry

"New" computer Industry

Distribution	Computer dealer	Value added resellers	Direct Mail / Mass Consumer / Superstore / Other		Layer 5

Applications Spreadsheets Word processors Graphics Database E-Mail	← Spreadsheets → Lotus 123	Microsoft Excel	Borland's Quattro	Layer 4

Operating System Software	MS-DOS	Windows	Unix / OS/2 / Apple	Layer 3
	Novell NetWare	Barryan / IBM	Other	

Computer Platforms	IBM / Compac	Other Intel based personal computer	Apple Macintosh / Other	Layer 2

Micro Processor	Intel	Motorola 68K / RISC / Other	Layer 1

Source: Intel

Finally, and perhaps more significantly, it was becoming clear that the boundaries between once distinct sectors of the information industry would increasingly shift, with computers and telecommunications moving closer together. The same trend applied to computers and entertainment, media and publishing, distribution, education, consumer electronics and office equipment. Figure 4.4 is a diagram based on work at Harvard University, provoked by the extent to which semiconductor technology and embedded intelligence was coming to dominate other information industries.

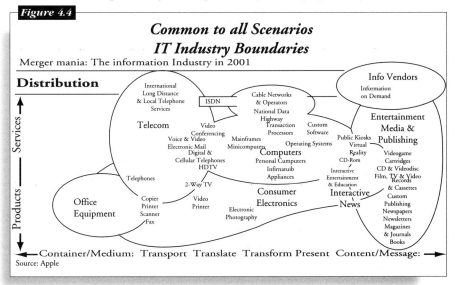

Figure 4.4

Common to all Scenarios
IT Industry Boundaries

Merger mania: The information Industry in 2001

Source: Apple

COMMUNICATION OF THE SCENARIOS

At the end of the scenario building project, the team had a much clearer view of the world and the underlying trends affecting us.

But we had great difficulty in communicating this clarity. The first problem was that initially the scenarios were presented in table form, spread over three pages in very small type. These took several hours to talk through in detail and we did not have a useful summary form (see Part IV, Scenarios Developed by ICL in 1993).

We had been discussing the Vision 2000 work with SRI International, and tapped into its scenarios expertise. It had found that a useful analytic framework for scenarios in technology based industries was using the axes of consumer needs/demands, business needs/demands, the macro-environment and delivery structures.

When we rated each of the three scenarios in terms of the rate of change (very high, high, medium, low) on these axes we produced Figure 4.5. This approach helped to begin to tease out the significant differences among the scenarios. They had acquired a different characteristic footprint and could no longer be thought of as "high/baseline/low".

The Technogrowth scenario scored showed high or very high rate of change in consumer and business demands, but only medium economic growth in Europe.

The Baseline scenario was very low in terms of changing delivery structures, it had medium growth of consumer needs/demands, static or declining business needs/demands and a less healthy macro-environment in terms of growth.

In the Stagnation scenario, business needs/demands would be very high, but it would be about reducing costs, with particular demand for outsourcing. Consumer demand would be very flat, while the macro-environment was low growth and delivery structures were relatively stable.

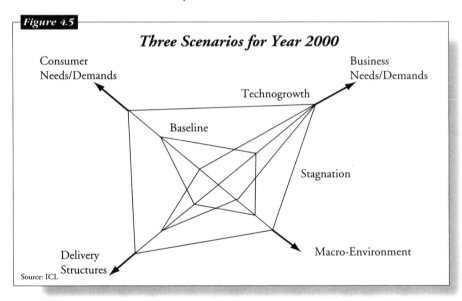

Figure 4.5

Three Scenarios for Year 2000

Consumer Needs/Demands

Business Needs/Demands

Technogrowth

Baseline

Stagnation

Delivery Structures

Macro-Environment

Source: ICL

Using these scenarios we were able to discuss a number of aspects of the industry we had not explored before from this angle. They allowed us to make mental jumps and examine how different elements are connected and predict that some areas would be more resilient than others. For example, we could see that outsourcing could be viable when the economy booms because people had discretion to rethink their business, and it could be viable when the economy was bad because people were trying to get efficiencies. So outsourcing would be driven by different forces in different scenarios. Though that was not a devastating conclusion, it was a useful one at the time.

This format highlighted the differences between the scenarios and helped us in discussing them with management teams. But they did not "live", and it proved difficult to include the scenarios into planning.

However, on the whole, we were happy with what we had learned from the pilot.

Lessons learned

With hindsight we saw a number of reasons that we were less successful than we would have liked.

- We had not started with a focused question we were trying to answer. You need a question to answer to put the scenario into context.

- Presentation was initially very unhelpful (the scenarios were spread over three pages in very small type, with far too much detail but lacking any explanation of the essence of the scenario - see Part IV).

- The scenarios representation using the axes suggested by SRI (consumer needs/demands, business needs/demands, delivery structures and macro-environment) made us also realize the importance of using graphical techniques. It allowed us to home in on the delivery structures as an area of major change, and to see that the demands on IT would be severe in both the Technogrowth and Stagnation scenarios: but we found that it required a very detailed commentary and reconciliation of the axes to use for exposition.

- We did not have a framework in which to place the results. There was little way anyone who had not been through the exercise could get a feeling for what we had understood.

- Having three scenarios proved to be dangerous, particularly in an industry where it can be assumed that people are reasonably numerate and literate. They will usually make what seems to be the sensible assumption that the middle one is the forecast - which limits the value of the scenario thinking.

- Because we held the sessions in the office, we probably did not think as laterally as we should have.

OUTCOME OF VISION 2000

Overall, Vision 2000 proved its worth in helping ICL to draw up a coherent picture of where the industry was moving. In January 1994 the company was reorganized into three main business streams: systems integration for project-based business, a services-based business specializing in outsourcing, and the technology/product divisions.

We integrated the trends analysis but not the variable part of the scenarios into the other strands of Vision 2000.

Although we had experimented with scenario planning, it was other tools like competitive benchmarking and the SWOT analysis that laid the foundation for the changes in 1993. Our understanding of the trends proved important later. But for the time being we parked the scenarios because the importance of other factors like the changing structure of the industry exceeded the impact of the variability included in our scenarios.

Software 2000

During the Vision 2000 project we found it easy to find forward projections for hardware capability. This contrasted with a lack of projections for, or discussion of, what would be happening with software in the year 2000. There was a belief that a set of discontinuities would be hitting software in terms of technology, techniques, skills and applications in the next few years, but there did not appear to be any coherent external body of analysis or thought on these issues.

So, we brought together an international team from industry, academics, suppliers and users for two days in April 1994 for a workshop sponsored by ICL and Esprit*, to discuss these issues. There was a notable degree of unanimity that software was facing dramatic changes, for instance:

- Powerful and cheap processing, storage, networking, and software, have created the potential for the global information infrastructure and changed our definition of what software is, how it is delivered, who writes it and who uses it.

- The Internet was at that time still perceived primarily as an academic tool: Software 2000 predicted that it would "imminently" burst into the mainstream and would have a far-reaching impact on software.

- Software is now embedded in most environments such as cars, traffic systems, medical equipment and is mission-critical in many instances which means that the centre of gravity is shifting.

- It is likely we will see massive changes over the next few years, causing the initial PC revolution to pale into comparative insignificance.

The conclusions, particularly on Internet, were formative in our decision-making over the next year, and provided input to the next scenarios project.

A SECOND SCENARIO PLANNING PROJECT IN 1995

Late in 1994 we talked to Laura Raymond of Shell about our views of the IT industry. In return the Shell scenarios team under Ged Davies briefed us on how they do scenario planning. Much of this has now been published by Kees van der Heijden (see Part III). In particular, their emphasis on the importance of credible scenarios which could plausibly evolve from "where we are now" was very helpful. And we took their advice on the number of scenarios to generate.

---

* Esprit was the name of the research programme of the European Commission.

HOW MANY SCENARIOS?

Shell had experimented with four, three and two scenarios for strategic planning.

What it had found was that:

- four scenarios encourage divergent thinking and are useful for creating vision

- three scenarios lead to the expectation that one is "the forecast"

- two scenarios allowed two very distinct (not necessarily "low" or "bad" vs "good" or "high") to be developed.

This approach is very different from the "baseline, high, low" approach, in that it concentrates on creating credible, but different, worlds for each scenario.

Meanwhile, since 1993 we had established a better framework for our futures work. This was to participate in external collaborations and consortia, with the aim of extending the range of ideas accessible to us: and to use scenarios as one way of "packaging"

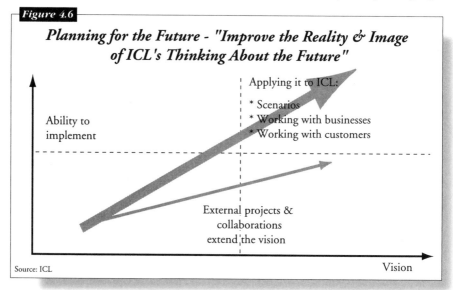

Figure 4.6

Planning for the Future - "Improve the Reality & Image of ICL's Thinking About the Future"

Ability to implement

Applying it to ICL:
* Scenarios
* Working with businesses
* Working with customers

External projects & collaborations extend the vision

Vision

Source: ICL

the most important ideas in the best way to help managers and planners in ICL to think about the future (Figure 4.6).

We investigated a number of sources of inspiration and ideas and discussion of the forces on the world. Two organizations in particular proved very helpful in extending our vision:

Global Business Network (GBN). This is an organization that aims to provide senior people in industry with stimulus through unusual ways of looking at the world and the future. One of the services provided is the "Network" of remarkable people; another is a bi-monthly mailing of a book selection. GBN was extremely useful in helping us to think about the social and individual contexts of the future (see Part II).

Business in the Third Millennium (BIT3M) is a programme planned to run over five years, to examine the effect of IT on business through its effect on consumers, government and society. It has sponsors like ourselves in Europe, and also in the US and Asia, since one of the aspects we are interested in is the cultural differences in the use of IT. One of the useful early outputs was a report on the nature and timescale of the IT infrastructure - what will these networks look like and when? (Part IV includes a description of scenarios for the Telecoms industry, developed as part of BIT3M.) The programme is run by SRI.

Methodology

In planning our methodology we investigated several sources:
GBN - which also runs training courses, and holds workshops several times per year.
Battelle Institute - which focuses around the health sciences/chemical industry axis, but has a general purpose methodology.
SRI - which has a well developed methodology and consulting practice.
IDON - which has a methodology oriented towards interactive, short timescale workshops, and a consulting practice.
Strategic Planning Society - which runs training workshops and conferences on topics including scenario planning.

The best overall guide to process that we found was the checklist in Peter Schwartz's "The Art of the Long View". (see Box below, and the full text in Part II.)

CHECKLIST FOR DEVELOPING SCENARIOS

Step One: Identify Focal Issue or Decision
Step Two: Key Forces in the Local Environment
Step Three: Driving Forces
Step Four: Rank by Importance and Uncertainty
Step Five: Selecting the Scenario Logics
Step Six: Fleshing out the Scenarios
Step Seven: Implications
Step Eight: Selection of Leading Indicators and Signposts

STARTING THE PROJECT

Scenarios for Information Markets in 2005.

Why Information Markets?
It had become clear to us that an information industry was being formed from the computer, telecoms, education and entertainment industries. We felt that the impact of this would revolutionize our markets over the next decade, as microprocessors have revolutionized the computer and electronic industries over the last decade.

Why 2005?
Our corporate planning period, the timescale over which the individual businesses plan, is three years. We plan at HQ over five years. What we wanted to do was to take a timescale that would not allow us to extrapolate forward, that was long enough to look afresh, but was not beyond imagination. In addition, to change the culture of a company of ICL's size takes ten years. So we voted for 2005.

Who would use the Scenarios?
The purpose of the project was to provide a framework for analysing the ICL portfolio, and for orienting it towards the areas in which our customers would be looking for help. This meant

that one audience was the Managing Directors and headquarters staff concerned with strategic planning. However, we decided that we also wanted the output to be accessible to managers who make day to day decisions; in ICL these manage units of 30-100 people.

A crucial step was to decide just what questions we wanted to answer about the future to help us in this. But even before that we had to gather a group together to do the project. The process we planned to follow was as shown in Figure 4.7.

In some environments it might be more suitable for a senior management team, or management team of a business unit, to engage in the process. What we decided was best to meet our aims was pull together a group of staff from HQ who could work with the businesses to explain and exploit the scenarios once they had been created, if necessary modify or extend them, and explore the implications.

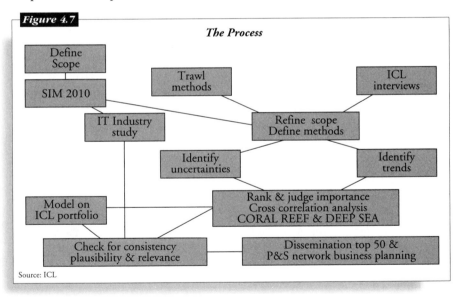

Figure 4.7

The Process

Source: ICL

The group consisted of:

- Paul Clayton: a business analyst who had done research into outsourcing and the changes in the computer services industry, with a MBA from Cranfield Institute of Technology.

- Laurent Douillet: a stockbroker and financial analyst from France who was on a mid-term break from an MBA at The Wharton School.

- Jane Dowsett: an economist by background with specialist experience in market research.

- Steve Parker: a business analyst with specialist expertise in the computer and telecoms industries.

- Gill Ringland: Group Executive with specialist expertise in software and the services industry.

Steve and Paul had done a short project (SIM2010) earlier in the year to look at the changes in the telecom industry: this was part of our background database. In fact, networking and the changes associated with increased bandwidth and decreased cost had the same central technology push role in the 1995 project that the decreasing price of processing had in the 1993 project.

We wanted the group to encompass diversity but also be reasonably empathetic to the concerns of the company, so that the company's assumptions and concerns were a central part of the scenario-building exercise. We decided to take the risk that having mainly ICL people might mean that important issues remained unidentified because of cultural blindness, since we wanted to explore the process, the methods, and crucially, how to use the scenarios with the two audiences, the HQ staff, and line managers.

The main project to build the scenarios ran over three months, with the group meeting twice a week for half a day, as well as carrying out research between meetings. No outside consultants were used, although we did discuss some of the outcomes during the project with Professor Gareth Price of the St. Andrews' Institute of Management.

The scale of the project seems typical of those creating broad spectrum scenarios, and is qualitatively different from that needed for the workshops used to create common vision and vocabulary and for team building. And since we were concerned to link to corporate planning we focused on two "near in" scenarios, rather than more diverse scenarios.

DEFINING THE QUESTION

One of the scenario team, Jane Dowsett, carried out a round of interviews with some 50 senior staff, both old timers and those new to ICL. Some were carried out over the phone, others were face to face. They were normally timed at half an hour: some interviewees got interested and discussed a range of ideas for several hours, others lasted only twenty minutes.

PRACTICAL TIPS ON THE INTERVIEW PROCESS

Consider carefully the number of interviews.
We aimed to get a range of views from different parts of the business, different countries, a mixture of senior board members and identified high flyers. The volume of information generated from these interviews made the analysis very time consuming: allow at least 2 hours per interview.

Plan how best to feed back the "internal" issues.
Much of the information concerns internal organization and culture. This needs to be packaged and fed into the relevant areas in the company, so that interviewees know that these ideas are not lost. But we decided to exclude these from the scenarios.

Confidentiality.
To get the best ideas and thoughts from people it is advisable to stress that individual comments will not be attributed. Some people were nervous about the fact that we taped the interviews, and asked for assurances on the security of storage of the tapes and the control of identification of the source of each script.

Setting the scene.
Ideally it is best to get people away from their desk and in a different environment, so they can think creatively. In practice,

> *the interview will be slotted into a busy senior managers schedule. In order to get people in the mood to think about the future and express their ideas, the interview needs to be relaxed and enjoyable. Most people find they jump around from one topic to another. It is best to try and encourage them rather than make the interview seem like a set of questions with right or wrong answers.*

The interviews had two objectives: to get management buy-in for the project and to understand what was the burning question for the organization.

In other words, sitting in 2005, what would we have liked to have known about in terms of political, economic, societal, environmental, technological and lifestyle trends ten years earlier? What was the "if only we had known that..." fact?

To unlock the answers, a set of seven questions was used. These questions were suggested by Gareth Price at a training session on scenario planning run by the Strategic Planning Society. The questions are those used by Shell. We amended question 7 slightly to ask:

"Imagine you are currently in 2005 and looking back on 1995:

a) What three things would you like to know?

b) What would you like to have done if all the constraints had been removed?"

We also added a question:

"How do you see ICL in the future?"

The reason for adding the ICL question was that many of the topics raised in pilot interviews concerned internal issues. Having an understanding of the person's view as to the type of company ICL would be in 10 years' time made analysing the internal issues easier.

SEVEN QUESTIONS FOR THE FUTURE

Most people have an understanding of how their world works, but often it is not voiced or shared. This questioning technique works on the basis that people know a great deal, but do not always know what they know.

These questions are to trigger thinking - the key is to understand the person's perceptions and unlock their strategic thinking. The technique could be used on an organization, a company, an industry or even a country. It should be done for a specific area of interest and over a relevant time scale.

The Vital Issues (the Oracle)
1. *Would you identify what you see as the critical issues for the future? (When the conversation slows, continue with the comment) Suppose I had full fore-knowledge of the outcome as a genuine clairvoyant, what else would you wish to know?*

A favourable outcome
2. *If things went well, being optimistic but realistic, talk about what you would see as a desirable outcome.*

An unfavourable outcome
3. *As the converse, if things went wrong, what factors would you worry about?*

Where culture will need to change
4. *Looking at internal systems, how might these need to be changed to help bring about the desired outcome?*

Lessons from past successes and failures
5. *Looking back, what would you identify as the significant events which have produced the current situation?*

Decisions which have to be faced
6. *Looking forward, what would you see as the priority actions which should be carried out soon?*

If you were responsible
7. *If all constraints were removed and you could direct what is done, what more would you wish to include? (The 'Epitaph' question.)*

Source: *Shell; Gareth Price, St. Andrews' Institute of Management*

The interview process referred to many external trends and other areas where staff were uncertain. Many of these could have come from a search of the literature. However by asking ICL senior management we were able to ensure they had covered what they considered as the key uncertainties for ICL. The resultant scenarios would then be relevant and challenging but not "shocking" enough to get in the way of their use.

We reviewed the interview scripts and created a list of 60 factors. When we analysed them we found that one-third of the interviewees explicitly raised, as a critical concern, what will be ICL's source of added value? And the question was implicit in the answers of another third of the interviewees.

We thus decided that in terms of the scenarios, we should focus on the question:

What added value will we provide to our customers in 2005?

We added the hypothesis that one source of added value would be working with our customers to "innovate to improve their business". The "opposite" to this would be to "minimize their risk".

SOURCES OF EXTERNAL DATA - THE DRIVERS

We found that the main problem was identifying the relevant data from the mass available. In the Vision 2000 and Software 2000 projects we had identified good sources for a wide range of IT industry data, telecoms research and on technology in general. For economic data, the Economist Intelligence Unit and the OECD provided good background.

The key to relevance is having a mental model of the factors which will be important, and populating the model with values for these.

In our case, we understood that our future would be in a restructured information industry. So data relating to consumer electronics, telecoms, publishing, media and professional services were important, in addition to the traditional computer industry.

We also knew that, although the business is global, being based in Europe is different from being based in the US. So data relating to the development of Europe, and its social model, was key to our scenarios.

Thus, populating the model with data should be straightforward. But, the problem is spotting which factors change radically when a paradigm changes, and which new dimensions or concerns may turn out to dominate a scenario. For instance, when do the changes in behaviour of individuals as the Information Society takes shape change the value chain for our customers? Are there other new developments which could change the rules?

The areas we found difficult were those relating to the wider information industry and to new developments like digital cash. For these consumer related sectors, we found that often the financial analysts were the best source of both data and opinion.

SCOPING THE DATA

We found that it was easy to get carried away in researching interesting trends, and following up ideas from futurists and newspaper or journal articles. We needed a discipline to constrain this: but we felt that to confine ourselves to issues explicitly identified in the interviews would have run the risk of missing major forces for change. So we decided to range fairly wide in our searches but, in developing the storyline of the scenarios, use examples which our target audience would recognize.

Two examples:

We read Huntingdon's "The Clash of Civilizations and the Remaking of World Order", with its argument that, following the end of the Cold War, the balance of power will change to one in which cultural communities are replacing the Cold War blocs, and the fault lines and conflicts are becoming those between civilizations rather than national states.

The implication of this for our scenarios was expressed in terms like *"The US and China continue trade hostilities over Chinese non-recognition of IPR, and the denial of US markets to China"*, and *"On the other hand the distinction between countries is blurred, with many sharing similar employment and inflation indicators. Fragmentation of regions along ethnic and cultural boundaries has been a feature"*.

We could see changes in social attitudes arising from the changing role of women and the disappearance of much traditional "heavy" man's work. We expressed the effect of this in the scenarios in ways which were directly relevant to ICL's markets e.g.

"Low economic growth has increased the gap between the unemployed and those in Mac jobs, and those in long term employment. Unemployment, especially among the young, who may be third generation unemployed, is increasingly a problem for governments, both as a financial burden and in terms of social unrest" and *"The level of economic growth and pace of change has eventually created a more mobile work force. More people are working but often less hours and in more flexible, less secure jobs. In some industries such as retailing and increasingly in financial services the majority of the workforce is made up of contract staff with no guaranteed income. The gap between the haves and have nots has increased. The bottom 10% of the population who are unskilled have found it increasingly difficult to get out of the poverty trap, and the social security safety net is weak"*.

On the other hand we tried to include in full the topics raised in the interviews, and to expand on them.

Developing the list of relevant factors

We added to the 60 factors that the interviewees had identified a number from our researches, e.g. the effect of 2 billion teenagers.

Figure 4.8

Sources and Methods

Data Sources	Methods
• Battelle	• Paul Schoemaker
• Shell	• GBN
• WEFA Group	• Shell
• CCA/ITC/Zenith	• IDON
• Market Analysis	• St Andrews' Mgt Institute
• Chatham House	• Battelle
• IDC	• SRI
• OECD	
• Vision 2000 & sources	
• Software 2000 & sources	

Source: ICL

We categorized the factors as either trends or uncertainties.

A view of the trends is derived from the best available sources, and from wide agreement. "Uncertainties" in the jargon, are *"factors over which there are major question marks"*. So, for instance, the continuing increase in processing power at a given price is a trend. However, it is uncertain whether consumers will switch from TV to PCs as a result.

The trends were collated from a number of sources and reflected "best educated guesses" about directions. These would be common to all the scenarios. A judgement was taken on which trends were already incorporated in ICL's thinking and processes. For instance, the decreasing role of national governments in Europe and the increasing reliability of hardware are all significant, but perhaps no longer needed spelling out.

Even with a well-understood trend, there could be surprises in the pace at which the trends would develop. So that forecasting, even based on trends, is a fraught exercise.

Figure 4.9

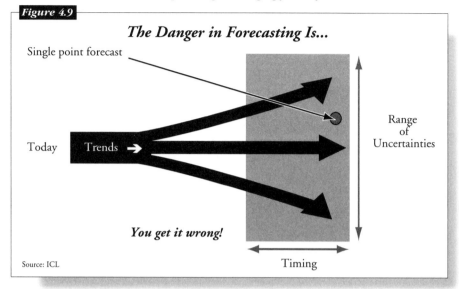

The Danger in Forecasting Is...

Single point forecast

Today Trends →

Range of Uncertainties

You get it wrong!

Source: ICL

Timing

THE TRENDS

Trends are more likely to be seen in two areas: those related to demographics and those related to technology. While surprises can occur - for instance between censuses in the US, the size and pattern of Catholic immigrant families changed the predicted demographic balance significantly - these are rarer than in the political or social arenas.

Economic/Geographic Trends

1. *Increasingly sophisticated and demanding customers.*
   More and more educated consumers ask for up-to-date, high performance and competitive products. The mass market will be fragmented into many niches. Competition will be fierce and based on price and quality of service.

2. *Growth in South East Asia/India/China, with an expanding middle class.*
   In 2010, the middle class in South East Asia (about 700 million) will be larger than that of Europe (about 300 million) and the Americas (about 200 million) combined.

3. Two billion teenagers.

In 2001, there will be two billion teenagers world-wide, most of them in Asia and Latin America. That is fifty times the number of teenagers in America in the peak years of the baby boom. Many of them will be in constant contact with each other through technology.

4. Increase in the older population in industrial countries.

Medical advances and better life conditions leads to the ageing of the population, mainly in developed countries where the birth rates are low. The demographic shift to an ageing population will require adjustment in many service industries like healthcare, leisure and travel. As the costs of the elderly, particularly with health, increases, service industries and governments will look for areas of productivity through IT.

5. Continuous restructuring of corporations.

The restructuring of corporations will be dominated by the following trends: globalization of markets, outsourcing of non-strategic jobs, and investments directed to the regions which offer the best profit potential. An increasing number of small companies will be linked through networks. Competition for customers will be intense and delocalized.

6. Outsourcing of IT is used by half of all Fortune 500 companies.

This trend will change the structure of the IT industry: there will be large potential growth for outsourcing and technology used as a support of outsourcing businesses.

7. Increasing environmental concerns.

More environmental concerns force companies on occasion to do business differently. It has positive implications in the sense of more business and some negative ones with possible increases in production costs to conform to environmental pressures.

Technology-Related Trends

1. Bandwidth explosion and development of the Internet.

Large infrastructure investments to increase cable and wireless networks. Both the volume of traffic increases due to price decreases, and the opportunities for exploiting high bandwidth networking. The Internet continues to grow.

2. *Processing power increases and processing becomes pervasive.*
Moore's law of the power of processing on a chip doubling every 18 months continues to apply for products shipped over the next decade. New generation of more powerful microprocessors emerge. However, the costs of developing those new chips are high. Processing will be used in more mission-critical applications. There will be an increasing use of embedded systems, and more IT devices will be available.

3. *Ease of use.*
Computers and electronic devices will be more and more friendly.

4. *Digitalization of content and growth of multimedia.*
Information is held digitally, whether context is text, video or audio. Games, videos, media will be delivered either on electronic storage as an alternative to paper, or increasingly through on-line services.

5. *Changes in sources of value added in the IT industry.*
As the industry matures, IT will be increasingly embedded in products. New sources of value added relate to ease of use, access, information security etc.

6. *Litigation in IT increases.*
The risk for IT providers of being sued for misperformance or non-performance increases.

7. *Semiconductor content of electronics increases.*
The content of electronics devices changes from 7% semiconductor to 27% semiconductor over 15 years to 2000. This changes the power and added value in the information industry.

DEALING WITH UNCERTAINTIES

Scenarios are constructed from a number of trends - as above - and a number of uncertainties. For instance, while the change in processing power or bandwidth is clearly a trend, the question of whether a consumer market will open up can be treated as an uncertainty: we need to think about the effects if it does, or if it does not.

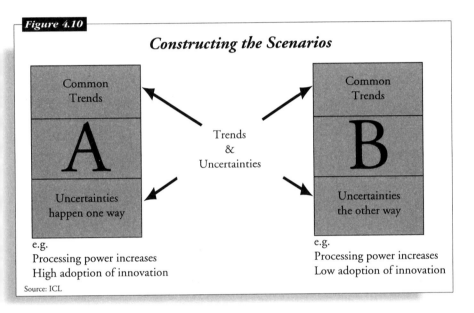

Figure 4.10

Constructing the Scenarios

Common Trends

A

Uncertainties happen one way

Trends & Uncertainties

Common Trends

B

Uncertainties the other way

e.g.
Processing power increases
High adoption of innovation

e.g.
Processing power increases
Low adoption of innovation

Source: ICL

Figure 4.10 represents this difference, using as an example our core uncertainty - will customers want to take advantage of the technically feasible innovations or will there be a backlash? Figure 4.11 shows the factors that we regarded as uncertain, and how we grouped them.

Some of the factors that we had initially identified were seen to be important to us, but with an unpredictable outcome in ten years' time. For each of these uncertain factors we built a correlation matrix looking to see how they related to each other. For example, did one increase, decrease or remain unaffected by another?

The intellectual activity to correlate these was one of the hardest of the project. For each factor, we determined whether it was positively correlated against every other (on a scale 1 to 3), negatively, or not at all (0). Then the factors were sorted, giving the list below in Figure 4.11.

Figure 4.11

Grouping The Uncertainties

Shift in technological innovation to SE Asia	5.1	Fragmented industry	-2.9
Loss of government control on info flows	4.3	No terrorism	-1.8
Economic power shift to SE Asia	4.1	No hostilities	-1.1
Greater economies of scale in technology	4.0	Monetary instability	-0.5
Consumer marketing dominates	4.0	Individualism	0.5
Chance of major breakthrough in technology	3.8	No immigration backlash	1.0
High adoption of innovation, e.g. multimedia	3.3	No earthquake	1.3
Major IT disasters	3.0	Large professional services organizations	1.7
High economic growth	2.8	EU same	2.7
Bigger and deeper EU	2.7	Low growth	2.8
Boutiques	1.7	No IT disaster	3.0
Major earthquake in USA or Japan	1.3	Low adoption of multimedia	3.3
Immigration backlash	1.0	No major changes in technology	3.8
Move towards community values	0.5	Business to business marketing	4.0
Monetary stability	-0.5	Same economies of scale in technology	4.0
Hostilities evolving major trading blocks	-1.1	No economic power shift to SE Asia	4.1
More terrorist actions	-1.8	Gvt keeps control of info	4.3
Full range suppliers strong	-2.9	No technical innovation shift to SE Asia	5.1

Some of the factors were inherently unknowable and not causally linked to any of the others - for instance, the occurrence of a major earthquake in the USA was not caused by any of the other factors - though it could contribute to a factor like "more terrorist actions". The factors which were not linked were called "wild cards". We found that the best way of treating these was to identify where in the organization the policy for dealing with these should rest, and discussing them, exploring the processes and responsibilities, and getting policies established, rather than building them into the scenarios.

We then saw a pattern, in which four themes emerged.

1. The degree of influence/power exerted by governments.
- What will be the balance between government-imposed

regulation and self-regulation?

- Will governments regulate to protect national cultures?

- Will government be able to control cross-border information flows and electronic commerce?

2. Social values.
- How important will be environmental concerns?

- Will individual or community values predominate?

- What will be the level and forms of security threats?

3. Consumer behaviour.
- Willingness to take on risks

- What will be the buying points in large organizations?

- Will consumers become tired of constant change?

- How IT literate will they be or need to be?

4. The shape and degree of global trade.
- What will be the degree of intra-block trade? Of inter-block trade?

- What will be the impact on the West of economic growth in Asia?

The major ranges of uncertainties could be grouped into these four broad headings i.e.

- regulation/deregulation,
- community values/individualism,
- innovation/technophobia,
- open cultures and trading/closed cultures and restricted world trade.

GROUPING IDEAS

Grouping ideas into connected themes is an important precursor to building a storyline. One technique which is widely used has been developed by IDON (see "IDON Scenario Thinking: How to navigate the Uncertainties of Unknown Futures" by Miriam Galt et al 1997). IDON uses coloured, magnetic hexagons, on which topics can be written. The hexagons can then be moved around on a whiteboard until the team are happy with the groupings and can name the themes. This turns out be a very effective way of morphing a shape for the eventual scenarios.

As Arie de Geus explains in the book's foreword, *"Scenarios are internally consistent stories of possible futures - they are the scenery into which the actors walk. The walk is initiated by the meeting addressing the question 'What would we do if this scenario came about?' The many answers to that question become the options that are open to the company under a variety of futures. Those options are expressed by the meeting in words - they create a language for them. Henceforth they can talk about these options in quite precise terms and they will remember the words - they have created a memory of their future! This memory will be extremely useful when the future comes - as it invariably does. The company knows what to look out for and it is better prepared for action.*

Talking and creating language in a meeting of corporate individuals is not as easy as it sounds. Many things can go wrong, and do go wrong. People talk but do not listen. Power positions are abused. Emotions take over.

This is where hexagons/idons have a proven track record. They help people calibrate the way they are thinking about the present. They help the group to see relationships and dynamics that are essential to understand the options that are open to them. With attention focused toward the whiteboard, on the idons and not on individual people, thinking is convergent - language becomes concise. Hexagons are powerful tools to help develop the language in which the institutional learning is embodied and which will form the institutional memory. A well-developed memory of the future is a pre-condition for the company to be pro-active rather than reactive - to make its own future rather than submit to it."

BUILDING A STORYLINE

These groupings helped us to begin to build up the storyline of how the world might look in two different scenarios. We linked open cultures and trading, deregulation/less government, individual values, and innovation, because of their correlations, and built up scenarios of two different worlds, shown as inner and outer circles in Figure 4.12.

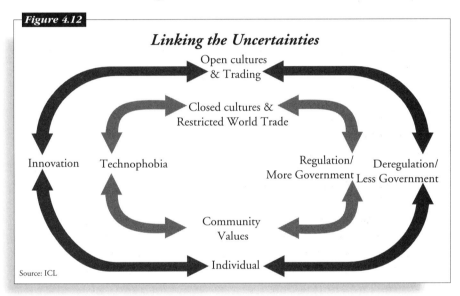

Figure 4.12

Linking the Uncertainties

Open cultures & Trading

Closed cultures & Restricted World Trade

Innovation   Technophobia

Regulation/ More Government   Deregulation/ Less Government

Community Values

Individual

Source: ICL

While having reached a set of themes helped us, it would not have been enough to communicate either to headquarters staff or to management. To provide hooks for engagement we adopted two illumination aids:

- populating it with a storyline, relating to events, geographies, people;

- offering early warning signs or indicators of each scenario.

So for instance a pair of alternative answers to an uncertainty about the style of marketing, either "consumer marketing dominates" vs "business to business marketing" (see Figure 4.11) became in the scenarios:

"Consumer style marketing techniques dominate, smaller boutique style companies are successful. Added value through innovation and marketing as seen by the customer.

Products and operational services - e.g. help desks, maintenance - are marketed to those who will use them. Purchasing decisions will be made by the individuals for themselves or possibly on behalf of a small group, whether for business or leisure use. This applies for smaller new systems too, driven by cost factors. Only for large infrastructure projects, and complex roll-outs, are business-to-business marketing techniques used.

Innovation in products and marketing are mostly introduced by small companies and quickly copied or bought out by the global players. Innovation in marketing and distribution is as important as innovations in technology. Small boutique style companies specialize - maybe globally - in detailed knowledge of an area, and establish presence through electronic marketing and word of mouth.

Advertising over the network subsidizes payment for content.

Outsourcing of information systems is booming as many organizations find that managing information systems is a management distraction. Start-ups using facilities in Asia dominate this market through their front men in North America."

The "business to business" polarity became:

"Business to business marketing style across the information industry.

Long term customer-supplier relationships are cemented through frame agreements and loyalty schemes.

The big full-range vendors dominate the Fortune 1000 and government, using direct and indirect channels. Outsourcing is concentrated in these organizations, and profit margins are vanishingly thin, with the full range vendors taking their profits on hardware and software supply.

Smaller companies are served by small value added resellers who supply hardware and software primarily based on price criteria.

Individual consumers find that vendors regard them as poor relations."

We discuss the early indicators below.

All in the name
We believe that one reason that this project worked better than our 1993 project was that we came up with names for the scenarios which described the essence of what they were about. The names had to act as metaphors so that when we were talking about a scenario we could use the name as an evocative short-cut, to give people an instant and intuitive picture of each scenario, thus providing a framework into which detail could be added.

At first we toyed with names like "Chinese meals" versus "Hungarian Hot Pot". The Hungarian Hot Pot was stodgy and could describe the scenario without much innovation, while the Chinese meal could apply to the more short-lived scenario.

However, these were not really satisfactory and after much discussion and brainstorming the names emerged: Coral Reef and Deep Sea.

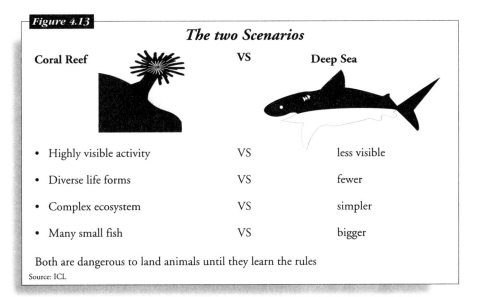

Figure 4.13

The two Scenarios

Coral Reef	VS	Deep Sea
• Highly visible activity	VS	less visible
• Diverse life forms	VS	fewer
• Complex ecosystem	VS	simpler
• Many small fish	VS	bigger

Both are dangerous to land animals until they learn the rules

Source: ICL

They seemed to fit well because of the intuitive behaviour which each describes. The Coral Reef world is very diverse, with much visible activity and complex food chains. There are many small fish. The Deep Sea world is less diverse, with fewer species of mainly larger fish. It is a simpler world in many ways. And for people who have reflexes formed on land, both the Coral Reef and Deep Sea can be dangerous places unless the reflexes are retrained: for instance, the natural response to danger under the water is to hold the breath and come to the surface. But if you have been breathing from a scuba tank, this is a way to die painlessly with an ascent of even less than 10 feet.

The moral is: training for the new environment is what scenarios are about, i.e. trying out for a possible future environment.

Figure 4.14

Deep Sea Characteristics

- Economic Background

  - Restricted economic growth due to:

    - Protectionist economies

    - Environmental and/or security threats

- Competitive Environment

  - Regulation and high barriers to entry

  - Major mergers between content/telecom

    companies

  - Niche high value segments

  - Local champions

Source: ICL

- Telecoms Infrastructure

  - Closed networks

  - Broadband only in some major centres

    of population

- Strongest Players

  - Best balance between content/

    network/access

INFORMATION MARKETS IN 2005

In creating the scenarios we developed separate storylines for each. This took as much effort as the step to correlate the factors: and it needed a divergent style of thinking rather than pure analysis. The storylines and early indicators proved to be the second major tool for communication and engagement, after the names of the scenarios. See "Composing a plot for your scenario", (Schwartz, 1992).

The full scenarios are given in Part IV.

Figure 4.15 is a summary of the characteristics of the Coral Reef, and Figure 4.14 of the Deep Sea world.

Figure 4.15

Coral Reef Characteristics

- Economic Background

  - High economic growth

  - Globally interconnected

    economies

- Competitive Environment

  - Highly competitive - survival

    of the fittest

  - Global specialist players

  - Many local niche players

- Telecoms Infrastructure

  - Open, high bandwidth networks

  - Universal broadband

- Strongest Players

  - Highest quality content

  - Best price/performance

    networks

  - Most convenient devices

Source: ICL

We then applied these scenarios to the Information Industry.

Coral Reef

Under the Coral Reef scenario the demanding and sophisticated customer outsources or purchases systems integration because of the potential for IT to change the business and is interested in new technology. Coral Reef is largely deregulated or self-regulated, while Deep Sea is regulated. Coral Reef exploits energy and innovation, with growth from Asia and new businesses in new areas.

An example of the differences is how information would be supplied to customers over networks. In Coral Reef, a multiplicity of devices would connect to a number of competing services, with price wars and confusion (see Figure 4.16).

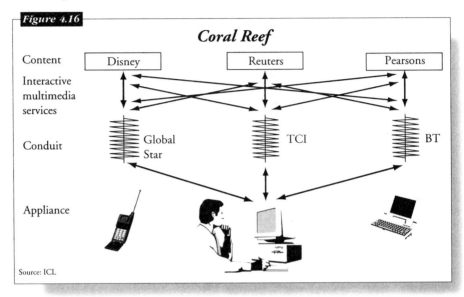

Figure 4.16

Coral Reef

Source: ICL

We thought that early indicators of a world behaving like the Coral Reef could include:

1. Bill deregulating US markets passed in 1995, European countries meeting their deadlines, and Japan deregulating in 1999.

2. AT&T sells NCR, or Siemens sells SNI, or Olivetti sells the PC business.

3. Spin-offs increase relative to mergers in the media business.

4. Digital sells its semiconductor business to Texas Investments (TI), and TI sells its software business to Computer Automation.

5. Semiconductor market share (for companies with HQs) in Asia

Pacific (including Japan) exceeds that of Europe and North America in 1996.

6. Fabrication capacity in Asia (excluding Japan) exceeds that in Japan, Europe and North America combined by 2000.

7. US and China establish a trade treaty in 1996

8. Microsoft and Intel have been constrained by anti-trust legislation.

Deep Sea

In this scenario, we see Europe and the US reacting somewhat negatively to changes in world balance. Under Deep Sea, the demanding and sophisticated customers outsource or purchase systems integration because it is not their core business. They are interested in a full range supplier taking the risk and reducing cost.

What the consumer might see in the Deep Sea world is shown in Figure 4.17. Here the range of offerings is smaller, with a lower bandwidth offering as the norm - so less possibility of movies on-

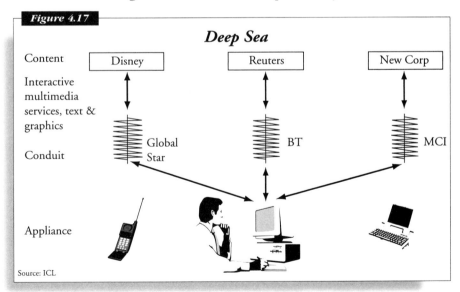

Figure 4.17

Deep Sea

Content

Interactive multimedia services, text & graphics

Conduit

Appliance

Disney   Reuters   New Corp

Global Star   BT   MCI

Source: ICL

line. The devices would be packaged with the network, and only work with one service provider.

Early indicators of Deep Sea could include:

1. The early indicators of Coral Reef are not seen, e.g. the number of mergers increases relative to the number of spin-offs.

2. UK, Spain & Denmark isolated at the 1996 Maastricht conference. US imposes punitive tax on a very visible Japanese export.

3. Successful lobbying of European governments to introduce tough new penalties to combat crime

4. Windows 95 fails to meet expected shipments in Europe, compared to its take up in the US.

But of course, neither scenario is a forecast, and so neither will happen. There will be elements of both scenarios in the actual outcome, while they may also co-exist in different segments and geographies, For example, the US may be more like Coral Reef while Europe may be more Deep Sea-like.

COMMUNICATING THE SCENARIOS

In communicating the scenarios, we have already discussed the importance of a name which conveys the right picture and associations for the scenarios.

Additionally, we prepared and circulated back to the group of managers that we had interviewed:

- a summary, with an offer to come and talk through the scenarios;

- a slide set;

- a glossy booklet, using images to convey the excitement and dangers of taking a view of the future.

TIMESCALE AND RESOURCING

January 1995
- start of project with work on the "new" information industry - Paul Clayton and Steve Parker

March
- Strategic Planning Society course - Jane Dowsett

April
- GBN workshop on building scenarios - Jane Dowsett

May
- start data collection - Steve Parker, Laurent Douillett, Gill Ringland, Paul Clayton

June
- start interviews - Jane Dowsett

July
- start building lists of factors, divide into trends and uncertainties - group working, several half-days per week

- analyse interviews - Jane Dowsett & Gill Ringland

August
- build correlation matrix - group working, half-days

- research on key topics e.g. electronic cash - Paul Clayton

- define the names and factors in each scenario, build storylines & early indicators - group working, half-days

- extract "wild cards"

September
- discuss with other HQ & senior staff, external experts

October
- feed back to interviewees and management team

We gave briefings to a number of groups inside ICL, e.g. the Policy & Strategy Network of corporate planners, the Client Managers and the Board, and included questions relating to dealing with uncertainty in the planning guidelines.

Lessons learned

In setting up the Information Markets project, we had learned some lessons from the project in 1993. These included:

- Take time and do enough research to make sure the right questions are being asked.

- The group should combine discipline with free-thinking, and work on the principle that no one is right or wrong. That discipline can come from a strong leader or from a shared vision, which is the way ICL works. That shared vision of what it is you are trying to do, and how exciting and even fun it is, is only effective if you are going to be able to tell other people about it, which means getting to an outcome by a defined time. Someone needs to own the process and outcomes.

- The group needs to be made up of a fairly disparate set of interests and backgrounds and approaches but be capable of sharing a language. Not only do you need experts on your industry, but it is also helpful to have different nationalities. We were too UK-oriented: the ideal balance for us would have been 50% UK, with representatives from the US, perhaps Japan and the Nordic countries.

- The scenarios must be relevant to the business in order to convince what can be sceptical line managers about their usefulness in creating fresher mental models.

- Use of a name for the scenarios which helped understanding at an intuitive level.

- Developing a storyline to help add dimensions to the scenarios, and to emphasize that they are not forecasts.

Even with the extra emphasis on communication of the scenarios, we found that none of the communication mechanisms worked without personal input from a member of the team. With that ingredient, we were able to tackle a range of situations.

In the next chapter we will look at how the scenarios have been used. This will bring out some more lessons.

CHAPTER FIVE

Linking Scenarios to Strategic Planning

SUMMARY

This chapter discusses using the scenarios, built as described in Chapter 4, in ICL's strategic planning. Four applications are discussed: applying the scenarios to Information Markets; a sensitivity analysis/risk assessment of an investment portfolio; linking scenarios to a PIMS and MA/C analysis; and using the scenarios to build a more robust strategy

APPLYING SCENARIOS

Scenarios are about ideas, and ideas are notoriously difficult to communicate. The techniques which will work depend on the intended audience and the environment in which they are operating. The methods used to communicate the scenarios will depend on who is going to use the scenarios and for what.

Kees van der Heijden, in his "Scenarios, the Art of Strategic Conversation", emphasizes the central role of scenario thinking in providing laboratories in which different models of the future environment can be tested: see Figure 5.1.

Within this framework, we see five different uses for scenarios (see Box "Using Scenarios Strategically", below).

• Sensitivity/Risk Assessment: using scenarios as a "wind tunnel" for projects or investments, as was needed with Managing Directors who had an investment portfolio of new projects;

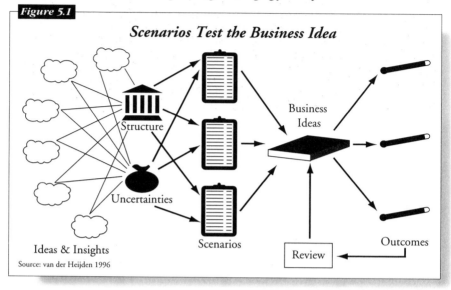

Figure 5.1

Scenarios Test the Business Idea

Source: van der Heijden 1996

- Strategy Evaluation: testing a strategy made on the basis of forecasts against possible other outcomes, as in the case of proposed disposals;

- Strategy Development: Using a "Planning-Focus" Scenario within a management team to build a more robust strategy, as with the HQ staff looking to improve the overall portfolio;

- Strategy Development: Without using a "Planning Focus" Scenario - taking a wide range of scenarios and testing strategies against them;

- Skills: using scenarios to reduce fear, uncertainty and doubt (FUD) and help formulate training and recruitment needs (e.g. ICL's Project Leonardo discussed below).

The form of representation of the scenarios needs to be different from the first two essentially analytic uses - and the last three - where the task is to synthesize strategies.

USING SCENARIOS STRATEGICALLY

In "How Companies Use Scenarios: Practices and Prescription", an SRI Business Intelligence Programme Report, Thomas F Mandel and Ian Wilson write that the scenarios should not be seen as an end in themselves but as a management tool to improve the quality of decision-making. However, this skill requires considerable sophistication and takes time to acquire. Corporations need a primer, a step-by-step guide for using scenarios to make strategic decisions (see Table 5.1).

TABLE 5.1 USING SCENARIOS STRATEGICALLY: A COMPARISON OF SELECTED APPROACHES.

Application	Steps	Evaluation
Sensitivity/Risk Assessment • Best use: Evaluate a specific decision (such as a major plant investment or new business development). • Approach: Use computer modelling (with scenarios providing assumptions) or simple judgement assessments to evaluate the strategy's resilience or vulnerability to differences in business conditions.	• Identify key conditions in the future market/industry environment (such as size/growth of market, changes in regulatory climate, or a technological breakthrough) that would be necessary for a "go" decision. • Describe and assess the state of these conditions in each scenario. • Compare the scenario conditions with the desired future conditions, and evaluate the likely success/failure and resilience/vulnerability of a "go" decision in each scenario. • Evaluate the overall	• Offers relatively simple, straightforward application in a series of descriptive and judgemental steps. • Depends on a very clear and specific "decision focus" that lends itself to a "go/no go" decision.

Application	Steps	Evaluation
	resilience or vulnerability of a "go" decision, assessing the desirability of hedging or modifying the original decision.	
Strategy Evaluation •Best use: Use scenarios as "test beds" to evaluate the viability of an existing strategy (usually one that derives from a single-point forecast). •Approach: Play a companywide, business unit or competitor's strategy against the scenarios to assess the strategy's effectiveness in a range of business conditions; identify modifications and/or contingency planning that require attention	•Disaggregate the strategy into its specific thrusts (Focus on consumer market segments in etc,) and state objectives and goals. •Assess the relevance and likely success of these thrusts in the diverse conditions of the scenarios. •Analyse the results of this impact analysis to identify: 1. Opportunities that the strategy addresses and those that it misses. 2. Threats/risks that the analysis has foreseen or overlooked. 3. Comparative competitive success or failure. •Identify options for changes in strategy and the need for contingency planning.	•Offers natural first use of scenarios in company's strategic-planning system. •Quickly identifies "bottom-line" issues and provides senior managers with immediate evidence of scenarios' utility (particularly when the company links it with competitive analysis.
Strategy Development - Using a "Planning-Focus" Scenario •Best use: To accommodate	•Review scenarios to identify strategic	•Flies in the face of strict scenario theory (by

Application	Steps	Evaluation
management culture, use as a starting point for strategy development. •Approach: Develop strategy to deal with the conditions of one scenario and then test it against other scenarios to assess resilience and the need for modification, "hedging", and contingency planning.	opportunities and threats for the business - in each scenario and across all scenarios. •Determine what the company should do and not do in any case. •Select a "planning focus" scenario (usually the most probable one). •Integrate the product of the preceding steps into a coherent strategy for this scenario. •Test this strategy against the remaining scenarios to assess its resilience or vulnerability. •Review the results of this test to determine the need for strategy modification, "hedging" and contingency planning.	dealing with probabilities) but can be a useful intermediate step in weaning executives from reliance on single-point forecasting •In its step-by-step process, addresses many key questions that scenario-based strategy should ask; avoids the pitfall of focusing on only one scenario.
Strategy Development - Without Using a "Planning Focus" Scenario •Best use: Takes all scenarios at face value, without judging probabilities. •Approach: Develop a "resilient" strategy that can deal with wide variations in business conditions.	•Identify the key elements of a successful strategy (such as geographic scope, market focus, basis of competition or technology). •Analyze each scenario to determine the	•Most closely approximates the goal of strategizing within the scenarios framework and makes optimal use of scenarios in strategy development. •Provides management with the maximum

Application	Steps	Evaluation
	optimal setting for each element (What would be the best marketing strategy for Scenario A? For B?) •Review these scenario-specific settings and determine the most resilient option for each strategy element. •Integrate these options into an overall, co-ordinated business strategy.	feasible range of choice and forces careful evaluation of these options against differing assumptions about the future. •Requires effort and patience; works best when the decision-makers participate directly in the scenario process.
Source: SRI International		

For analytic uses, where the scenarios have been based on extensive political, economic, social and technology (PEST) data gathering and analysis, and the scope chosen to fit the potential audiences, the task is somewhat easier. This is the realm in which integration with a planning process, the use of checklists, and quantitative approaches, is considered feasible.

But even in this environment, Shell finds it useful to produce well-written, colour publications to describe the scenarios, as a prelude to working in detail with the businesses.

Our experience accords with this, as discussed in Chapter 4, we found that it was essential to have:

- a "lift (elevator) speech";

- vivid names, and a glossy "storyline" booklet helped;

- clear representation of "the question";

- memorable incidents on the timeline;

- a good storyline and coherence that people found credible;

- a process by which the scenarios can be used by the organization.

The latter point, the lack of a process including scenarios, was in many ways our immediate hurdle: the organization's strategic planning process could be extended to include scenarios, but was this right for all nine businesses?

Instead of trying to apply scenario thinking with each of the individual businesses across the organization we decided to apply Coral Reef and Deep Sea to specific problems, or to issues in specific businesses.

APPLYING THE SCENARIOS TO INFORMATION MARKETS

Before we began to apply what we had learned from the scenarios to the business portfolio, we analysed the sectors of the digital Information Industry in 2005 (as in Figure 4.4) in the context of the scenarios.

There were a number of findings, some of which surprised us - for instance delivery and logistics organizations thrived under the "innovative" and electronic Coral Reef scenario (see Table 5.2) and less so under the risk-averse Deep Sea scenario.

TABLE 5.2 THE EFFECT ON THE INFORMATION INDUSTRY SECTORS

Office equipment: Under Coral Reef that market disappears into the computer and consumer electronic markets. Under Deep Sea the same happens, but revenues do not decline as quickly.

Telecoms: Under Coral Reef voice profitability decreases, with many new entrants and a high growth in non-voice traffic. With Deep Sea, voice profitability holds, with few new entrants and lower growth in data traffic.

Distribution: Under Coral Reef, the number of broadcast channels increase, and mail is largely electronic although parcel mail increases. Revenues grow, whereas under Deep Sea they decrease.

Marketing and Advertising: Coral Reef shows high growth of

---

electronic commerce in business and consumer sectors, with huge growth in on-line advertising: $37 million now to $2 billion in 2000. In Deep Sea, the growth of electronic commerce is limited to the business sector.

Computer Systems and Services: *Coral Reef shows high growth and rate of change, with more companies restructuring, and increase in mobiles and a growth in complex devices. PCs may have different architectures. In Deep Sea, there is lower growth and pace of change.*

Consumer Electronics: *Coral Reef shows huge growth which is innovation-led. Deep Sea has lower growth.*

Media and Publishing: *In Coral Reef business use increases, with high growth among the connected and CD-ROM and Networks prominent. There is a move to transaction pricing from product pricing. There is lower growth in Deep Sea, with home use stabilising on CD-ROM.*

LINKING TO A NEW INVESTMENT PORTFOLIO

One of the ICL Board, John Davison, had spent the previous two years with a remit to develop starter skills and market knowledge to enter a range of new markets associated with multi-media and the Internet. At the time we were finishing the scenarios work, he had a portfolio of seven possible projects. We tried several techniques for analysing the projects in terms of the scenarios. The purpose of the exercise was to help resilience-test the new venture business plans, which had been written with a knowledge of today's environment and technology.

First we used the factor analysis (as given in Chapter 4) to "mark" each of the projects. For each of the factors (seven social/economic, seven technological) we looked at each project to see if it was very much accelerated by the trend, in which case it was scored +3, or alternatively it was very much hindered, in which case it was given -3. For lesser effects we used lesser scores. And for each of the six headings in each of the scenarios we did the same.

As Table 5.3 shows, the projects had very different profiles. All, as might be expected, were assisted by the technology trends. And some, like Project 6, were resilient against the choice of a scenario and did well in both. But others, like Project 2 and Project 3, were negative or neutral against Coral Reef or Deep Sea criteria: while Project 5 was a much better investment choice in a Coral Reef world.

TABLE 5.3 SCORING THE PROJECTS					
	Social economic	Technology	Coral Reef	Deep Sea	Total
Project 1	3	14	9	0	26
Project 2	3	13	-1	1	16
Project 3	4	11	0	-2	13
Project 4	12	14	9	1	36
Project 5	3	11	8	0	22
Project 6	12	16	8	9	45
Project 7	7	14	10	8	39

Having spent several hours discussing each of the projects in relation to each of the points, and coming up with a view of which were the strong contenders, and which were very dependent on one scenario or another, we were able to see which of the projects we would forge ahead with and which ones we could only consider doing some other way such as merging with another business.

We realized as a result of this discussion that it was quite difficult to apply all the factors captured in a particular paragraph of the scenario to a whole business because there were many factors and multi-faceted businesses.

So when we started to look at the total ICL portfolio of businesses, we instead used the Market Attractiveness/Capability (MA/C) matrix, which described the constituents of a business. This meant more analysis but a more accurate overall assessment.

LINKING TO THE PIMS AND MA/C ANALYSIS

Two businesses had been proposed for disposal after analysis of their competitive position using PIMS, and the MA/C matrix, as discussed in Chapter 3.

The case of D2D.
The first was D2D, our contract manufacturing business which among other things makes the terminals for the UK's lottery company, Camelot, and for a number of PC, telecoms and computer suppliers. At the time we had just finished the scenarios, D2D was primed to write a business plan that would be a realistic guide to a potential purchaser, following the work described in Chapter 3 to assess its fit within the ICL portfolio.

When we discussed the business plan with the management team, we realized that the plans were based on a default scenario which was very like Coral Reef. This reflects the attitude of many people in the computer business: they are enthusiastic and have often joined the computer business because they enjoy innovation and find the pace of business in information technology to be fun.

So we then asked the question - what happens if the world is more like the Deep Sea scenario? Are the customers of subcontract electronic manufacturing mostly in markets which are very innovative or are most of the markets characterized by risk-avoidance, outsourcing of manufacturing to minimize risk in existing business? This would be more like the Deep Sea scenario.

Obviously there are customers who follow both paradigms but the overall shape of the subcontract electronic manufacturing business when we looked at it in more detail was dominated to an extent by risk minimization. So a number of the characteristics that D2D had assumed had very high value were of less interest to the customers than the business had supposed. The likely direction of the business was further away from innovation, and more towards low risk manufacturing.

The business plan was rewritten, and the business was sold to a multi-national contract manufacturer in December 1996.

The case of volume products

As Chapter 3 showed, ICL's volume products (PC) business was in ninth place in terms of size. Analysis with PIMS highlighted the fact that the cost and profit structure of volume products was almost exactly what the PIMS database said it would be. The results also showed that a PC manufacturer has to be in the top four to make money.

Further work analysing the critical success factors of volume products backed up this view that PC manufacturing demands global scale, a global brand and low cost production. At the same time, applying the scenarios to the business provided confirmation that the environment for PCs was clearly moving to dominance by a few global players. This is more like the Deep Sea environment and made Fujitsu a more natural home for the business, i.e. a better parent.

Fujitsu took over the ICL PC business in July, 1996.

Assessing the total portfolio

We had previously created a matrix for our businesses as in Figure 5.2.

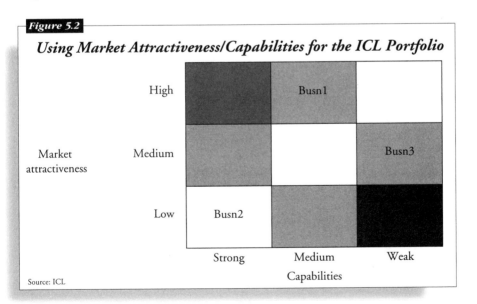

Figure 5.2

Using Market Attractiveness/Capabilities for the ICL Portfolio

Source: ICL

In applying the Coral Reef and Deep Sea scenarios to the ICL portfolio of businesses, we had seen in general terms (see Chapter 4) that there were some major differences.

For instance, under the Coral Reef scenario, demanding and sophisticated customers outsource or purchase systems integration because of the potential for IT to change their business, and are interested in new technology. Under Deep Sea, the demanding and sophisticated customers outsource or purchase systems integration because IT is not their core business. They are interested in a full-range supplier taking the risk and reducing cost.

So we decided to investigate, as a headquarters team, the different effects of the scenarios on our business portfolio. We used a staff training event for senior people to work as a task force on the analysis of the portfolio against the two scenarios.

The group was divided into two teams, one a Coral Reef world management team and the other a Deep Sea world management team. Each was asked to assess the ICL portfolio in 2005 using questions about the Market Attractiveness and the Capabilities (see Figure 5.3).

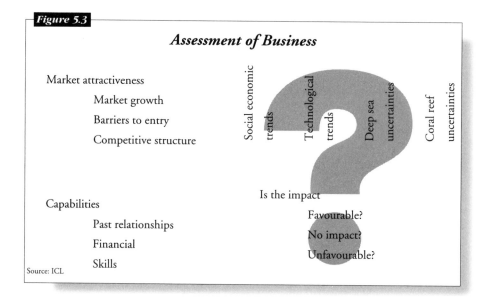

Figure 5.3

Assessment of Business

Market attractiveness
- Market growth
- Barriers to entry
- Competitive structure

Social economic trends • Technological trends • Deep sea uncertainties • Coral reef uncertainties

Capabilities
- Past relationships
- Financial
- Skills

Is the impact
Favourable?
No impact?
Unfavourable?

Source: ICL

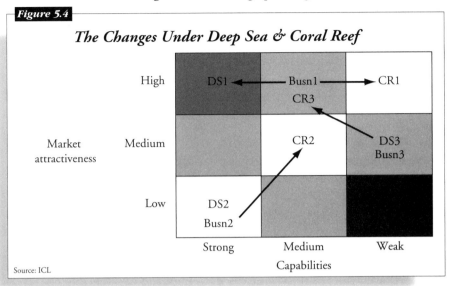

Figure 5.4

The Changes Under Deep Sea & Coral Reef

Source: ICL

The changes in markets and capabilities, and the changing resultant positioning of our businesses on the matrix, were significant (see Figure 5.4). This provided impetus into the skills planning activity in particular, as discussed below.

Figure 5.5 shows how this links into Strategic Planning, for a portfolio of businesses.

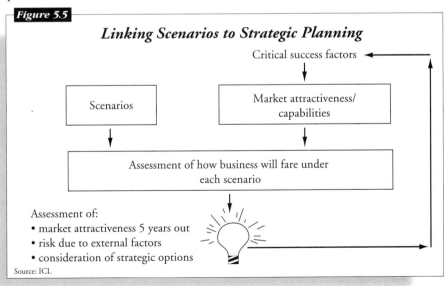

Figure 5.5

Linking Scenarios to Strategic Planning

Source: ICL

USING SCENARIOS TO BUILD A MORE ROBUST STRATEGY

We found that in an organization working in a very competitive environment, with many immediate pressures, it was difficult to get mind share in the businesses for the general concept of scenarios. It was easier for people to understand how to use Coral Reef and Deep Sea. The scenarios were always greeted with great interest, and discussed very animatedly in any group where they were presented, with every group asking for more detail about their precise part of the business, whether it was local government, the consultants, law and order, or servers.

Rather than extend the scenarios, we adopted a format which would allow us to work with a business unit, basing the thinking on Coral Reef and Deep Sea, encouraging discussion and expansion of the scenarios to cover the unit's world in more detail.

The question we wanted to answer was whether, for instance, a one-day forum to introduce the idea of scenarios was sufficient to give the management team a view of how the scenarios would affect their business plans and to provide them with a framework for a discussion about their future strategy. We found that once the scenarios were presented at a briefing at the beginning of the day, time was needed for the group to identify the additional issues particular to their business in each of their scenarios, in order for them to start adopting the scenarios.

It was also useful to divide up into two groups, one for each scenario, in order to define half a dozen extra issues that were important for the business in each scenario, and for the group as a whole to define half a dozen additional trends which were specifically important for its business. After that level of immersion, the group was in a position to talk about strategic planning and the implications arising from the scenarios. These workshops have now been run for a number of business units.

WORKSHOP ON MARKETS OR SKILLS IN 2005: OUTLINE AGENDA

Aim: Start to plan for skills needed in 2005

Method:
- Envisage the futures
- Brainstorm the changes
- Plan development programme

Attendees: Functional group (e.g. Distinguished Engineers, Consultancy Managers), management team (e.g. Criminal Justice Department), planning team (e.g. High Performance Systems)

Pre-reading: Scenarios for Information Markets in 2005

Provided: Vocabulary for process skills

Duration: 2 x 1/2 days or one day

Agenda
First module:
- Briefing on ICL in 2005
- Brainstorm: events & trends specific to the business or function
- Build list of services for 2005 (syndicates Coral Reef/Deep Sea)
- Report back

Second module:
- Assess for each service or market: effect of trends & scenarios, size of market, key skills, core/bought in
- Report back from syndicates
- Five top process skills (CR, DS)
- Report back
- Action planning

Partly as a result of our portfolio analysis, we became conscious of the need to get a clearer view of what sorts of skills would definitely be needed in 2005 and what the skills profile and the personality profile were if the business should turn out to be operating in a Coral Reef or a Deep Sea scenario.

The format we used for the skills workshop was very much like the one used with the business units, which was

- circulation of material beforehand, including the written scenarios;

- an initial briefing at the workshop on the scenarios as a reminder;

- a brainstorm on the trends specific to the particular group;

- separate work groups to concentrate on skills needed within each scenario;

- the formation of a combined picture, which formed the basis for deciding what actions to take.

This framework has since been used in relation to technical skills, consultancy skills, and management teams. In most of the workshops we found that there were one or two people who were absolutely clear at the beginning of the workshop that they knew what the future was, and therefore found the scenarios unacceptable. The best technique for dealing with this was to find confirming evidence for both scenarios in current behaviour so that people could understand that the future was likely to be as confusing as the present and that it was a question of understanding commonalties and differences and focusing the business on competencies.

There were a number of these workshops. In Project Leonardo, for technical skills, for example, workshops consisted of ICL Fellows and Distinguished Engineers and business unit managers in leading edge businesses. They also had personnel people and those with responsibility for training. The consultancy work was done with the managers of the various consultancy practices: Figure 5.6 shows the output from one of the workshops.

Figure 5.6

Core Competencies

Category	Project mgt	Costing metrics & models	Cons on impact of env, pol, econ	Tech to bus transfer	Od & change mgt	Future visioning	Mgt services & sla's	Systems thinking	Innovation & info soc	Technical knowledge	Net-working & telecoms	Knowledge mgt	Bid skills
Growth required	CR+++ DS+	CR+++(1) DS+++(1)	CR+ DS++	CR+++ DS++	CR+ DS+++	CR++ DS+++	CR+++ DS++	CR+++(1) DS+++(1)	CR++(1) DS++(1)	CR++ DS+++	CR+++ DS++	CR++ DS++	CR++ DS++
Delivery	In-house	In-house	In-house/ sub	In-house	In-house	In-house	In-house	In-house	In-house/ sub	In-house/ sub	In-house/ sub	In-house/ sub	In-house
Role	B	E/G	G	G/J/E	E/J	J	E	E/G/J	J/G	E/G/B	G/B	J	G
Number	10-100	10-100	10-100	100+	10-100	10-100	10-100	100+	10-100	100+	100+	10-100	<10

Key:
i) CR = Coral reef DS = Deep sea
ii) + or ++ or +++ + Extent of competency growth required for this scenario
iii) In-house or subcontract = Probable capability strategy
iv) E = Expert/catalyst role; G = Guru role; B = Body shopping; J = Jester/facilitator role
v) Number = likely number of consultants requiring this competency

CONCLUSIONS

Our experience

We first used the scenarios we developed, Coral Reef and Deep Sea, to run in parallel with strategic planning. PIMS and MA/C analysis of two businesses - the contract manufacturing and volume products businesses - suggested we should divest them. The question was: how do these businesses look in future markets? In the case of the manufacturing business, we found that the default scenario of the management team, which had driven their business plans, was near to the scenario in which customers quickly adopted innovation. A consideration of the structure of their market allowed us to reposition the business. On the volume products business, the analysis suggested that a larger parent, more suitable for a market where global sales and support are the characteristics of the leaders, would be better in the future. The business is now owned by Fujitsu.

We also used the scenarios to evaluate a set of potential new businesses. We had seven "at the starting gate" and could not invest in all, so we used the scenarios to evaluate the ability of the potentials to operate under either scenario. One is the business which now runs BBC On-line. The other, which won the European IT Prize in 1996, helps financial services companies develop Internet services for home banking, allowing banks to build up a picture of the customer's behaviour.

Links to strategic planning
In terms of linking strategy to scenario planning, the discussion above highlights three different roles.

One is the "wind-tunnel" role, of examining particular options, given a set of potential investments. This is normally used within a particular business.

The second is the strategy evaluation role, in which the analysis based on historic or current data is evaluated in the light of trends or uncertainties. So for instance the plan for D2D was found to be much less viable in a Deep Sea world than a Coral Reef world.

The third role is strategy development, in which a portfolio of businesses is evaluated under the scenarios for a future date, and the necessary actions planned - improvement of capability, or investment in markets or divestment of businesses - to improve the overall portfolio.

So, thinking of scenarios in the context of the strategic planning cycle (see Figure 5.7), it is clear that the role of scenarios is within the "Strategic Options and Intent" bubble. This provides the focus for any use of scenarios with strategic planning.

Introducing the thinking
We found that working with the teams responsible for a particular function or market was the only way that we could introduce the thinking into the organization - it is a new way of thinking in an action-driven company. So we learned (again) from Shell and brought out a glossy brochure. We trained ICL consultants to work with customers using our scenarios or creating tailored scenarios for the business and our Senior Executive Programme

(which works with customers on strategic and team building events). And we worked with teams that had specific problems at the time: for instance, using the scenarios to help the consultants and the technical community to plan for a skills portfolio in the future.

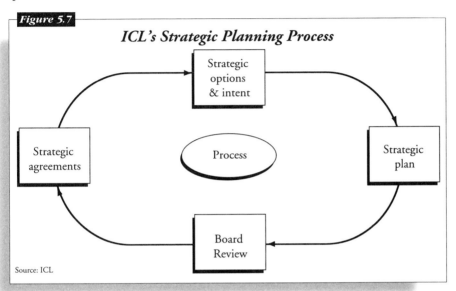

Figure 5.7

ICL's Strategic Planning Process

Source: ICL

And we concluded that (as seen earlier), to communicate scenarios in organizations not steeped in scenario thinking, the following are needed:

- a "lift (elevator) speech" which describes the use of the scenarios in relation to a specific concern, or a success story, or reference sell;

- clear representation of "the question";

- vivid names, and a glossy "storyline" booklet helps;

- a good storyline and coherence that people found credible, memorable incidents on the timeline;

- a process by which the scenarios can be used by the organization to decide what to do next.

CHAPTER SIX

Scenarios to Influence Public Attitudes

SUMMARY

This chapter focuses on the use of scenarios to create a framework for a shared vision of the future, by promoting discussion and building consensus, outside a business environment. Looking at the similarities between organizations which report success in using scenarios, and the way in which, for instance, the South African or Canadian governments have used scenarios to create coherence, suggests the importance of communication via storyline and image.

SCENARIOS CREATED TO INFLUENCE PUBLIC ATTITUDES

One of the first uses of scenarios outside the military think tanks was to influence public attitudes, as when Herman Kahn built scenarios about the effect of a possible nuclear war as a way of preventing it happening (see Chapter 1).

The common thread among the scenarios described below is the desire to provoke discussion, to examine alternatives, to provide input to policy, or to help a system cope with change.

The Copenhagen Institute for the Future's scenarios for the post-industrial city of 2010 were developed to help identify what policies would make life tolerable or better for the half of the world's population expected to be living in cities by then (Jensen, 1996). The "Mont Fleur" scenarios were created in South Africa in 1991 at a time when the negotiating process among the different political groups was at a critical stage: the shared vision created through the scenarios is credited with helping the peaceful transition (GBN, 1996a). In Canada a group of senior public sector officials, private sector executives and researchers have used scenarios to look at the implications of the emergence of the global information society on organization and governance, prompted by a sense of crisis in how countries govern themselves in the face of complexity and change (Rosell et al, 1995).

Scenarios have been used to explore the connection between a successful Europe and a common currency (Currie, 1997), and Peter Schwartz's global scenarios for the future were written to focus attention on the challenges which will need to be met for the optimistic scenario to prevail (Pine, 1995).

Three scenarios for the Industrialized World were created by the Chatham House Forum to spark debate on the future of the UK as part of the industrialized world, and Glen Peters' "Beyond the Next Wave" (Peters, 1996) explores changes in society underlying consumer behaviour. And an event hosted by ICL produced the Hedsor Memorandum as an input to industrial policy in Europe based on the Information Society.

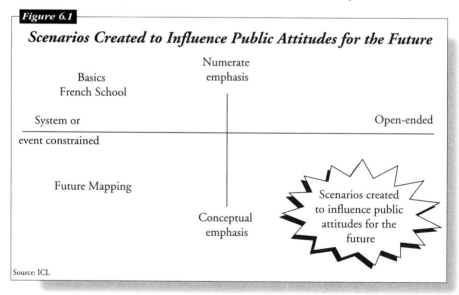

Figure 6.1

Scenarios Created to Influence Public Attitudes for the Future

Source: ICL

132

Figure 6.1 compares the scenarios in this section discussed elsewhere. The emphasis is on concept rather than numbers (although, for instance, the Mont Fleur scenarios were worked through into the implications for the economy) and on uncertainty rather than trends. As the methods and examples in Part II suggest, the organizations most associated with this type of scenario are the Copenhagen Institute, the Global Business Network, and (historically) SRI.

Why does a discussion of these scenarios belong in a book on scenario planning - managing for the future? For two reasons:

- the techniques for communicating the scenarios will often be a help in the strategic planning environment;

- the scenarios show the type of differences in emphasis depending on their scope.

HOW MANY SCENARIOS?

Scenarios intended primarily to create a shared public vision often use more than two scenarios. Many of the examples in this chapter have used four to explore very different futures, in order to understand the range of choices and also to explore evolution paths.

In the Hedsor event, the intention was to move to recommendations: so we decided to use just two visions, one - what we would like world to be, the other - if things went badly.

Another factor which influences the number of scenarios is the time factor. In a 24 hour event, the extent to which a group can work with four scenarios is limited. In a two-day event, the larger number can be managed.

THE POST-INDUSTRIAL CITY 2010

In 1996 the Copenhagen Institute for the Future held a conference entitled: "Four Futures: The Post-Industrial City 2010" to analyse the range of likely or possible futures of the city in the light of future economic, social and environmental changes. Reproduced in a special issue of the Institute's publication, "Future Orientation" in 1996, the Director of the Institute, Rolf Jensen, pointed out that according to World Bank statistics on urbanization, over half the world's population will be living in cities within the next one to two decades, something he calls a "historic event" since until modern time rural living has been the norm.

The four scenarios developed focus on the service-oriented, post-industrial cities of Europe and North America, although they have been done from a global perspective. They are extreme visions of possible futures and, although there could be a future with elements from each scenario, it is more useful to regard them as distinct and mutually exclusive scenarios.

SCENARIOS FOR THE POST-INDUSTRIAL CITY 2010

The Green City:
Green thinking, or ecological concerns, becomes a dominant factor in attitudes towards food, packaging, the environment, products and services. It is both technical, or concerned with striving towards a sustainable environment, and emotional, manifested by concerns such as animal rights and love of nature. This affects transport, including cars and roads, a revitalization of parks, alternative energy sources and a new approach to architecture.

The High-Tech City:
The use of electronics becomes so pervasive that it transforms the way we live. Home working/mobile communications cuts rush hour traffic, home shopping brings a halt to the growth in shopping malls, while roads will have in-built chips to react with cars, not only regulating distance from other cars but establishing road routes and automatically registering speeding cars.

The Blade-Runner City:
The cities are badly affected by violence, decline, fear, theft and

street gangs. People move out, leaving the inner cities to street gangs, while the demand for more private security increases. This takes place against the background of a collapse of faith in authority and a collapse of social control. Cities are now the home for gangs.

The Story-Telling City:
This is a city where material needs have been satisfied to such an extent that people want stories and experiences, and where they could play parts in the theatrical settings of central squares. There will be much more travelling between cities around Europe for weekend breaks, shopping and so on, because of faster transport and lower prices.

SOUTH AFRICA - THE MONT FLEUR SCENARIOS

In 1991 a group of academics, politicians, administrators, trade unionists and business people met at Mont Fleur in South Africa to create scenarios about what the country could look like in 2002. Facilitated by Adam Kahane of Shell International, the group met twice more, in 1991 and 1992, while a lot of additional work was carried on in between meetings. The group analysed the country's social, political and economic crises and compiled 30 possible stories about the course of events during the next decade. These included stories of revolution, economic growth through repression, right-wing revolts and free-market utopias. The 30 stories were carefully scrutinized and sifted in terms of criteria such as plausibility and internal consistency. Nine stories survived, which were reduced to four by the end of the second meeting (Figure 6.2).

These four scenarios described what might happen in South Africa, using as a point of departure the negotiating process then in place among the different political groups. The group had concluded before creating the scenarios that there were a number of critical elements underlying political, economic and social crises.

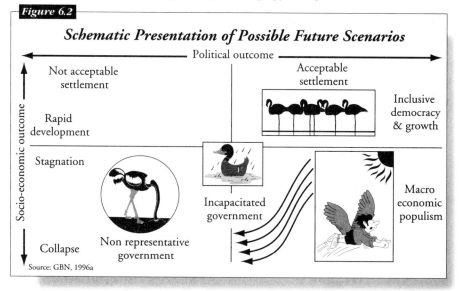

Figure 6.2

Schematic Presentation of Possible Future Scenarios

Source: GBN, 1996a

The main factors in the political crisis were seen to be as follows:

- The present system lacked legitimacy.
- Widespread mistrust of the security forces.
- Lack of faith in the judicial system.
- Repression, intimidation, intolerance and political violence.
- Increasing exploitation of ethnic and regional divisions.
- The collapse of black local authorities and the breakdown of services in many areas.

The country's economic crisis was characterized by economic stagnation, declining investment, falling per capita incomes, growing unemployment and large economic disparities. These stemmed from:

- The unsustainability of South Africa's traditional growth path based on primary exports (gold and minerals) and cheap labour.
- Failure to develop a broad-based manufacturing sector.
- Unified production of capital goods (such as machinery) needed for manufacturing.

- South Africa's isolation from the international technological revolution.
- Lack of investor confidence.

The social fabric in many communities was disintegrating because of:

- High unemployment.
- Escalating political and criminal violence.
- Inability of the health and education systems to meet the demands made on them.
- Collapse of many rural communities.
- Rapid urbanization.
- Alienation among the young.

The team foresaw four possible outcomes of the negotiating process depending on the answers to the issues shown in the Box: Four Scenarios for South Africa.

FOUR SCENARIOS FOR SOUTH AFRICA

1. If negotiations do not result in a settlement, a non-representative government will emerge (Ostrich).

2. If the transition is not rapid and decisive, the government that emerges will be incapacitated (Lame duck).

3. If the democratic government's policies are not sustainable, collapse is inevitable (Icarus).

4. If, however, the government adopts sustainable policies, South Africa can achieve inclusive democracy and growth (Flight of the Flamingos).

Even more powerfully, by exploring possible future paths from one scenario to another they concluded that inclusive democracy was the only viable route (Figure 6.3).

Figure 6.3

Possible Future Paths

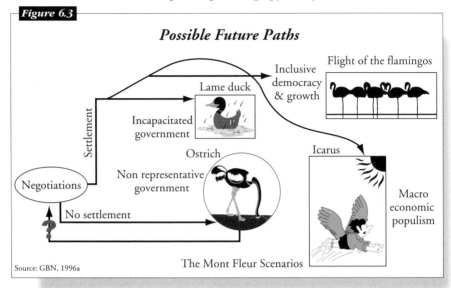

The Mont Fleur Scenarios

Source: GBN, 1996a

CANADA - THE INFORMATION SOCIETY

At the beginning of the 1990s a group of senior Canadian public sector officials, private sector executives and researchers began to look at how to develop more effective ways of governing in the context of the emerging global Information Society. Their context was a sense of crisis in how countries govern themselves in the face of complexity and change. The first phase, as described in Steven Rosell's "Governing in an Information Society" (1992) concentrated on gathering information to identify the social, economic and technological changes that were leading to the creation of the Information Society. There was then a formal meeting to consider how the Information Society was changing governance in those areas. It was concluded that the most important elements in relation to governance were:

- globalization,
- atomization/democratization/fragmentation,
- end to the bureaucratic model of organization,
- the growing importance of human resources,
- the loss of boundaries and fundamental restructuring among not just industries but the private and public sectors,

- the decreasing possibility of secrecy.

Backed by more than a dozen federal government departments, the project turned into a series of meetings attended by senior government officials who discussed views with external experts as well as sharing case studies from their own departments. Steven Rosell (1995) noted, *"Initially, the roundtable focused on the disintegrative effects that the information society appears to have on established instruments and practices of governing, and on the crisis in governance that results. But gradually that focus shifted to a search for new ways of governing, new ways of integrating, more appropriate to the realities of the information society."* The recommendations covered topics such as information-based ways of organizing and forging consensus in the Information Society.

It was then decided to build on the success of the first part of the project and hold more roundtables, with additional government officials and four executives from the private sector. The goal was to establish shared frameworks and construct scenarios of how Canadian governance could be shaped from the impact of the Information Society over the next decade. With Kees van der Heijden as a guide, the group began to look at the key issues that needed to be addressed. It was finally agreed that four broad issues should be examined:

- The new information (or knowledge-based) economy;
- The social contract in the Information Society;
- People, culture and values in the Information Society;
- The changing relationship between the governors and the governed.

Those issues were explored in more depth using experts to build up the knowledge base. A two-day workshop was then held to construct scenarios that would describe different ways in which the emergence of a global Information Society could reshape the environment for governance over the coming decade. Before the workshop, smaller sub groups had been meeting to consider critical certainties and uncertainties. The full meeting then agreed a final list.

Facilitated by Adam Kahane (see the section on the Mont Fleur scenarios for South Africa), the group then began to build up a collection of what Kahane called snippettes, which were brief causal sequences showing how the key elements might link up. (For example, education focuses on technology → skills surge of young people entering Information Industries → Canada becomes key player in software.) Combining those then produced "mega-snippettes", or collections of a number of snippettes, and these were developed into four scenario stories.

SCENARIOS FOR CANADA

Starship:

This scenario envisions a booming economy coupled with the development of new social consensus. The difficulties of the early 1990s turn out to be transitional and as institutions learn to adapt to the requirements of the Information Economy, a new, global, secular economic boom develops in which Canada plays a leading role. Institutions and individuals have reached the point in their learning curve where they can begin to realize the full potential of the new information technologies. Measures are taken to enhance social cohesion, while strengthening the work ethic.

Titanic:

This scenario envisions a world with low or no economic growth, coupled with growing social fragmentation. The Information Economy does not produce nearly enough high-paying jobs to replace those being lost and there is persistent high structural unemployment and low or no growth. Some countries have been successful in recognizing and adapting to the new realities, but Canada is not among them. Canadians become increasingly inward-looking and cling to visions of the past, as the situation deteriorates. Canada falls behind.

HMS Bounty:

A booming economy is combined with continued (and growing) social fragmentation and polarization. One image is Los Angeles:

high tech and dynamic, with many people doing very well, but with society very polarized and very difficult to govern. As in the Starship scenario, the Information Economy ushers in a new global secular economic boom. IT transforms the economy and work, and Canada is well-placed to take advantage of this and is a success story. The scenario sees that by 2005 the social and regional disparities, and conflict between haves and have-nots, is threatening to smother further economic growth, and tensions are increasing.

Windjammer:
This envisions a new social consensus emerging around a low or no-growth economy, at least as conventionally measured (it had been agreed that there could be a high degree of growth - including personal and non-material growth not captured by conventional measures). As in the Titanic scenario, the Information Economy does not produce enough high-paying jobs to replace those being lost, and there is low or no economic growth. But, unlike Titanic, a series of events triggers growing public awareness and concern, and action is taken in time to change course.... (The government) leads a national process, involving the public, private and voluntary sectors, to develop and implement a new national strategy to take Canada into the 21st century.

The scenarios, once created, were recognized to be related through an economy/society matrix, with low/no growth versus a new secular boom along the horizontal axis, and social fragmentation versus new social consensus along the vertical. The resulting matrix is represented in Figure 6.4.

Steven Rosell writes in 1997: *"On the question of what has happened since the 'Changing Maps' scenarios, the short answer is that we seem to have spawned a small epidemic of scenario-based work. Activities have been essentially of two types.*

The first has involved applying the scenario methodology to other public policy issues. For example, a special task force of Deputy Ministers (Permanent Secretaries) was set up to explore the future of the public service in Canada and adopted a scenario

Figure 6.4

Scenarios for Canada

New social consensus	Windjammer	Starship
Social fragmentation	Titanic	HMS Bounty
	Low/no growth	New secular boom

Society

Economy (as conventionally measured)

Source: Rosell, 1995

methodology patterned explicitly on what we did in 'Changing Maps'. Resulting scenarios have been used to encourage strategic conversation and to test policy proposals in several Federal departments and in at least one Provincial government. Another of our roundtable members organized a very large scenario process on the future of the Americas, with meetings in Latin America, the U.S. and Canada. Those scenarios have been used for development programming in the region, and several countries are planning to replicate the approach at the national level (e.g. Colombia, Guatemala). There are several other examples.

The second sort of activity spawned by 'Changing Maps' has involved using our scenarios as a focal point, or starting point, for a policy development/strategy exercise. This has been done for example, by a team that included senior human resource executives and union leaders to develop a new approach to staffing and human resource management within the government. New legislation, based on the results of their work, is now being developed. In another example, the Environment department used the scenarios to undertake a review of approaches to sustainable development, drawing on outside experts and stakeholders as well as departmental officials. Their work opened up a range of new strategic issues for the department and the government in this area, that now are being woven into the work and planning of the department. The department found the approach to be very valuable and is planning to use it again. There are lots more examples, but these should give you a sense."

THE FUTURE OF EUROPE

In a research report published by the Economist Intelligence Unit, outlining the pros and cons of European Monetary Union (EMU), author David Currie (Currie, 1997) emphasized the uncertainties facing the attempt to create a single currency by constructing four scenarios based on a two dimensional spectrum of possibilities: Europe stagnates or prospers, EMU happens or is abandoned.

Figure 6.5

Four Scenarios for Europe's Future

	Europe stagnates	*Europe prospers*
EMU abandoned	Scenario 1 Europe stalled, EU divided	Scenario 2 Single market triumphant, EU unified
EMU happens	Scenario 3 The core humbled, EU divided	Scenario 4 EMU triumphant, EU unified

Source: Currie, 1997

THE FUTURE OF EUROPE

Scenario 1: No EMU: Europe stalled, EU divided.
- *Most countries fail to meet the Maastricht criteria.*
- *Increasing popular discontent with the prospect of the euro, especially in Germany.*
- *EMU is initially postponed and then indefinitely postponed.*

- *The high-debt countries experience sharp rise in short and long term interest rates, worsening fiscal problems.*
- *Considerable acrimony among EU members.*
- *Lack of progress in further implementation of single-market provisions and in liberalization of EU telecoms and energy markets.*
- *Failure to tackle problems of structural rigidities in Europe.*
- *EU countries stagnate amid mountains of debt.*
- *EU loses its direction and momentum.*
- *EU failure to address the issue of enlargement to the east.*

Scenario 2: No EMU: single market triumphant, EU unified

- *Increasing lack of support for EMU leads EU countries to defer EMU and concentrate on other policy initiatives.*
- *The move to fiscal responsibility continues, reducing problems of excessive deficits and debt.*
- *All countries succeed in achieving low inflation, despite the abandonment of the euro.*
- *Major moves to liberalize European telecoms, energy and airline markets and to pursue energetically the implementation of all single market directives.*
- *Reform of European benefit systems and undue labour market regulation leads to greater flexibility of labour markets.*
- *Result is a dynamic growing European economy, with falling unemployment.*
- *A more confident EU addresses the issue of enlargement to the east.*

Scenario 3: EMU: the core humbled, EU divided

- *6-10 countries join EMU.*
- *EMU works badly.*
- *Instabilities in transition; European Central Bank hits technical problems in running euro monetary policy.*
- *Conflicts between ECB and Ecofin (the group of EU economic and finance ministers) lead to instability of the euro against other currencies, and dollar/yen volatility.*
- *Unemployment high and rising in some areas, because of structural rigidities strengthened by EMU.*

- *Debt levels climb; debt traps re-emerge.*
- *General European stagnation.*
- *Excessive bureaucracy; failure to tackle rigidities.*
- *Enlargement issue avoided, so that Europe as a whole is divided.*
- *The "outs" fare better than the "ins" but still suffer from the stagnation of the EMU core.*
- *Political pressures build for the abandonment of EMU and the restoration of national currencies.*
- *Growing disenchantment with EU integration undermines commitment to the single market.*

Scenario 4: EMU triumphant, EU unified

- *6-10 countries proceed to EMU in 1999 and others follow: most EU countries adopt the euro by 2002.*
- *Transition to euro works smoothly.*
- *No major macroeconomic problems: the European economy revives and unemployment falls.*
- *ECB establishes an early and strong reputation.*
- *No institutional conflicts between ECB and Ecofin.*
- *Euro widely adopted as vehicle currency.*
- *European competitiveness tackled by flexibility and deregulation.*
- *No creeping protectionism, debt and deficit problems solved.*
- *Some limited accretion of powers to Brussels, but no great federalism: an open decentralized Europe (on the Swiss model).*
- *A strong EU addresses the issue of enlargement, avoiding conflicts to the east.*

Source: © The pros and cones of EMU, the Economist Intelligence Unit Ltd. Reproduced by permission of the Economist Intelligence Unit Ltd.

These scenarios show very clearly their use to rehearse the future, at a time when the debate is still very much live across Europe. By separating consideration of a successful future for Europe in terms of unification from that of a common currency, the issues which are important can be more easily be unpacked.

However, the unexpected is always hard to predict: the scenarios were written in 1997 but did not predict that the French elections would be called early and cause a major change in policy, with the new government showing signs of being willing to dump the move towards the common currency.

TWO GLOBAL SCENARIOS

Peter Schwartz has constructed two different scenarios, one taking an optimistic look at the future and one conveying a much more pessimistic note (Pine, 1995).

The drivers of the optimistic scenario include the following hopeful signals:

- US productivity growth
- Pervasive new technology
- Increasing growth potential
- Increasing multilateral co-operation
- Falling global trade barriers
- Take-off of Asia
- South American economic growth
- Improving conditions in Central Europe
- Increasing perception, response to environmental problems.

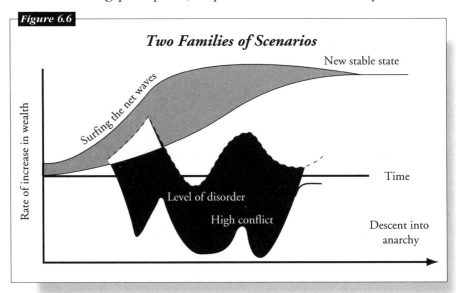

Figure 6.6

Two Families of Scenarios

The pessimistic signals include:

- Slow job growth
- Widening income gaps
- Rising crime and terrorism
- Mounting environmental decay
- Weak political leadership in OECD
- Mounting trade disputes
- Currency volatility
- Ethnic cleansing in Bosnia and Africa
- Anti-immigrant fever
- Politics of identity

PETER SCHWARTZ OFFER TWO SCENARIOS FOR THE FUTURE

The scenarios are from (Pine, 1995) and are reproduced by permission of The Planning Review.

The first scenario is "Descent into Anarchy", in which there is conflict between the US and Russia because of upheavals in central Asia, drug lords control large areas of the developing world, ethnic conflicts increase, and terrorism rise in the US. However, this is in the context of a healthy, growing global economy, although one divided into haves and have-nots. According to Schwartz, in this scenario pessimism is growing not because things are getting worse but they are getting less stable for a number of reasons:

- Economic struggle and change
- Accelerating technological change
- Widening income gap
- Growth in Asia
- Collapse of Africa and Russia
- End of Cold War restraints on conflict.

However, he paints a more optimistic picture in "Surfing the Net Waves" where the sheer power and reach of technology creates many new opportunities for people everywhere. But to reach this state a number of challenges have to be met:

1. Joint peacekeeping efforts in Central Asia and the Middle East driven by the Security Council.

2. Managing economic structural change, including making technology easier to use and hence more accessible, and an emphasis on improving education everywhere.

3. Low tolerance for violence and war, based on quick multi-lateral action.

4. Using the World Trade Organization effectively.

5. Domestically, resolving crime at its roots.

6. Finding ways to include Asian countries such as China and India in the first order of nations.

7. Discovering new methods of environmental conflict resolution, particularly in relation to China.

THREE SCENARIOS FOR THE INDUSTRIALIZED WORLD

The Chatham House Forum, a foresight group of business and government representatives, was established at the UK's Royal Institute of International Affairs in 1995 as a vehicle for exploring the implications for the longer term of the complex challenges, opportunities and threats facing organizations. It operates on an annual cycle, with teams exploring chosen themes. These themes, with additional information from other sources, are woven together to create a synthesized view.

In 1996 the Forum published "Unsettled Times", which describes three different scenarios for the year 2015, dwelling chiefly on the concerns of the industrialized world. The scenarios, built over three months by a team of three Institute staff plus Forum members, are reproduced below, by permission of the Royal Institute of International Affairs. They were communicated through the book and through slide-set presentations.

The Forum identified a number of drivers of changes and coupling forces. The industrialized world is already feeling the impact of the technology explosion, an ageing population, an over-stretched welfare system and the transformation of once stable institutional structures. Economic coupling continues to occur, as marketplaces merge across borders which makes talent and skills more widely available but also sharply increases competition. Cost-cutting and market liberalization undertaken by both companies and governments reinforce the effects of the coupling forces. The rate of commoditization in many industries is accelerating, which lead to declining profitability with adverse social impact.

POSTCARDS FROM THE FUTURE

Scenario 1 - Faster, Faster (FF):

This points to a world of starkly accelerating change, in which industrial transformation is rapid and innovation is ceaseless, but commoditization is even swifter and profits are never quite sufficient to cover the risk which is involved. Industry condensation proceeds quickly across the industrialized world (IW), with the population falling into three groups; those considered essential to the firm; a larger group working in affiliation with it; and a substantial group who work only occasionally or not at all.

This said, a general "solution" to the issues of national governance is recognized which spreads swiftly around the IW. Social cohesion is generally maintained. The generic nature of the solution permits other nations to learn from it. The convergence of the industrializing nations upon the IW is accelerated. Nations can easily be ranked as the criteria for success are more clearly understood, and markets become even more prone to amplifying success and penalizing failure. Information technology serves as the conduit through which ever more complex work is "posted" to global marketplaces, in which the low-wage areas play an ever-expanding role. Those with the lowest skills are the most penalized.

This is a scenario which perpetually threatens to spin out of control.

Scenario 2 - The Post-Industrial Revolution (PIR):

A small shift in the balance between the rates of commoditization and economic differentiation will have a profound effect on the tone of the times. As commerce finds itself able to resist competitive erosion, it feels confident. This confidence is communicated to the rest of society. Nations are able to exploit the smooth, endless technological explosion. They can begin to offset the coupling forces that lead to commoditization. Unlike in the first scenario, in this one relative knowledge and potential is found to occur best in physically connected, specialist networks. Detailed and protracted human interactions are needed in order to achieve success. It proves impossible to carry this out with the same degree of success across IT systems or between remote locations. It takes the complex societies of the IW to create such centres of excellence. Nations tend these sources of distinctive competence with great care. They are given the local regulatory and institutional support that they need.

Relative economic success among the IW nations also creates the conditions for positive partnerships and thus supranational collaboration develops. The forces which dominated Faster, Faster remain potent, however, and their demands have to be met. The need to co-ordinate a response to this, across these levels of scale, dominates the re-creation of the tools of government. Each IW nation emphasizes its distinctive competence, doing so within a common framework of knowledge-centred commerce. Societies too, change rapidly. Pluralism offers identity in a complex world.

Scenario 3 - Rough Neighbours (RN):

The third scenario is one in which Faster, Faster, slips off the treadmill. The nations of the IW fall into a period of general difficulty, from which they emerge in the next decade to find that Rough Neighbours have arrived on the scene. In the initial stages of this, politics responds to social stress by shifting its base, such that within the IW, a rejectionist majority confront a capable minority. Adjustment processes are derailed. Joint initiatives, designed to slow the pace of change, are co-ordinated across the IW. A wide range of measures is attempted, none going so far as outright protectionism and all based on entirely worthy aspirations.

The effect is, however, a decade of muddled strife, from which the IW emerges fragmented and bruised, with any claim to global leadership compromised. It is confronted by an Asian economic region, revolving around China's predominance and answering to different ethical and political imperatives to those with which the IW feels familiar. A political centre of weight has developed around a number of the Islamic nations. The low-income world is cross-hatched with competing ideologies. Many of these alternative views find enthusiasts among the less capable within the IW, linked together by IT.

Figure 6.7 represents the dynamics of the three scenarios.

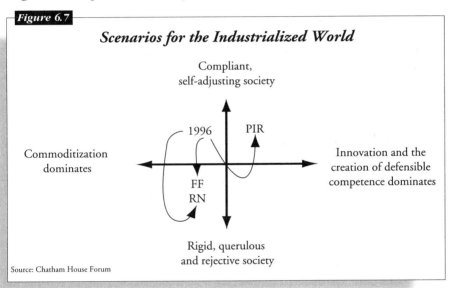

Figure 6.7

Scenarios for the Industrialized World

Compliant,
self-adjusting society

1996   PIR

Commoditization
dominates

Innovation and the
creation of defensible
competence dominates

FF
RN

Rigid, querulous
and rejective society

Source: Chatham House Forum

BEYOND THE NEXT WAVE

Glen Peters, in communicating two scenarios for consumer behaviour in 2015 (Peters, 1996), has used illustrations, plays and newspaper front pages to communicate his two scenarios. In "The World in Mid Life Crisis", the relatively ageing population of the developed word points to both a growing conservatism but also a search for lost youth, while challenges from the younger population in the developing world creates tensions. In "The Two-Tier World", the split deepens between the haves and the have nots. For each vector of change which Peters identifies, a newspaper front page has been developed to convey the ideas colourfully. For example, Figures 6.8 and 6.9 show the front pages for the vector of change associated with the family under each scenario. The aim is to get the scenarios to become part of consciousness, to be worlds in which people can immerse themselves.

Peters has also experimented with plays as a communication tool. Plays are sometimes used, for instance at GBN, as a tool for developing a storyline, where they work well. Peters has used professionals to act out a playlet to communicate scenarios to a business audience although it has proved difficult for the audience to make the transition to a dramatic approach. It could be that this format would work after dinner, as the briefing for a workshop next day intended to apply the scenarios to a specific business, market or skill set.

THE HEDSOR MEMORANDUM

In 1994 the European Commission published a report entitled "Europe and the Global Information Society", otherwise known as the Bangemann report. It represented the findings of a group of senior business people and community leaders, including the then-chairman of ICL, Sir Peter Bonfield, under the chairmanship of European Commissioner Dr Martin Bangemann. The report has formed the basis of much of the European Commission's work programme in strategic planning for the Information Society. It also influenced the subsequent G7 Global Information Society conference held in Brussels in 1995, and is reflected in programmes such as the UK government's Information Society Initiative launched in 1996.

However, perceiving that there were still a large number of difficult issues to be addressed, ICL hosted a seminar in July 1996 at its executive training facility, Hedsor Park, to examine:

Figure 6.8

 The DOUBLE STANDARD,

===== January 1, 2015 =====

O'MALLY HOMES ARE "SAFER THAN HOUSES"

The building company O'Mally Homes announced that its new range of up market family homes was the safest house that anyone could buy today for under half a million dollars.

The newly designed homes are part of a refocusing of the company's operations on those looking for security in these crime-ridden times. A company spokesperson for O'Mally said, "Market research has told us that safety from burglary and violence is the major concern for knowledge professionals. These homes have been designed to be impregnable to external intrusion by undesirables."

The homes are clustered in groups of 12 with high-voltage protection wire ringing the 12-foot walls which surround each mini-estate. The entrance gate is operated by a remote controller fitted to a car. At night an armed guard occupies the gate-house as added protection, and each house is fitted with an emergency alarm connected to the local rapid-deployment police center.

Most of O'Mally's new homes have been sold before a single brick has been laid.

SAVVY SUPERMARKETS ACT TO CUT SHRINKAGE

Last year the Savvy supermarket chain lost 15 percent of its stock through shrinkage, which its CEO, Harry Johnson, said would "bust the company." Today Johnson and his managers are fighting back with an aggressive plan to combat the light-fingered customers and workers.

Savvy is taking a step back in time to the days when shopping assistants served people from behind a counter. Customers asked for what they wanted and were handed the items requested upon payment.

Customers will be able to browse through the entire range of products on display, with dummy products on show. The cans of baked beans will be empty, loaves of bread will be made of plastic look-alike material, and meat will be sprayed with a formaldehyde to render it inedible.

Customers will tick their orders on special order forms and hand them to the sales assistants who will then pack the items requested. When payment has been made, the customers will be able to collect their goods from a collection kiosk.

Savvy hopes that the plan will cut shrinkage and improve profitability. Although the initiative will increase costs, with labour at $2 an hour it could recover its investment in a few weeks with shrinkage being reduced by 80 percent.

STUD MALLS A CRIME-FREE HIT

The Shop Till 'U Drop malls have been pulling in record numbers of shoppers this Christmas due to its ingenious way of cutting crime in our shopping centres.

To visit the STUD malls you have to insert a gold or silver intersmart payment card to get through the entrance. One hundred smart-points are awarded to every first-time visitor and 50 points for every subsequent visit.

A spokesperson for the STUD Development Company said, "Our malls are appealing to the top 5 percent of the population, who wish to spend their hard earned income in a quality, trouble-free, crime-free environment. With the record of theft and physical violence to high net-worth individuals in our city-based shopping centers, STUD is the only sage alternative."

The malls feature a range of entertainment facilities, a top restaurant, a cinema, and franchise retail outlets operated by the world's most famous brand names.

FAMILY PROTECTION CORPORATION HIT BY SCANDAL

The Family Protection Corporation has been alleged to employ illegal aliens in its personal protection unit. In view of the national security implications of significant numbers of these individuals, who possess arms in connection with their protection duties, an injunction has been issued for FPC to cease trading until it has been cleared of these allegations.

No one was available yesterday at the Cayman Island registered company for comment.

The Family Protection Corporation has provided armed bodyguards for wealthy businessmen and their families over the last five years and has grown into an international business with a turnover of $150 million.

Figure 6.9

THE MID-LIFE TIMES

=== January 1, 2015 ===

MARRIAGE STAGES MAJOR COMEBACK – DIVORCE RATE FALLS FOR FIRST TIME THIS CENTURY

The office of census and survey revealed one of the best set of statistics for countries in the North Atlantic as a special new year present. For the first time since the middle of the last century the number of recorded marriages rose by 5 percent over the last year.

A spokesperson for the authority was quoted as saying, "These figures would seen to vindicate the aggressive family values programs pursued by governments since the beginning of this century, when the number of marriages had fallen to an all-time low."

Romance is in the air once more

Evidence that the compulsory counseling program for couples considering divorce has succeeded was also borne out by the fourth year's consecutive fall in the number of divorces granted by the courts.

Under current law couples with children aged under 16 have to apply to a government tribunal for divorce. Only in exceptional circumstances will a tribunal allow a divorce unless it is satisfied that the couple have undergone a cooling-off period of at least one year and have agreed to attend three residential counselling sessions with a government approved counsellor.

Although the news was welcomed by community and church leaders, Action Against Males, a feminist organization, dismissed the report as being a fabrication to hide the deep injustice being perpetrated against women. "We have lost the woman's right to choose her own future. Many women are having

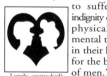

Lonely, unattached?
Call 0800-FAM 1 LY

to suffer the indignity of both physical and mental torture in their homes for the benefit of men."

GRANNY FLATS HOLD PREMIUM

Despite the recent slump in house prices those with customized facilities for the elderly or live-in parents have held their prices up well according to a survey by the Moynihan Institute, a research-based foundation promoting family values.

Most families seeking to support their parents make do with a spare room in the house with the two children having to forfeit a bedroom of their own.

"Homes that offer self contained accommodation for parents are at a higher premium as there is more space for the three different generations to get on with life without falling over each other."

LOVE IS A MANY SPLENDOURED THING SCOOPS OSCARS

The remake of the 1950s Hollywood romantic tear-jerker made a comeback 65 years later as the best film of 2014.

Worldwide audiences on Twenty-First Century Entertainments interactive channel were independently audited at 247 million, the highest since records began.

CLUB 4+2 LAUNCHES EXOTIC DESTINATION PROGRAM

One of Club 4+2's exotic destinations

Club 4+2, the highly successful vacation company which has targeted the extended family segment with its Mediterranean resort program, has extended its new season offers to long-haul destinations in Asia.

The company, founded in 2006 by entrepreneur and former Catholic priest, Michael Shannon, has been successful at targeting the fast-growing sector of families which have invited mum and dad to live with them. The company discounts heavily the price of

the two additional adults provided at least two full-price holidays are purchased.

Michael, himself a married man with parents who live in, was the centre of criticism by the church in Ireland last year after he published a series of advertisements in the Irish press calling for the "primitive" abolition of the restrictions imposed on priests not to marry. Shannon claimed that the position taken by the church was anti-family and against the teachings of Christ.

- issues of regulation in the light of new technological advances;

- issues arising from the implementation of the Information Society in Europe such as public awareness/education, skills training
- the most appropriate regulatory/institutional environment to encourage entrepreneurship and innovation.

Participants in the Hedsor seminar included Dr Martin Bangemann, Commissioner for Industry in the European Commission, Keith Todd, ICL's Chief Executive Officer, and twenty participants from the media and the Open University, public administration, telecoms and computing, and entrepreneurs. The workshop was facilitated by Peter Schwartz of GBN, and the participants represented 13 countries.

The format of this event was very successful and has been used many times since (see Box).

SCENARIO THINKING TO HELP REDUCE FEAR, UNCERTAINTY AND DOUBT (FUD)

Location: Country House or other location removed from pressures

Players: Owner: person who is hosting the event and is expecting recommendations from the Group
Facilitator: in charge of process

Size of Group: Up to about 30 to have good group dynamics, more than 10 to get diversity of interests

Agenda: Start late pm
Introductions and agree aims
Presentations - defining the terms
Round table discussion after dinner

Next morning, syndicate work (a maximum of four syndicates) on aspects of the question:

e.g. for the Futurescope event (see below) the groups tackled work, education, leisure and the family
Create a picture of the desirable future
Create a view of what happens if nothing changes (or, as in the Hedsor event, the undesirable future)
Informal lunch or lunch with visiting speaker

In plenary, syndicate groups report back using hand-written (or computer captured) summary points on foils
Syndicate groups brainstorm actions/recommendations
In plenary, agree on actions or recommendations
All participants take away hard copy of summary points and actions/recommendations.

Leading and Trailing Scenarios

As part of the discussions, the group developed two visions for Europe; a leading and a trailing scenario.

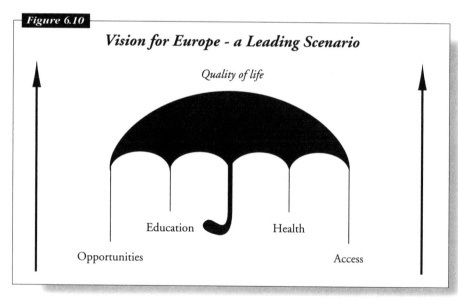

Figure 6.10

Vision for Europe - a Leading Scenario

Quality of life

Education   Health

Opportunities   Access

The leading scenario described a society with an improved quality of life. Contributing to that would be choice: opportunities for employment rather than jobs as such, opportunities for education, choices over lifestyle, health and medical care, and choice to use information technology or not - based on there being no barriers to access.

There are a number of things that have to happen for this scenario. First is infrastructure: it is said that the cost of building the information highway in Europe could be estimated at 67 billion ECUs. The second is the attitude of mind, which should be about using technology to solve problems, rather than installing technology for the sake of it. Another essential element of this scenario was the private sector, which should contribute to the bulk of the 67 billion ECUs of infrastructure plus help create all the ensuing services. This scenario is based on a model somewhere between the US approach driven by the stock market and a highly government driven approach. It could be called a financial breakthrough, where the banks and the financial institutions are prepared to take incremental risks to invest in this scenario for the future.

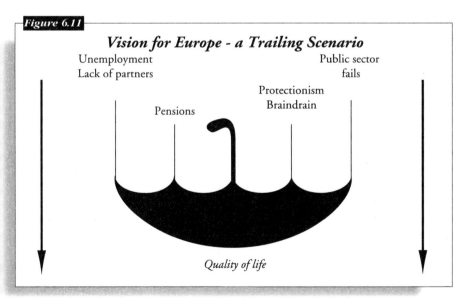

Figure 6.11

Vision for Europe - a Trailing Scenario

Unemployment
Lack of partners

Public sector
fails

Protectionism
Braindrain

Pensions

Quality of life

One problem in Europe is that many countries are heading for a huge pensions crisis. The only hope of solution rests with creating more employment to fund this yawning gap. In the trailing scenario, Europe fails to provide these additional jobs and opportunities and there is a pensions crisis of astronomical proportions. Educational opportunities shrink, and hence potential new jobs do not emerge. Europe becomes the poor region of the world, with an exodus of talent, leading to fortress Europe mentality. The high standards of health and education which Europe now enjoys would shrink.

The group concluded that to achieve the leading scenario three elements had to be in place:

- The capacity of Europe to improve the relationship between entrepreneurship, education and the financial system;

- Education, helped by IT, needs to become a critical factor in growth in Europe. Secondly, Europe needs world class companies such as a Microsoft of Europe. Overall, the whole attitude toward risk-taking and management has to change;

- A new approach to regulation and deregulation in the light of technological developments. For example, while getting rid of monopolies is important, the completely deregulated model might not always be appropriate.

What came to be called the Hedsor Memorandum was a call for Europe to move forward resolutely and embrace the full potential of the Global Information Society. The group concluded that the premise of the original Bangemann Report that the formation of the Information Society represents as major a change and challenge as the formation of the industrial society, with the same or greater global implications, remained absolutely valid.

Nor can Europe isolate itself from the rest of the world. But there is still not enough awareness in Europe generally about the potential of the Information Society, although Europe's strength in education, literature, media and the arts means it could make an effective contribution. Nor is there the entrepreneurial approach to make European companies into global players.

The recommendations made by the meeting focused on areas for action which would use the infrastructure of communications, and which could be carried out over the next two years to take effect over the next decade. It was argued that attention should be shifted to spreading awareness of the impact of the Information Society from large organizations to individuals, so they understand the potential to increase their skills, to small and medium sized enterprises which will play a critical role in advancing the Information Society by extending their global reach through technology, and to local governments as catalysts and providers of local networks with a bridge to global resources.

The Future Scope Group

Following the Hedsor seminar, we were concerned that perhaps the Hedsor participants might have a systematically different view of life from the next generation, who would be living in the Information Society. So we invited a group of seventeen young graduates from throughout ICL, from a wide range of backgrounds and nationalities, and with differing knowledge, skills, attitudes and experience, to attend a $1^1/_2$ day "Future Scope" workshop to consider Europe in 2006: what should we want and expect from the Information Society? After an initial brainstorming session to collect views about Europe and the Information Society in 2006, three main themes were extracted for break out groups to consider in more detail; work, education, leisure and the family.

It was concluded that there can be no single definitive picture of the Information Society in Europe in 2006 because too many uncertainties remain about what this society will look and feel like. The group decided that although the uncertainty in itself does not necessarily have to be a bad thing - it can open up exciting opportunities - it would be useful to reduce some of the uncertainty and steer the Information Society in a certain direction.

The discussion brought forth a number of predictable and uncertain factors (see Box).

WHAT IS UNCERTAIN AND WHAT PREDICTABLE ABOUT THE FUTURE?

Leisure and the Family

Uncertainties: The return to original values; fragmentation of social patterns, the convergence of work and leisure; the response to the deterioration in the environment; the choice of homeworking; the re-emergence of the importance of religion and the censorship of information.

Predictable: Increased levels of travel for leisure purposes/ activities; increased number of women in the workplace; social interaction with particular reference to the advent of technologies that reduce society's need to interact during certain activities (i.e. home shopping).

Education

Uncertainties: Society's attitude to education; the use of languages; cultural and social values; teaching skills; legislation; the role of parents and the funding of education.

Predictable: Integrity of information (information control); the advent of PCs and network computers; lifelong, self and distance learning; the Internet; understanding the capability of and exploiting IT; flexibility and the impact that commerce may have on education.

Work

Uncertainties: The style of leadership, the ability for people to change, geographic boundaries and the effect of European politics on jobs; company loyalty vs company change and commoditization vs target markets (niche).

Predictable: The increased rate of change; new working roles and their complexity; the change in the job mix and the increased importance of marketable multi-skilled employees; more women in the workplace; working smarter; increasing levels of competition; less interaction with colleagues; culture awareness and skills; the use of technology for communication and job insecurity.

The Group's vision of the Information Society differed from that of the Hedsor Group in one important particular. The emphases that they placed on leisure, on working smarter not longer, on education (see Figure 6.12) were significantly higher.

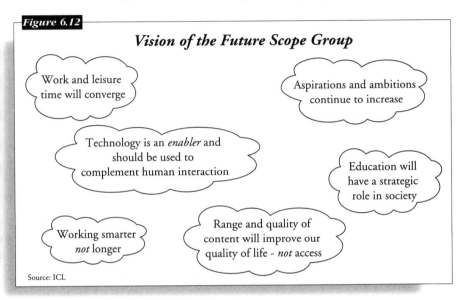

Figure 6.12

Vision of the Future Scope Group

Work and leisure time will converge

Aspirations and ambitions continue to increase

Technology is an *enabler* and should be used to complement human interaction

Education will have a strategic role in society

Working smarter *not* longer

Range and quality of content will improve our quality of life - *not* access

Source: ICL

At the end of the workshop the Group made a number of recommendations.

- More information should be provided on EU discussions in all nations in a format that is easy to understand and read. This could be helped by a structured EU awareness/advertising campaign. Also, forums, particularly involving the younger generations who are growing up with the assumptions and aspirations of the Information Society, should meet to establish a vision of Europe.

- In schools and colleges career advisors should actively promote the increasing need for a flexible workforce that is willing to and can accommodate change.

- In industry companies should provide "management of change" training to prepare its workforce for the need for transferable skills and a flexible attitude. They should also make flexible working easier by offering the choice of working from home, providing the means (technology) and by measuring performance on realistic results, not hours worked.

• The younger generation should have a more valued role in the creation of the Information Society, in recognition that they foster different ambitions and approaches that are relevant to decision-makers.

These recommendations were included in the Hedsor Memorandum.

The communication technique chosen for the Hedsor Memorandum was in two steps. First, a short write up of the event and its recommendations was posted on the Internet asking for comments and additional areas for action. The focus was on recommendations rather than the scenarios which had been used to develop the recommendations, though the leading scenario did start to create a vision of why and how we might enjoy an Information Society. Then the Memorandum was written to include the comments from the consultation on the Internet, and given wide circulation to policy makers.

COMMUNICATING SCENARIOS

The differences between communicating scenarios for influencing public attitudes as opposed to business planning, arise in part because the audiences are different. Although top-level communication for portfolio managers, for example, is important to get the concept across, communication of scenarios in business planning also demands a level of detail. A discussion of the differences appears in the proceedings of an IIR conference (Ringland, 1996).

The Chatham House Forum project discussed earlier is a good example. In 1996 the Forum published "Unsettled Times", a book about 200 pages long and a presentation. The presentation was a slide set on disk with the use of build up to show the systems' effects.

There were three scenarios which were positioned on two axes. One is whether the industrialized world is or isn't successful in the new environment, while the other axis is whether the industrialized and industrializing world manages to converge or doesn't, in which case there would be social disaffection. Distilling what can be a number of uncertainties into two basic axes makes the message easier to grasp.

However, while both the book and the slide set have been good techniques to communicate the findings to audiences such as economists, senior people in business, and government organizations, the lack of storylines or dynamic characters make it more difficult for wider audiences to hook into the ideas easily.

In retrospect, it could have been useful to find additional techniques for communicating the essence of the scenarios: other possible methods include videos, newspaper headlines, or plays. We considered videos of the presentation, which used slide build up techniques to show evolving systems graphically, but perhaps newspaper headlines would have been the most appropriate for this audience. These can not only bring the storyline to life, but it can also help monitor potential signposts, as Glen Peters showed in his headlines.

CONCLUSIONS

The use of scenarios as a way of developing recommendations for public policy has proved its worth: by providing a range of possible plausible futures, the effect of actions can be made explicit in a non-threatening way.

This chapter focused on the use of a set of scenarios to create a framework for a shared vision of the future, to promote discussion and build consensus, outside a business environment. Looking at the similarities between organizations who report success in using scenarios, and the way in which, for instance, the South African or Canadian governments have used scenarios to create coherence, suggests the importance of communication via storyline and image.

The scenarios produced by the Chatham House Forum, the Economist Intelligence Unit, and Glen Peters' "Beyond the Next

Wave" explore dilemmas for governments and business as the world evolves.

This chapter takes the Hedsor memorandum event as an example of an event which used scenario thinking in a diverse group to formulate recommendations for actions, in a 24 hour timescale. This pattern has been successfully followed on a number of other occasions.

CHAPTER SEVEN

Scenarios for Learning

SUMMARY

This chapter starts by reviewing the learning aspects of some of the scenario projects discussed so far or described in the case studies in Part III. It then discusses three examples of the use of scenario thinking events designed with the aim of increasing the capability of the individuals rather than immediately linking to policy or to business planning. It concludes that, while scenario building events in workshop mode create shared vocabulary and stimulate thought, working with scenarios over a longer period leads to significant learning.

INTRODUCTION

Many of the case studies and examples, replies to the Conference Board Europe poll, and discussions with experts, highlight the importance of scenarios as a learning environment. By providing a framework for a disciplined but open-ended "what-if?" or "how could it be?" discussion, scenarios support the learning process for groups or individuals. This was a common and prevalent theme.

Learning takes time and space, for experimentation and exploration, so most of the examples are of projects with a duration of months rather than days. But in some environments, step functions of learning can take place within a few days: two examples are discussed below before, later in the chapter, the dynamics of short events are analysed in more detail.

LEARNING EXPERIENCE WITH SCENARIOS

In Part II, the use of scenarios at Statoil is described in the SRI section. There, scenarios were used to prioritize R&D projects initially - but the example suggests that the enduring benefit for Statoil was the adoption of the thinking process.

The Hemingford Scenarios are described in Part IV and their use is discussed in Part III. They plot four possible futures for health care, and were developed in a two-day workshop based on input from polling expert opinion. The scenarios have been used by many units of the UK Health Service: the application at North West Anglia Health Authority describes how the localization, adoption and learning has taken place over several months.

United Distillers have used scenarios to help the Indian and South African Management teams deal with the political and economic uncertainties affecting the business in their country. The South African experience particularly identifies the need for and achievement of *"having the scenarios in the blood"* and *"you can't (in United Distillers) think about South Africa without thinking about the scenarios"*.

In ICL we have used scenarios for portfolio management, risk assessment, and skills planning. In each application, the scenarios have been the framework within which the relevant managers could "play" in the future and experiment with options and the consequences of actions. The skills workshops described in Chapter 5 allowed a group of people, with a shared concern and vocabulary (e.g. consultancy managers), to learn to think about alternate futures in a very short space of time, and develop action plans for their businesses.

The 24-hour event organized by ICL to consider the evolution of the Information Society used scenarios to create a common vocabulary and shared vision to underpin the recommendations. During the event, we come to a realization of some of the significant differences between the Information Society and the Industrial Society-relating to the increased role of the individual, of small businesses, and of local government (see Chapter 6).

The Chatham House Forum scenarios were outlined in Chapter 6 (Three scenarios for the Industrialized World). The working method which contributed to the scenarios has some similarities to the Information Society work in Canada, and some interesting differences.

Organizations belonging to the Forum through a subscription are represented at working meetings by individuals from a range of departments - Personnel to Corporate Planning to Quality - and levels from very senior to quite junior. The meeting tackled a topic or aspect - for instance the effect of information technology on brand, the management of complex systems - which were fed into the emerging scenarios. During the year of discussions the individuals created a vocabulary and approach which now supports the addition of new members with ease. The learning process was slow at first, and the issues complex. The communication level after a year is startlingly more effective than at the beginning.

The process described in Steve Rosell's books "Governance in an Information Society" (1992) and "Changing Maps" (1995), on work in Canada on the Information Society, was achieved with a more homogeneous group of participants than the Chatham House Forum. But, as he emphasizes, the roundtable of senior civil servants met with a number of international authorities and looked for case studies in their own departments, as part of the process leading to building scenarios. The scenarios were then used over time to consider the implications for policy, and this was the stage at which they "lived".

Since the scenario construction workshop is a central aspect of most of the approaches described in this book it seemed worth taking a look at the dynamics of these events through three examples.

SCENARIO WORKSHOPS

The common theme in the following sections is the use of scenario building to create a shared language among a small group of people. The data gathering stage for these types of scenarios may be negligible or even non-existent, with discussion based on the knowledge already in the group's heads. The output may or may not be presented outside the group. So the examples are based on events I have been part of, and concentrates more on the dynamics of the process than the outputs.

So for instance, the Global Business Network (GBN) Workshop on Electronic Commerce described below used a set of scenarios as a starting point to get a diverse group of people to think through some of the effects of electronic commerce on their home organizations. This is similar to the use of the Coral Reef and Deep Sea scenarios in Marketing 2005 - a workshop held under the auspices of the Worshipful Company of Information Technologists to look at the shape of Marketing in the IT Industry in 2005

The University of Loughborough event on "The Future of Manufacturing" brought together a diverse set of academics and industry players, and did produce a report; but the participants commented that the value they got from the event was the individual and group insights relevant to their research programmes.

BRAINSTORMING AND SCENARIOS

Our use of scenarios followed the exploration of a range of techniques for thinking about the future, with our ICL 2020 Group. This group consists of people who are in their late twenties or early thirties, so have been with the company for typically about five years, and have been nominated as "people who could be running the company in the year 2020".

We first began these meetings with pure brainstorming, but found that counter-productive. It was very difficult to get any sort of coherence of vocabulary and vision and tended to result in people arguing about whether they were right about the future.

We have now run a series of scenario-based workshops with them to focus their thinking on the potential challenges in 2020: these have looked at technology, at markets, and at skills and have directed the energies into outputs which help us in Strategic Planning.

GLOBAL BUSINESS NETWORK WORKSHOP ON ELECTRONIC COMMERCE

In July 1996 GBN held a workshop on electronic commerce. The purpose was to create an environment in which people from a range of organizations could consider the characteristics of the electronic commerce battlefield. It was a two-day event with about 100 participants. There were initial briefings by academics and researchers, and the aim was to use examples and vivid images to aid adoption of a new vocabulary and enable the discussion of issues.

The framework laid out was based on the two major driving uncertainties below. These affect the environment of companies developing strategies to profit from market restructuring, either as successful attackers or successful new entrants.

1. Ease of entry. This is the set of criteria that determines the ease with which new entrants can enter the marketplace, even those whose market share and infrastructure might once have provided sustainable competitive advantage and where there have been strict regulatory restrictions such as telecommunications and banking. New technology and new means of reaching customers erode the value of existing infrastructures.

2. Degree of customization. This is the set of criteria that determines the degree to which companies are able to tailor their product offerings to the needs of individual customers, including product design and pricing so as to attract (or not attract) profitable (or non-profitable) customers. This may be high or low in the future depending on the availability of information to support customization and the degree to which privacy regulation or other factors limits the ability to tailor designs and pricing strategies. This also determines how easy new entrants might find it to attack existing industry participants, particularly where those have not carried out customer profitability analysis.

The first driver thus reflects the ease with which new entrants can develop the infrastructure, distribution channel, and regulatory approval to enter the market. The second driver reflects the ease with which new entrants can target their desired customers, and thus can capture desirable market share and the associated profits away from established players.

The drivers were combined to create four scenarios.

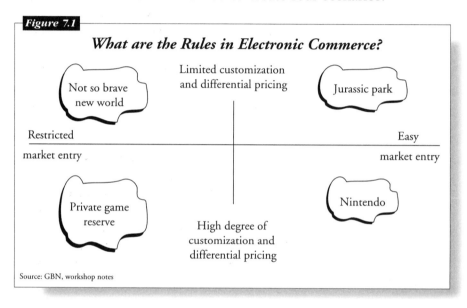

Figure 7.1

What are the Rules in Electronic Commerce?

Not so brave new world

Limited customization and differential pricing

Jurassic park

Restricted

market entry

Easy

market entry

Private game reserve

High degree of customization and differential pricing

Nintendo

Source: GBN, workshop notes

FOUR SCENARIOS FOR ELECTRONIC COMMERCE

Jurassic Park:
It is easier to get into the market here than it is to succeed. Once in the marketplace, new entrants find that they have no distinctive advantage over the incumbent firms and that the dinosaurs they encounter are surprisingly capable of defending themselves. Change is slow, and new entrants either fail, or come to resemble existing industry participants.

Nintendo:
This is a "shoot em up" scenario. It is easy to enter the marketplace and, once in, new competitors are free to develop

new and more effective strategies for targeting customers through differential product offerings and differential pricing strategies. These strategies are used to attack both each other and the incumbents that previously dominated the industry.

Private Game Reserve:
Regulatory restrictions or restricted access to resources needed to enter the marketplace limit the number of new entrants. However, once in the market these new competitors are able to perform whatever degree of customization they believe will optimize their profitability. They may also find that the industry's incumbents are ill-equipped to withstand attack due to their poor customer service, inappropriate pricing policies or other factors. New entrants initially pick off previously dominant players the way poachers hunt down tame deer in a protected forest.

Not So Brave New World:
Here the future looks very much like the present. Market entry is difficult to achieve, new competitors cannot employ new targeting strategies, either for product design or differential, and find themselves forced to act much as the existing incumbents have acted.

During the workshop, breakout groups considered the competencies, opportunities and threats these scenarios posed for individuals, businesses and industries. The conversation was wide ranging, with contributors from small aggressive institutions, from large corporates, and from academia. The group did not attempt to converge, but could assess the ways of competing under each scenario. Each participant took their own lessons from the discussion for their organization.

A WORKSHOP TO THINK ABOUT MARKETING IN 2005

This Workshop was organized for the Worshipful Company of Information Technologists, a Livery Company of the City of London. The Company acts as a network of senior people in the industry and related industries, and engages in projects which relate to Information Technology and the City of London, as well as taking a wider role in charitable works.

This workshop was designed to see if a group of people who had not used scenarios before could immerse themselves enough to move into creation mode by thinking about the role of marketing, in a Coral Reef or Deep Sea world, in 2005. It was a one-day event, following the same sort of timetable as the workshops on Skills in 2005 described in Chapter 5.

The group of 12 people found that after the first hour of initial presentation, they were able to imagine the worlds sufficiently to start the discussion on how marketing would be different. The next hour involved a fair amount of definition of a vocabulary for the group, before moving into syndicate mode to develop alternate business models for the two scenarios.

When each syndicate reported back to the other, both groups revised their views to some extent. The similarities and difference in marketing in the two environments was discussed.

The group concluded that as a result of the Workshop they were in a better position to make decisions in their own organizations, and that the day had provided good value.

UNIVERSITY OF LOUGHBOROUGH

A two-day workshop was organized by the Manufacturing Systems Integration Research Institute of Loughborough University to look at the future of manufacturing systems knowledge of the UK in light of global competitive forces. The participants were from the Institute, a range of manufacturing companies in the UK, government officials, and ICL, and mostly knew at least one or two of the other participants.

The workshop was oriented to developing scenarios as a way of unravelling a number of influences on the future. It was intended to supplement conventional analysis and forecasting, to provide input to:

• research strategy

• business strategy

• national policy

It was facilitated and designed by IDON, which also produced the report.

Their agenda followed a typical pattern (see Box).

AGENDA FOR A TWO-DAY WORKSHOP

Day 1:

am: meet, introductions
                questions for the Oracle
                review process to be followed
                brainstorm factors

pm: separate out the likely givens from the trends and uncertainties
                cluster the uncertainties
                decide on the interesting combinations

Day 2

am: review the combinations
                write a scenario story for each chosen combination

pm: describe an evolution sequence for each
                look for turning points
                review Oracle questions
                discuss the implications.

They took as the time span ten years, i.e. to 2006. Each member of the group started by sharing questions for the Oracle with each other. The Oracle, as in the Greek myths, knows everything. For instance one question was "Worldwide, is the demand for manufactured goods greater or less than current levels?" With these in mind, the group saw in the timescale to 2006 a number of things which would stay relatively constant. The group identified these factors, as "Likely Givens".

The group also separated out some trends which were likely to affect the future of manufacturing systems. While each of these individually are very visible, the rate of change of each of them can vary and there could be cross-impact. However the environment for the scenarios is assumed to consist of these "Important Trends" with the Likely Givens forming a uniform backdrop.

Then the group concentrated on the factors where they were even less certain about the outcome. This was for one of several reasons e.g.:

- lack of information at the time;

- experts "know" the answer but they disagree;

- factors which are too complex or subject to the laws of chaos.

Figure 7.2

Likely Givens

- A higher need globally for manufactured goods

- Environmental issues will play a larger part

- A critical role for information systems in manufacturing

- Less man hours per unit of production

- Greater variety & number of products

- Fully global communications

- More just-in-time at the point of consumption

- A higher proportion of old people (in the West)

- More self-employed people

- High proportion of home working

Source: IDON

Figure 7.3

Important Trends

- Increasing telecommuting for work
- Products becoming more complex
- Systems becoming more modular
- Increasing computer use skills
- Decreasing number of people in manufacturing work
- Increasing electronic modelling of processes & products
- Falling product life-cycles

- Increasing leisure markets
- Growing service component
- Increasing home shopping
- Increasing electronic trading
- Growing gap between "haves" & "have nots"
- Increasing proportion of manufacturing being assembly based
- Growing use of virtual rapid prototyping

Source: IDON

The factors were clustered, and for each cluster a central question was posed, which expressed the uncertainty through an answer "yes" or "no". These are referred to as "flip-flops", and those identified by the group are shown in Figure 7.4.

Figure 7.4

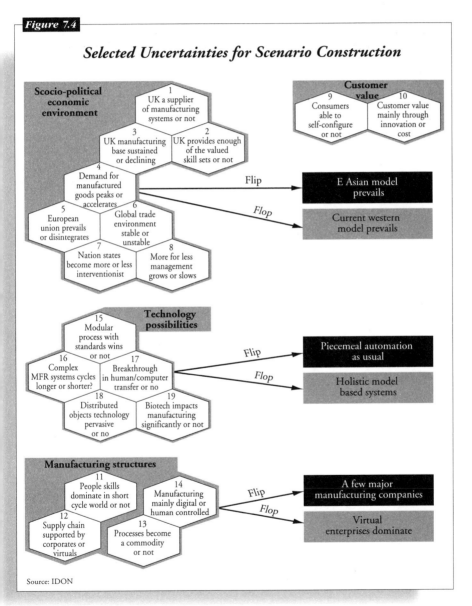

Selected Uncertainties for Scenario Construction

Source: IDON

Out of the eight possible flip-flop combinations, four combinations were chosen which seemed plausible but interesting. These were all different from the group's current forecasts or default scenarios, since the aim was to extend the range of possibilities considered.

FOUR SCENARIOS FOR 2005

All Quiet on the Western Front:
- in which East Asian business goes slowly and quietly virtual and emerges unexpectedly the winner.

During the decade 1995-2005 we have seen the West taking on board an Asian culture at the same time as Asian companies have bit by bit come over to the West in increasing numbers and gradually achieved a dominant position in the market place. Their culture has become the driving force shaping the way industry and companies develop, their gradual development of how to combine virtual enterprises with holistic model-based manufacturing eventually paying off.

Enter the Dragons:
- in which the East Asian Corporations permeate and exploit the chaos in the West until they dominate and acquire.

Over the last decade we have seen a world emerge that is dominated by virtual enterprises, retaining the piecemeal automation and a lack of standardization - the East Asian model for manufacturing industry has become the operating industrial model. This was achieved largely by the increasing dominance of Eastern corporations outright in a scheme in which virtual enterprises were set up world-wide on a transformed Keiretsu model.

How the West was Won:
- in which East Asia, especially China, ends up ruling the West though economic conquest.

By now the West has become excluded from Far East markets. Although access to these markets was already difficult, the Chinese ensured that it was almost impossible to get European goods or USA goods into China and the Eastern markets by influencing that sector of the community. It did this in two ways - creating fear amongst its neighbours and eventually combining politically with Taiwan, thus creating its current domination of world markets.

West stays Best:
- in which the West plays the East-West "partnering game" and sustains its dominance.

The West won the partnership game with the Western culture becoming predominant, holistic model-based systems being implemented and virtual enterprises becoming the norm. The West clawed back its lead from the East, Western business culture prevails, model-based systems became possible and virtual enterprises became the norm.

The scenarios would evolve through different routes, for instance the scenario "All Quiet on the Western Front" turned out be very dependent on high technology developments and their adoption (see Figure 7.5).

The workshop closed with this piece of work, since there was not time to review the Oracle questions. The consideration of the implications was left for a later discussion, mostly within the Institute. A report was produced later, though the participants felt that the main benefit had been in expanding their range of ideas for use in their own organizations.

It was significant that the group had not worked together as a whole before, even though most participants knew one or more of the others. As often happens with new groups, it look a while to develop a common vocabulary: and this meant that the progress was slower than might be expected in, say, a management team.

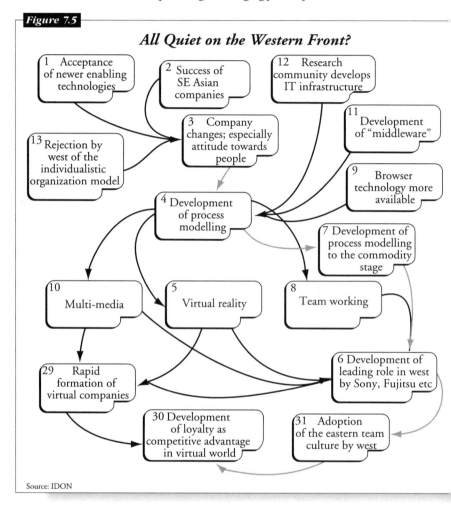

Figure 7.5

All Quiet on the Western Front?

Source: IDON

DURATION OF WORKSHOPS

The two-day workshop described is hard work, and it is often difficult to reach the storylines early enough to start thinking about the implications. However it is possible in two days to develop scenarios from scratch.

At ICL we have tried out one-day workshops to develop scenarios. These seem to be only feasible with a relatively narrow topic area and a group which is used to working together. So, for instance, we ran a successful workshop with our ICL 2020 Group, which tackled the topic of "what will be the most disruptive technology up to 2020", and captured some useful ideas. The group managed to compress much of the two-day agenda, including thinking about time lines, into one day. On the other hand, we ran a one-day scenario workshop on "work" with a group of participants who had not developed a common language by working together before. This group followed the first day agenda of the two-day workshop, and a subgroup was needed to take the combinations away to develop a storyline and recommendations.

Workshops spanning 24 hours - e.g. 4pm to 4pm - provide a way of extending the informal time when participants can develop their ideas off line, and can be successful in developing scenarios.

GBN uses a longer time period - the best part of a week - for the training workshops it organizes, which develop scenarios around one of the participants' area of interest. This provides time to try out techniques like imagining characters, developing playlets, and newspaper headlines of events, to enrich the scenarios.

The time difference seems to be important not just for the working hours: relaxation time for the group, allowing a rethinking of ideas, seems to play a considerable role.

One-day workshops based on existing scenarios, such as the Coral Reef and Deep Sea scenarios, work well, though a 4pm to 4pm format is often valuable to allow a break from day to day pressures and routine thinking.

CONCLUSIONS

In each of the workshop events the discussion and building exercise was deemed by the participants to be at least as useful than the scenarios actually generated.

The GBN Workshop on Electronic Commerce used a skeleton set of scenarios as a starting point to get a diverse group of people to think through some of the effects of electronic commerce on their home organizations. We similarly used the

Coral Reef and Deep Sea scenarios as input to a workshop held under the auspices of the Worshipful Company of Information Technologists to look at the shape of Marketing in the IT Industry in 2005

The University of Loughborough event on "The Future of Manufacturing" brought together a diverse set of academics and industry players, and did produce a report: but the participants commented that the high value they got from the event was the individual and group insights relevant to their research programmes.

The design of these events seems to suggest that to build a "new" set for a scenario takes at least two days because of the stages involved and the need to converge the vocabulary of participants: GBN typically takes most of a week for these. Workshops based on existing scenarios - as the Electronic Commerce Workshop - and ICL's workshops on skills development can achieve useful results in a working day, though a 24-hour event may provide more radical thinking.

CHAPTER EIGHT

Summary and Conclusions

SUMMARY

In this chapter we review the ground covered and summarize the answers to the question we asked at the beginning, viz.

"If I am a manager who is concerned to improve the chance of my business prospering in turbulent times, can scenario planning help?"

RECAPPING

Chapter 1
The book started by tracing the development of scenarios through to the present day. Scenarios are essentially a form of modelling of the future, in the same way as a wind tunnel is used to test new airframes or cars. While the concept is not new, the present range of techniques sometimes referred to as scenario planning mostly become visible just after the Second World War.

Figure 8.1 compares scenario planning with other forms of modelling.

Chapter 1 traces how some of them have arisen. The main schools found have been:

- High value/forecast/low value planning, where a plan is reworked with some major driving factors - e.g. market growth, or growth of market share - set to higher than or lower than forecast values. This is a useful and prudent part of strategic planning but is no longer normally thought of as scenario planning.

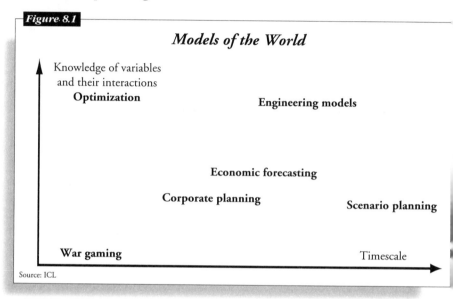

Figure 8.1

Models of the World

Knowledge of variables and their interactions

Optimization

Engineering models

Economic forecasting

Corporate planning

Scenario planning

War gaming

Timescale

Source: ICL

- Trend-impact analysis, which is concerned with the effects of trends, for instance in markets or populations, over a time period. The work done to isolate the important trends to consider, may well be similar to that used in what is more generally called scenario planning, but the basic assumption within scenario planning is that we are looking for the unexpected, i.e. what could upset the trends.

- Cross-impact analysis, which is a technology for analysis of complex systems. It concentrates on the ways in which forces on an organization, external or internal, may interact to produce effects bigger than the sum of the parts, or to magnify the effect of one force because of feedback loops. It has been used successfully where the dominant forces can be identified, and the modelling mechanism can be used to increase management's understanding of the relative importance of various factors. A recent example of its use is described in the book on 2015 by John Petersen (1994).

- What is called the "Pierre Wack" Intuitive Logics, as practised by SRI and Shell. ICL, and most of those organizations surveyed, are essentially using this approach. The essence of this is to find ways of changing mindsets so that managers can anticipate futures and prepare for them. The emphasis is on creating a coherent and credible set of stories of the future as a "wind tunnel" for testing business plans or projects, prompting public debate or increasing coherence.

This chapter also looked at the relation of scenario planning to strategic planning: for instance the rise in the use of both in response to the problems the West encountered in adjusting to the 1970s oil price shock. During the 1980s both fell comparatively into disrepute, with corporate staffs cut and a focus on cutting cost to survive.

Chapter 2
Chapter 2 surveys which companies or organizations are using scenario planning now, why and how. We took a poll of companies using scenario planning today, we looked at the literature, attended conferences and we listened hard.

We found a range of examples e.g.:

- at the Austrian insurance company, Erste Allgemeine Versicherung, to spot the results of political changes, e.g. the Berlin Wall coming down and so establish themselves early in former Eastern European countries;

- at British Airways, as a counter-weight to existing planning processes;

- at Electrolux, the consumer goods company, to see the opportunity for new businesses, e.g. a service business based on re-using consumer products;

- at wiring and cable supplier KRONE, to develop 200 new product ideas;

The published papers describe a range of uses:
- at Shell, for strategy building;

- at Digital, to understand the changing shape of the Information Industry and so restructure themselves;

- at Pacific Gas and Electricity, to dispel assumptions about the "Official Future" and cause them to work to reduce energy consumption;

- in the UK National Health Service, to provide a way for a very dispersed, large and disparate organization to think through new relationships, internally and to customers.

Most scenarios produced by the respondents to our poll through the Conference Board Europe took less than six months to build. The poll also identified that scenarios were thought of as a management development tool, as a way of creating shared vision as well as better plans, in a number of organizations; and that those who started by concentrating on the scenarios for portfolio management found this to be a valuable spin-off.

The size of organizations using scenarios ranges from KRONE UK, a medium sized organization using outside consultants, to Shell, using internal staff with some outsiders. The key seems to be "geared to the organization" which in some cases means taking a specific focus or topic. For instance in the construction industry, back of the envelope scenarios based on the effect of government regulations may be appropriate for the situation. But in some industries, and some companies in some industries, the need is to take a systematic and global view because of the nature of their business.

The chapter goes on to suggest that the turbulence caused by the paradigm shift which many futurists see occurring over the next few decades will push many organizations to look more widely for sources of help in planning for the new order.

A major source of change in the world today is the adoption of information technology. The changes visible in the last few years are expected to be dwarfed by the changes to come – in the way we work, play, shop, are governed, bank, and the communities we belong to. The impact of the Information Society could exceed those provoked by the oil price shock.

The Chapter concludes that successful organizations in this environment will be those which have found ways of looking for early warning signs that current assumptions may be invalid.

Chapter 3

Chapter 3 outlines strategic planning as performed in ICL to set a context for the discussion of our scenario planning. ICL is a company made up of (at the time of writing) nine businesses, with a small headquarters.

The chapter outlines the ICL Strategic Planning process, and discusses the use of Business Value to provide measures and create a common set of terms relating to our business targets. We also use tools like PIMS to benchmark businesses, and the Market Attractiveness/Capability matrix for portfolio analysis. Some examples are given of how these tools have been used to transform the business in conjunction with scenario thinking.

Chapter 4

Chapter 4 compares two scenario building projects that we completed two years apart. In both cases the projects were linked to strategic planning; in both cases we found that building the scenarios was a fascinating and mind-stretching project.

The first scenarios were built as part of the Vision 2000 project which was overall very successful. But the scenario project was flawed - we had failed to think through two important questions:

- what question are you trying to answer?

- how can you communicate the results and the implications?

In the second project, in 1995, linked to the examples of business transformation discussed in Chapter 3, the key question was:

- given ICL's strengths, where do we see our value to our customers in the future?

Our Coral Reef and Deep Sea scenarios described two different answers to this question: see Figure 8.2.

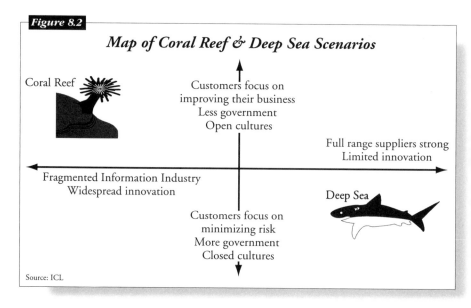

Figure 8.2

Map of Coral Reef & Deep Sea Scenarios

Coral Reef

Customers focus on
improving their business
Less government
Open cultures

Full range suppliers strong
Limited innovation

Fragmented Information Industry
Widespread innovation

Deep Sea

Customers focus on
minimizing risk
More government
Closed cultures

Source: ICL

Chapter 5

Chapter 5 describes how we have used the Coral Reef and Deep Sea Scenarios. We first used them to run in parallel with strategic planning. PIMS and MA/C analysis of two businesses - the Contract Manufacturing and Volume Products businesses - suggested we should divest them. The question was: how do these businesses look in future markets. In the case of the manufacturing business, we found that the default scenario of the management team, which had driven their business plans, was near to the scenario in which customers quickly adopted innovation - a consideration of the structure of their market allowed us to reposition the business. The analysis of the Volume Products business, suggested that a larger parent, more suitable for a market where global sales and support are the

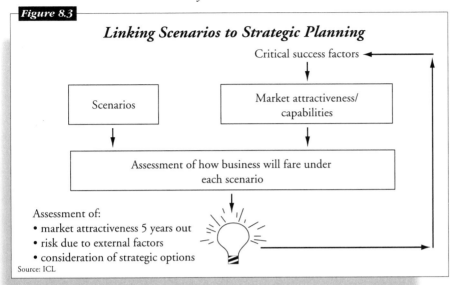

Figure 8.3

Linking Scenarios to Strategic Planning

Critical success factors

Scenarios

Market attractiveness/
capabilities

Assessment of how business will fare under
each scenario

Assessment of:
• market attractiveness 5 years out
• risk due to external factors
• consideration of strategic options

Source: ICL

characteristics of the leaders, would be better in the future: the business is now owned by Fujitsu. Figure 8.3 shows the relationship between the scenarios and the portfolio management process.

We also used the scenarios to evaluate a set of potential new businesses: we had seven "at the starting gate" and could not invest in all of them: we used the scenarios to evaluate the ability of the seven to operate under either scenario. One is the business which now runs BBC On-line, the other won the European IT Prize in 1996 and helps financial services companies develop Internet services for home banking and allows banks to build up a picture of the customer's behaviour.

In terms of communicating the scenarios, we found that working with the teams responsible for a particular function or market was the only way that we could introduce the thinking into the organization - it is a new way of thinking in an action-driven company. So we learned (again) from Shell and brought out a glossy brochure. We trained ICL consultants who work with customers, and staff from our Senior Executive Programme (which works with customers on strategic and team building events). And we worked with teams that had specific problems at the time: for instance, using the scenarios to help the consultants and the technical community to plan for a skills portfolio in the future.

And we concluded that, to communicate scenarios in organizations not steeped in scenario thinking, the following are needed:

- a "lift (elevator) speech" which describes the use of the scenarios in relation to a specific concern, or a success story, or reference sell;

- clear representation of "the question";

- vivid names, and a glossy "storyline" booklet helps;

- a good storyline and coherence that people found credible, memorable incidents on the timeline;

- a process by which the scenarios can be used by the organization to decide what to do next.

With these hooks, individuals or groups can start the process of "getting inside" The scenarios, even if they have not been part of their genesis.

Chapter 6

In Chapters 3, 4, and 5 we have been describing work in ICL to build and use scenarios for - broadly speaking - business planning. Chapter 6 focused on the use of a set of scenarios to create a framework for a shared vision of the future, to promote discussion and build consensus, outside a corporate environment. Looking at the similarities between organizations who report success in using scenarios, and the way in which for instance the South African or Canadian governments have used scenarios to create coherence, suggests the importance of communication via storyline and image.

Chapter 7

Many of the companies and people we polled on the use of scenarios emphasized their role in learning so in Chapter 7 we discussed the use of the process of scenario building for creating a shared language, for instance within a management team. In this environment, the building process is part of "getting inside" the scenario. Hearing - or reading - a scenario does not internalize it: phrases like "getting into the blood" were used to describe the process of working with scenarios in planning.

Since a central building block of many scenario planning processes is a workshop, three workshop events were analysed.

The Global Business Network (GBN) Workshop on Electronic Commerce used a skeleton set of scenarios as a starting point to get a diverse group of people to think through some of the effects of electronic commerce on their home organizations. We similarly used the Coral Reef and Deep Sea scenarios as input to a workshop held under the auspices of the Worshipful Company of Information Technologists to look at the shape of Marketing in the IT Industry in 2005

The University of Loughborough event on "The Future of Manufacturing" brought together a diverse set of academics and industry players, and did produce a report: but the participants commented that the high value they got from the event was the individual and group insights relevant to their research programmes.

The design of these events seems to suggest that to build a "new" set for a scenario takes at least two days because of the stages involved and the need to converge the vocabulary of participants: GBN typically take most of a week for these. Workshops based on existing scenarios - as the Electronic Commerce Workshop - and ICL's on skills development can achieve useful results in a full day.

PERSONAL CONCLUSIONS

As a result of the work and investigations described in this book I have come to four personal conclusions.

The first is that scenario planning, whether in the public domain or in business is an important technique for two reasons:

- in a time of uncertainty, it unfreezes intellect, allowing intelligent people a framework within which it's not only "OK" but even mandatory to admit that they do not know what the future will bring, but nevertheless to plan. The role of vivid image, storyline, of timelines, of anecdotal events in scenario are an important part of the method.

- it can be used to "wind-tunnel" analysis made using strategic planning techniques like PIMS benchmarking or portfolio management with Market Attractiveness/Capability matrixes. By looking at whether the decision would be the same under both scenarios, or the same in several years time, the danger of solving last year's problems with strategic planning is reduced.

The second conclusion is that successes in scenario planning are, like successes in strategic planning, hard to pinpoint. Would Shell have found ways of growing faster than Exxon if it had not developed a way of looking for early indicators, thinking through what to do if eventualities should occur, re-acting fast? What has been the case in all of the examples noted is that scenarios have been found to be a good management tool for creating new ideas, identifying opportunities presented by the new environment. Would they have found better opportunities by another route? It's hard to say.

The third conclusion is that, to communicate scenarios in organizations not steeped in scenario thinking, it needs all aspects of communication to be thought through, from lift speeches to storylines and from immersion exercises to processes. The purpose of this communication is to engage the individual or group, so that "thinking inside" the scenarios can start: it is only by working with the scenarios that learning is possible. This is the part that most often goes wrong.

And the final conclusion I have come to is in the importance of the people who lead and contribute to the scenario activity. While only 20% of large organizations use scenarios currently, the need for good thinking - to set content and process - is clear: it is a leading edge activity. It seems to be quality rather than quantity of effort that matters, in particular, finding ways of taking the organization outside its box. Some advocate the use of consultants for this: we used an MBA mid-term student as devil's advocate on our 1995 project in ICL. The advantage of consultants is that they will also bring process, and I have seen the difference in a group operating in a well-designed and facilitated process and a similar group without. But of course the need for involving people who understand the organization's culture is clear, unless the scenario exercise is seen as a bullet for a particular problem as in KRONE's case.

The question remains, of whether it is useful - as scenario planning becomes more widely used - to routinize it. It seems to me that the jury is out on this, though the right structured process can certainly help teams to extend their capabilities.

I hope that the previous chapters have shown how I have come to these conclusions.

Finally, some questions which are raised by the discussion in this book, but are beyond its scope to answer.

- About 20% of large organizations have experience of scenario planning: are there systematic differences between these companies compared with those that have not?

- The first wave of scenario planning in business followed the oil price shock of the early 1970s, and scenarios have been used over the past decade to think through uncertainties associated with political change, with environmental forces, and with industry restructuring. Which of the aspects of the paradigm shifts foreseen by the futurists will cause the next surge of usage?

As Philip Kotler says in "Rethinking the Future", (Gibson (ed) 1997), "*To prepare for the twenty-first century, companies need to imagine alternative scenarios for the marketplace of the future, and use these scenarios to stimulate their thinking about possible contingencies and strategies.*

My advice, therefore, is get busy building scenarios and determining what they imply in the way of strategic planning. Don't think 'business as usual'.

To quote Yogi Berra, 'the future ain't what it used to be'."

PART II:

Methods and Examples

The sections on each method/school/organization are intended to provide a brief introduction, and to include examples as illustrations.

The sections are in alphabetic order:

Battelle's BASICS
which uses a computer-based cross-impact model to derive likely scenarios.

Comprehensive Situation Mapping (CSM)
which is a computer-based system to go from concept to systems simulation to probabilities.

Computer-Driven Simulations - e.g. STRAT*X
is a computer based tool to assist management decisions.

The Copenhagen Institute for Future Studies
is an organization which develops scenarios concerned with social factors.

The European Commission
has developed a methodology called "Shaping Factors" which is an adaptive form of Delphi consultation.

The French School
is a tool-based approach to scenarios which uses an extension of cross-impact techniques to include high order interactions.

The Futures Group
who use trend-impact analysis to develop scenarios.

Global Business Network
which has benefited from Shell and SRI in developing methods to tackle scenarios with creativity.

NCRI
whose Future Mapping methodology is based on finite sets of events and end states geared to developing market strategy.

SRI
uses its experienced approach to create focused scenarios as the basis for strategy and decision making.

BATTELLE'S BASICS

The following is a quotation from an article by Stephen M Millett, Manager of Forecasting and Strategic Planning Studies at Battelle Institute, in *Planning Review,* Vol 20, 2, 1992. Reproduced by permission of the Planning Review.

"During the 1980s other organizations were developing their scenario planning methodologies using computer techniques. The US-based consulting group Battelle had begun performing scenario analysis in 1980, creating a methodology it calls BASICS (Battelle Scenario Inputs to Corporate Strategy). It is an adaptation of the cross-impact technique developed at the RAND Corporation and the University of Southern California. This, in turn, was coupled with Battelle's computer-based algorithm formulated in Geneva. An expert judgment methodology is another element of the system.

The process was then packaged into a user-friendly, personal computer software program at Battelle headquarters in Columbus, Ohio. Since then the scenario consulting team has worked with about 50 clients around the world applying scenario analysis to various market environments and investment questions."

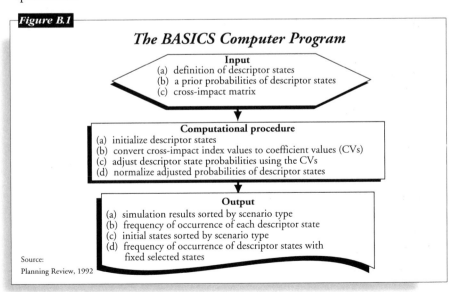

Figure B.1

The BASICS Computer Program

Input
(a) definition of descriptor states
(b) a prior probabilities of descriptor states
(c) cross-impact matrix

Computational procedure
(a) initialize descriptor states
(b) convert cross-impact index values to coefficient values (CVs)
(c) adjust descriptor state probabilities using the CVs
(d) normalize adjusted probabilities of descriptor states

Output
(a) simulation results sorted by scenario type
(b) frequency of occurrence of each descriptor state
(c) initial states sorted by scenario type
(d) frequency of occurrence of descriptor states with fixed selected states

Source:
Planning Review, 1992

Abbreviated from the same article is the following example:.

EXAMPLE: Changes in the European IT Market

In 1988 Battelle was asked to work with an American-based IT company and apply the BASICS scenario method to a forecast of the changing European IT market (including computer hardware, "smart" machines, software, databases and networks). The company already had a profitable business in Europe but was facing increasing competition from other American, European, and Japanese IT companies. While the company enjoyed a large market share of a few products in discrete niches, it was searching for the formula for wider success in the highly profitable but competitive European market. It wanted not only to defend its existing share, but to expand it if the circumstances proved favourable.

The CEO was very clear in his objectives to the scenario team, which was composed of both Battelle analysts and corporate managers. He did not want them to generate more data. Rather, he wanted their report organized into alternative sets of outcomes anticipated by the onset of the European Single Market in 1992, as well as proposals for alternative corporate responses to achieve business goals. He did not want a single summary of what the future would be. He wanted several possible views of the outlook for what was then called the European Community (EC), now the European Union, so that he could evaluate the different sets of likely future conditions and judge how best they might affect the IT business. By recognizing these alternative potential market environments, the company could begin to formulate the contingency strategies needed to meet the changing circumstances. Moreover, the CEO wanted company managers to adapt the scenario approach so that they could continue their own scenario analysis and strategic thinking without depending too much on external consultants.

There were three stages to the project.
1. Identifying the Issues.
The first step was to state the question as precisely as possible.

In 1988 the company needed to know:

- How likely was the EC to reach its single market cohesion goals by the end of 1992?

- Would an integrated EC market result in a "fortress Europe", with a policy of protectionism aimed at US-made products?

- How might a more integrated EC affect the overall growth and competitiveness of the IT market?

These answers would help the company decide whether to invest further in European-based manufacturing, or to consider whether other types of investments might buy greater local presence for marketing and service.

To identify the most important factors Battelle held a series of group meetings to elicit critically important issues using a group dynamics technique called the Nominal Group Technique, a round-robin procedure developed at the University of Wisconsin that polls opinion in a systematic, non-confrontational way. That technique was selected because results were needed quickly and the budget was tight. The technique is well-suited for managing the judgments of face-to-face participants and it has a record of producing excellent results even when both time and resources are limited.

Three sessions were held, two at the company's offices in Europe and the US, and one at Battelle's headquarters in Columbus, Ohio, with Battelle technologists, economists and market analysts. From this the scenario team distilled 20 critical factors for the scenario analysis.

2. Trend Analysis

An essay was then written on each of those factors by both Battelle researchers and knowledgeable company managers. In BASICS, these factors are called "descriptors" but they could also be called variables, issues or trends. Each essay defined the factor, explained its importance, reviewed its immediate history and current situation, and speculated on alternative outcomes by

1992. After being peer reviewed and critiqued, the essays formed the documentation for the judgements made for the alternative outcomes. The BASICS method, unlike other variations of cross-impact analysis for scenario generation, provides for two, three or four likely outcomes for each factor. The researchers who prepared the essays selected the outcomes and the a priori probabilities based on their judgement.

3. Cross-Impact Analysis

Using the BASICS PC software program, a matrix was composed with the factors and alternative outcomes arrayed on each axis. The cells of the matrix were filled with index values of how the occurrence of each outcome would change the a priori probabilities of all other outcomes. In purely statistical terms, the index values were used as easy approximations of conditional probabilities. A matrix of 20 descriptors of each axis, which would call for the completion of 3,600 matrix cells, was performed with relative ease on a PC using the software program.

The cross-impact matrix was completed and reviewed, with differences of judgement discussed and reconciled. The BASICS algorithm performed calculations for a variety of initial conditions and conditional probabilities. It organized outcomes with high probabilities into sets that were internally consistent. From these outcomes, the analysts detected a clear pattern of the most likely outcomes and prepared a report outlining the four principal scenarios which were delivered to the company's senior management in August 1989.

THE EC 1992 SCENARIOS

Scenario 1.
The first and most likely scenario was called "EC 1992 Works". That said that the EC would likely meet most, but not all of its single market cohesion goals by the end of 1992. While progress would be made towards the free movement of goods and the standardization of indirect taxes, the EC might not achieve banking centralization with a unified currency and monetary

policy. Nonetheless, EC government control would grow in strength. It was anticipated that East-West relations would become "friendlier", but in the summer of 1989 the collapse of the Warsaw Pact and the disintegration was not seen. The policy of the EC would be no more and no less protectionist than the rest of the world. In this scenario, the level of IT market growth would be medium to high.

Scenario 2.
This was called "EC 1992 Disappoints". It did not portray a failed EC single market, but it did show it evolving more slowly. In this version, IT growth would continue to be moderate, despite the slow pace toward cohesion.

Scenario 3.
Called "The EC Fails", it painted a gloomier picture than the second one. Little or no progress was being made towards achieving the 1992 goals, and the perception was that the EC had not just disappointed but fizzled. Only under these circumstances would EC trade policies be different from the rest of the world and be less protectionist. IT market growth would be low.

Scenario 4.
Called "The US of Europe", it expected the 1992 single market goals to be reached and perhaps succeeded. A centralized banking system would be in place and free movement of goods achieved. The EC would grow in power to the state of semi-sovereignty, and be no more or less protectionist than the rest of the world. IT market growth would be high.

Some general conclusions were drawn following briefings with company managers in the US and Europe. Among them:

- While the EC was unlikely to achieve all of its goals by the end of 1992, the momentum towards single market cohesion was strong. The concept of an integrated European market was to be taken seriously and must be included in long-term IT business plans (and this was before the Maastricht treaty in December 1991).

- The prospect of a "Fortress Europe" as a protected market was unlikely, at least for American-made goods.

- Being American-based, the company should definitely increase its presence in the EC in order to get closer to end-user customers. This did not necessarily mean manufacturing in the EC, but strengthening the presence at the marketing/servicing end of the value chain.

- IT growth in the EC would most likely be medium to high.

- There would be intense competition from European-based IT companies both in the more cohesive EC market and around the world.

The company took a variety of actions, including:

- Increasing its local presence within the EC by expanding marketing and service networks to be as close to the customer as possible.

- Made a commitment to maintain and expand an office in Brussels to keep close to the European Commission.

- Reaffirmed its appreciation of long-term business opportunities in Europe, and was expecting increased competition, not only in Europe but eventually from European IT companies in the US.

- Began to use the scenarios as a tool of communication from the company to customers. The scenarios were seen to provide "thought leadership".

- Revised and extended the scenarios to 1995.

COMPREHENSIVE SITUATION MAPPING (CSM)

CSM is a tool that can help in strategy design from the initial phase of building a model of the situation, to strategic analysis, to fully-fledged system dynamics simulation modelling. This description is based on that given in Georgantzas and Acar (1995).

It combines the advantages of cognitive mapping with an integrative desktop tool. It incorporates principles of system dynamics and systems thinking whereby relationships between strategic variables are not modelled piecemeal, but entire situations are captured at once. It acknowledges that the main parties involved in a situation are purposeful actors who can manipulate controllable levers or decision variables. Modelling the dialectical argumentation process is an essential component of direct or computerized group decision-support systems.

Features allow the diagramming of complex strategic situations and the computing of scenarios of change in the environment and in a firm's strategy. These are not just loosely based on assumptions but are the computational results of propagating change through an elegant yet simple modelling technique which stimulates the way environmental sources affect a firm's situation by activating both external triggers of change and the way internal levers might be pulled on decisively by a firm's management team.

Because it has features akin to computer simulation, it can serve as a bridge between qualitative thinking and quantitative operation research/management science simulation modelling.

EXAMPLE: Using CSM at Combank

Combank's team of top managers wanted to take advantage of the rise in the inflow of overseas investment to the US market in the context of its mission of achieving balance sheet strength while remaining a service business highly responsive to other requests. It was growing through both acquisition and staying close to its clients and providing advice on long-term global business plans. The proposal was that the bank build on its reputation and history of serving foreign corporations and institutions in the US market, while also helping the US subsidiaries of its foreign clients.

Led by the senior vice president of strategic planning, senior managers wanted to reach a better understanding together of the potential synergy among its products, and explore the relationships among profit, volume capacity and the importance of staying close to the customer. The goal was to make profit and profit potential the basis for future identification, measurement and performance evaluation.

The first step was to hold two meetings, one involving the vice presidents of finance and operations, and the other with the marketing and planning vice presidents. That enabled the formulation of both a technology- and marketing-centred view. The first meeting brought everyone together and was the basis for creating the integrated CSM of Combank (Figure CSM.1)

The CSM was then backed up by using the MICMAC variable classification approach (Godet, 1987) to verify higher order effects and to check the stability of the diagram. This confirmed what the Combank team had projected as the importance and relationship of the key variables, and led to the generation of scenarios which captured the behavioural patterns of profit

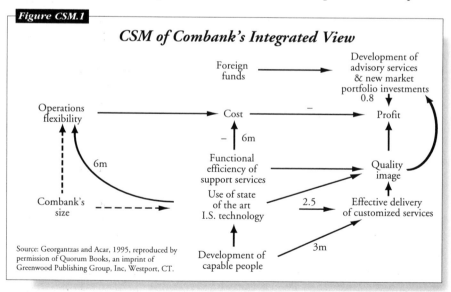

Figure CSM.1

CSM of Combank's Integrated View

Source: Georgantzas and Acar, 1995, reproduced by permission of Quorum Books, an imprint of Greenwood Publishing Group, Inc, Westport, CT.

Part II: Methods and examples

growth, and showed the potential synergy among Combank's services, volume capacity and the importance of staying close to customers.

This view also led to the creation of second and third creation of scenarios, based on more complex systems dynamics. The second set of scenarios were based on the two strands in the bank's possible responses: raise revenues and boost the effectiveness aspect of the CSM. Alternatively, the efficiency aspect of the bank could be highlighted with streamlined operations. This led to the creation of four sets of mixed change scenarios based on different values of the input variables, i.e. capable people, foreign funds and efficiency (Figure CSM.2)

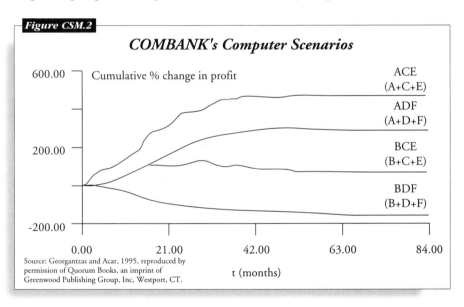

Figure CSM.2

COMBANK's Computer Scenarios

Source: Georgantzas and Acar, 1995, reproduced by permission of Quorum Books, an imprint of Greenwood Publishing Group, Inc, Westport, CT.

Then using BASICS from Battelle, the high/medium/low probability of each state that could occur in terms of potential profit as a result of a corresponding state affecting the influx of foreign funds into the US was assessed. As the authors write, *"To estimate the final outcome probabilities, we assigned three sets of a priori probabilities to the three possible states (high, medium, low) of each of the variables that Combank's planning group deemed critical. The three sets of the probabilistic weights assigned were:*

0.50, 0.33 and 0.17 for the best-case scenario or fast-growth potential,
0.33, 0.34 and 0.33 for the reference scenario and
0.17, 0.33 and 0.50 for the worst case scenario.

The cross impact matrix based on the CSM's deterministic causal graphing served as input to BASICS, which confirmed the CSM results."

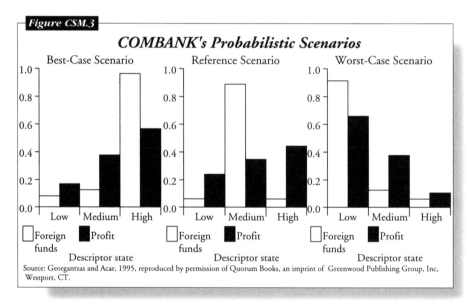

Figure CSM.3

COMBANK's Probabilistic Scenarios

Source: Georgantzas and Acar, 1995, reproduced by permission of Quorum Books, an imprint of Greenwood Publishing Group, Inc, Westport, CT.

These results represented in Figure CSM.3 formed the basis of strategic recommendations to the Bank, and showed the sensitivity of the Bank to the influx of foreign funds.

COMPUTER-DRIVEN SIMULATIONS - EG STRAT*X

This section is based on discussions with Mark Loveless of Strat*X and Adrian Kamellard, see Kamellard (1996).

The use of powerful simulation models is another approach being used by some companies to look at "what-if" questions about the future based on fairly robust assumptions. One such model is that offered by Strat*X, founded in 1984 by Jean-Claude Larreche, Professor of Marketing at INSEAD. It has developed a portfolio of Windows-based business simulations, each designed to bridge the gap between theory and practice across a variety of industries. The original MARKSTRAT, was developed in 1977 by Professor Larreche, then at Stanford University, and Professor Hubert Gatignon, then at the Wharton School, to use with their students.

The latest version, MARKSTRAT 3, is designed for use with groups of 16-30 managers split into teams of 4-6 people. Each team is responsible for managing a simulated services company in direct competition with the other teams. It gives people a risk-free environment in which to get some hands-on applications of the tools. Programmes are tailored to individual needs.

The simulation can run over 7-8 decision periods (years), with each decision taking approximately 2-2$\frac{1}{2}$ hours to complete. This is accompanied by lecture-discussion sessions on relevant tools, concepts, and frameworks.

Participants have to conduct several different types of analysis in the process of making decisions:

* Information and market analysis (by region), including total market size, market growth rate, segment size and growth rate, number of products, average price, product positioning, micro-segment behaviour.

* Competitive analysis (by region), including total market share, market share by segment/channel, number of products, brand equity, reputation, corporate initiatives, advertising and sales force expenditure by brand, revenues, R&D expenditures.

- Environmental analysis (by region), including GNP growth rate, exchange rate, inventory holding costs.

- Financial analysis (by region), including revenues, costs of goods sold, inventory holding costs, advertising, gross marketing contribution, R&D salesforce, market research, exceptional cost/profit, net marketing contribution, next period budget.

For example, after the context has been set and an understanding of scenario planning principles have been developed, each team manages a simulated company within an industry. They have a portfolio of products/services and have to manage the life cycle of that portfolio, adding new products to the portfolio, phase out older ones that are losing their effectiveness, make investments and plan the marketing mix, including the price, and send out the sales force to different market segments depending on where they see the best demand or competitive advantage. Within the simulation market research can also be purchased about competitors' activity, while perceptual maps can show perception of the team's company.

Participant performance is evaluated against a number of possible measures, based on a balanced score card approach:

Financial:
- Share price
- Sales
- Relative market share
- Net group profit
- Return on investment
- Brand contribution/profitability
- Country profit etc.

R&D Investment productivity:
- Leadership in certain markets
- Number of innovative products developed etc.

EXAMPLE: Using Computer Simulations in the Telecoms Industry

The MARKSTRAT Services - Telecoms Scenario (or MSS Telecoms) was developed in 1996 in response to demand for a sophisticated simulation specifically designed for Cable & Wireless. It was also the first time that scenario planning became an element in the MARKSTRAT process. It involved focused lectures and discussion sessions to address major issues and dynamics within the telecoms industry. The programme of lectures, discussions and simulations was complemented with keynote speakers from within the client company. The goal was to sensitize the managers to the need to plan ahead using scenario plans and to be prepared to make quick, yet sensible plans and decisions in the face of adversity or change. The simulation exercises were tailored to include a specific twist requested by the client: a series of discontinuities.

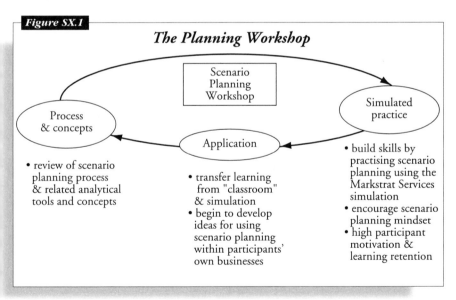

Figure SX.1

The Planning Workshop

Scenario Planning Workshop

Process & concepts
- review of scenario planning process & related analytical tools and concepts

Application
- transfer learning from "classroom" & simulation
- begin to develop ideas for using scenario planning within participants' own businesses

Simulated practice
- build skills by practising scenario planning using the Markstrat Services simulation
- encourage scenario planning mindset
- high participant motivation & learning retention

Overview of Proposed Scenario for a Workshop

- Five teams competing interactively, with each team taking over the strategic management of a fictitious services firm.

- Firms will have different characteristics (size, profitability, services offered, capacity, geographic coverage, cost structure and cost reduction capabilities, market positions).

- Five market segments with different needs which could change dramatically over time (e.g. stimulated by a technological breakthrough).

- Four areas with different market and competitive dynamics (market size, growth rates, segment mix, levels of competitive activity, industry capacity utilization).

- Firms will have a presence in an "area" (region/country) when they have a "network" in that area. Decisions at the network level will include coverage, capacity, pricing, and marketing priorities (segment focus). HR decisions (number of staff-customer-facing vs back-office, remuneration policy).

- Three core products (two existing and one emerging - with product substitution effects. Two associated products with more emerging over time (up to six). Products can have quite different cost structures.

- Firms to have full control over strategic decisions:
  Product portfolio and how the portfolio evolves through service innovation projects (investing to improve or cost-engineer existing services, develop new services).

- Bonus policy (linked to share price or profitability).

- Strategic alliances.

THE COPENHAGEN INSTITUTE FOR FUTURE STUDIES

This section is based on discussions with Rolf Jensen, Director of the Institute, and papers provided by him.

The Copenhagen Institute for Future Studies was founded in 1970 as a not-for-profit organization by the former Danish minister of finance and OECD secretary general, Thorkil Kristensen, in co-operation with a number of visionary companies and organizations which wanted to qualify their contemporary decisions through future studies.

Scenario planning began in 1984. The catalyst was an American company, 3M Denmark, which wanted scenarios of different possible futures to use as a method of helping its people become alert to new ideas and trends. Called "The Futures Game", the concept behind the exercise was creativity training with the participants encouraged to think in the future and compare tendencies in society with the development of the business by looking out for new tendencies and trends.

Through discussion, they had to choose which future they found the most probable based on three world scenarios giving a broad picture of Danish society in ten years' time:

- The green society where people want a clean environment and quality of life;

- The high technological or neo-bourgeois society, which is characterized by competition with an emphasis on the introduction of new technology and where the economy is a decisive measurement of value.

- The sub-culture society, where the population is split into many different lifestyles, both in domestic and working time and where business cultures are very strong.

The second half of the game was aimed at adapting the business to the future each person had chosen to believe in, using inspiration and creativity. This technique is still being used: although the scenarios have developed over time, taking society as a whole the basis for the exercise is still valid.

Based on a membership structure, the Institute is now involved in three areas:

1. Strategic planning for the future based on national and international analyses and scenario processes.

2. Reports, presentations, consultation, sparring etc. directed at those companies and organizations which are members of the Institute.

3. Seminars and conferences.

Methods used range from analysis of computerized statistics to the evaluation of international trends, values and a number of emotional factors shaping the future. It works with a number of other futures groups around the world, including the US-based World Futures Society, The Conference Board Europe, and the EUROCONSTRUCT group, which focuses on trends and forecasts in European construction and infrastructure and which has 19 European countries as members.

THE EUROPEAN COMMISSION'S METHODOLOGY

This section, contributed by Dr. Michael D Rogers of the European Commission's Forward Studies Unit, describes the *"Shaping Factors-Shaping Actors"* Methodology for Expert Consultations.

Background

As Michel Godet has frequently emphasized the future is not written and in principle cannot be forecast (Godet, 1993). However, the very process of thinking about the future and exploring the implications of alternative futures (which might be logically constructed in various ways) can have a profound impact on policy formation. In this sense the future can be influenced and this possibility lies at the root of prospective studies as practised by the Commission's Forward Studies Unit.

This prospect of shaping the future is fundamental to human behaviour. The earliest hunter gatherer improved his survival by continually positing "what if" (there is a sabre toothed tiger behind the next rock). The modern entrepreneur survives by anticipating possible changes in customer preferences or economic climates. The neglect of prospective (or foresight) studies by public bodies in the West during the 1970s and 1980s could have contributed to the lack of anticipation of many significant events during this period.

More recently there has been a welcome return to public support for such studies and "think tanks" once again provide useful inputs to the policy formation process. It is notable that think tanks themselves are considered to be an important shaping factor by some participants in our recent study of East Asia which is described below.

One of the earliest recorded foresight centres was of course the Delphi Oracle in ancient Greece (Herodotus, 1972). In essence the Delphi Oracle represented an expert consultation (interestingly the advice was usually ambiguous). In recognition of this early oracle the most common modern expert consensus method for prospective studies is called the Delphi Method.

The modern Delphi Method consists of a systematic

interrogation of a group of anonymous experts through the use of questionnaires. The process is repeated through several cycles in order to promote convergence and identify consensus. This method has been used over many years by the Japanese in their technology foresight programme (Japanese National Institute for Science and Technology Policy, 1995).

The Shaping Factors-Shaping Actors Method

The Forward Studies Unit's Shaping Factors-Shaping Actors Method is a different form of expert consultation. In contrast with the Delphi Method it uses smaller groups of nominated experts and does not involve questionnaires. It is a less formal and more adaptive approach to expert consultation.

The method consists of two main stages and was first used in our study of Europe Post 1992 (Jacquemin and Wright, 1993). The introduction to this comprehensive study gave the main elements of the method. However, there is no formal definition of the term "Shaping Factors", rather a broad description. They are the issues which are considered to be important in shaping future outcomes and as such can be global, national or regional in nature. They could even be sentiments, as in the case of the perceived importance of Asian values by some influential commentators:

*"...they are the long-run structural factors, be they socio-economic, socio-political or cultural, that are, **de facto**, influencing our European futures".*

These could include

"...sudden external shocks or brutal ruptures in previous trends".

In fact, the aim is to produce a rather comprehensive listing of shaping factors as the **first stage** of the process.

"Shaping Actors" are those players which are able to influence the Shaping Factors in an interactive fashion. The inclusion of Shaping Actors in any prospective study makes the study less deterministic than one which considers only the major Shaping

Factors. Thus the inclusion of shaping actors in the study is crucially important. Actors can be individual decision makers (political, economic, cultural) or groups of individuals.

*"...they themselves can become **environment makers** as opposed to **environment takers.** Therefore, the rhythm of change - and the process of change itself - are open to influence by the leading actors."*

In this **second stage** it is clearly important to identify the main (strongest) actor-factor linkages.

Thus the Unit's Shaping Factors-Shaping Actors prospective studies method is a form of Delphi but it is much less formal than the full Delphi Method. In this lies both its strength and weakness as a method. In engineering parlance it is to a certain extent "quick and dirty" i.e. it can produce results rather quickly but these results may lack the apparent precision of more formal methods. For policy makers this is clearly a strength. There is little point in producing studies months, if not years, after the policy requirement became apparent. Furthermore, the formal Delphi Method encourages convergence which may hide divergent views. The Shaping Factors-Shaping Actors Method should include such views. Its weakness lies mainly in the fact that each study draws on a restricted number of experts, so it is to an extent a partial view. Thus the selection of experts is crucial to the success of the method.

EXAMPLE: East-Asia Shaping Factors-Shaping Actors Study

Take the East Asia (Pape, 1996) study as an example. This involved four stages.

Data Collection
- A more or less continuous activity.

Shaping Factors
- The establishment of a list of the major shaping factors for the

region drawing on the knowledge of Commission experts on East Asia. These Shaping Factors constituted the Terms of Reference for the study.

Pilot Study
- The establishment of a first prospective study following the lines of the Terms of Reference. This study was intended to identify the main elements of the research and in particular the actor-factor linkages and thus to provide the essential stimulus for subsequent expert workshops.

Expert Workshops
- Critical meetings designed to improve, update and extend the pilot study. Brainstorming was encouraged and separate meetings were held with European experts on Asia and Asian experts (on Asia) (the former took place in Europe and the latter in East Asia).

This method lends itself to the production of scenarios. "Pessimistic", "Optimistic" and "Surprise Free" scenarios are readily derived from such expert workshops. (Surprise Free is a term coined by the Hudson Institute to represent expert judgemental extrapolation (Kahn and Weiner, 1967). The scenarios are of course to an extent intuitive but are none the worse for this.

Clearly, the whole process is iterative. In a sense this study is just the first iteration (data - shaping factors - pilot study of factors and actors - expert workshops). Given that many of the factors and actors are changing rapidly it is inevitable that a second cycle will be necessary in the future.

The East Asia study has been extended by focusing on the evolution of China up to the year 2010 (Canarelli, 1996a), using fuzzy logic to produce seven scenarios through the Method of Fuzzy Scenarios (Canarelli, 1996b). The results of this "pilot" work have been particularly interesting.

The Unit's Shaping Factors-Shaping Actors methodology has also been used for studies of Russia (to be published shortly), the Future of North-South Relations (European Commission, 1997), and a number of other topics.

The Shaping Actors concept is particularly useful within the Forward Studies Unit because it helps to stimulate the interest of our main stake-holder, the Commission. By identifying actors, we highlight the role and influences of particular power centres and of vested interests. (A key role of the Commission is to promote the common interest.) Furthermore, the pragmatism and flexibility of the method helps in harnessing the knowledge of different partners both within and outside the European Commission.

THE FRENCH SCHOOL

In the mid-1970s a French strategy specialist called Michel Godet began to do scenario planning work when he was in charge of the Department of Future Studies with SEMA Group from 1974 to 1979. During the 1980s the methodology was extended at the Conservatoire Nationale des Arts et Métiers with the support of institutions such as EDF, Elf and the Ministry of Defence. Now a Professor of Strategic Perspective at the Conservatoire, Godet's work has centred on the use of "perspective", based on its use in the fifties by the French philosopher, manager and civil servant Gaston Berger to underline the importance of having a future-oriented attitude. Like the Battelle BASICS methodology, this approach uses a probabilistic method to compute cross-impacts.

Writing in Long Range Planning in April 1996, Godet reflects that on the basis of more than 50 projects undertaken with companies and public administration, scenario planning has contributed to:

- Stimulating strategic thought and communication within companies;

- Improving internal flexibility of response to environmental uncertainty and providing better preparation for possible systems breakdowns;

- Reorienting policy options according to the future context on which their consequences impinge.

The Godet approach has evolved over the years and now consists of a number of computer-based tools, including MICMAC. This stands for "Matrice d'Impacts Croises Multiplication à un Classement", and is a variable classification approach. It allows for second-, third- and higher-order interaction effects to be assessed among the variables on a causal map pertinent to a firm's strategy design in a disciplined way. MICMAC is based on computers: it helps highlight interdependencies between inter-related variables that more simplified procedures may ignore and which managers and planners might overlook as neglected multiple interactions among the variable factors.

The scenarios approach based on a MICMAC structural analysis is divided into three phases.

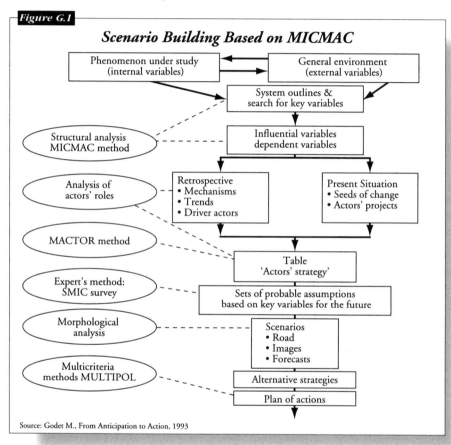

Figure G.1

Scenario Building Based on MICMAC

Source: Godet M., From Anticipation to Action, 1993

Phase 1: Building the database

The process begins by studying all the internal and external variables which characterize the company or organization and its environment to create a system of inter-related dynamic elements.

A structural analysis using the MICMAC method is used to define the system. A retrospective study, which should be as detailed and quantified as possible, should be carried out on the variables stemming from the structural analysis. After having listed the variables which compose the system, a cross-impact matrix is built to study the influence of each variable on all the others. They can be binary (existence or non-existence) or more usually, estimated through a scale from 0 to 4 (none, weak, medium, strong, very strong). Then their total influence and dependence are placed in a diagram (Figure G.2) which highlights their respective positions and roles.

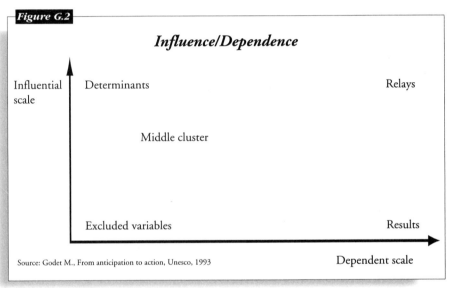

Figure G.2

Influence/Dependence

Influential scale — Determinants — Relays

Middle cluster

Excluded variables — Results

Dependent scale

Source: Godet M., From anticipation to action, Unesco, 1993

This retrospective analysis can avoid over-emphasizing the current situation, when it can be tempting to extrapolate the past into the future. Analysis of past trends can reveal the dynamics of the changing system and the productive or counter-productive role of certain actors. Moreover, each actor must be defined according to his or her objectives, problems and means of action. Then, to examine how the actors position themselves with respect to each other, a table is drawn up showing the actors' strategies (the MACTOR method).

Phase 2: Scanning the range of possibles and reducing uncertainty

Once the key variables have been identified and the actors'

strategies analysed, future possibilities can be listed through a set of hypotheses which could point to a continuation of a trend, a new one or the ending of one. A morphological analysis can then be used to break up the subject under examination into essential dimensions and study possible recombinations of the different dimensions, with those recombinations comprising as many visions of the future as possible. By using expert methods, based on software (SMIC), uncertainty can be reduced by estimating the subjective probabilities of the different combinations occurring or different key events for the future.

Phase 3: Developing the scenarios

At this stage, the scenarios are still embryonic since they are restricted to sets of hypotheses, whether implemented or not. The next stage is to describe the route leading from the present situation to the final vision.

EXAMPLE: Scenarios for the Iron And Steel Industry

The Godet method was used in 1990-1991, when, after several months of considering the future of the steel industry in France, a group of industrial experts built six global scenarios (Godet and Roubelat, 1996). They were based on three main hypotheses:

- H1: weak economic growth (less than 1.8%)
- H2: strong environmental constraints
- H3: strong competition from other materials.

The six scenarios, reprinted with permission from *Long Range Planning,* Vol 29, 1996, "Creating the future: the use and misuse of scenarios", were constructed from combinations as follows:

S1. Black: weak growth of GNP and strong competition from other materials.

S2. Gloom: weak growth of GNP without strong competition from other materials.

S3. Trend driven: continuation of the current situation.

S4. Ecology: strong environmental constraints.

S5. Optimistic steel: strong growth of GNP and competitiveness favourable to steel.

S6. Optimistic plastic: strong growth of GNP and competitiveness favourable to other materials.

At the end of the scenario workshop, experts were asked to discuss the probabilities of the three hypotheses. Processing those subjective probabilities using SMIC-Prob-Expert software showed that those six scenarios covered only 40% of the probable outcomes in the judgement of the experts:

- S5   14.8%
- S1   10.8%
- S6   7.1%
- S3   1.6%
- S2   1.6%

The experts had thus developed their views and now thought that three new scenarios, all including as part of the picture, the effect of the "green" movement, had a greater probability of happening:

S7. "Black" plus "ecology".
S8. "Ecology" plus "optimistic steel".
S9. "Ecology" plus "optimistic plastic".

The combination of the first two hypotheses of weak economic growth and strong environmental constraints had been eliminated because in the context, weak growth/strong environmental constraints did not seem probable. The combination of strong environmental constraints and strong competition from other materials had been eliminated because strong environmental constraints seemed rather more favourable to steel, which at the same time was not subject to strong competition with other materials. The initial thinking had neglected to imagine recyclable or biodegradable plastic.

Godet has also been associated with the Sensitivity Method, (Godet, 1992). The Sensitivity Method is a trans-disciplinary modelling approach. It has been developed by Frederic Vester (Vester, 1988) as an attempt to assist groups of experts from different reality domains to build a common language as opposed to the prevalent jargon of specific areas of expertise. In addition, by centreing on the interrelatedness of issues in the real world it puts strong emphasis on the analysis of its inherent causal structures. A fundamental assumption is that processes in reality can be described by applying circular causal logic, i.e. feedback thinking.

THE FUTURES GROUP

Taken from "Alternative Scenarios for the Defense Industry After 1995", Planning Review, May/June 1992 (Boroush and Thomas, 1992, reproduced by permission of The Planning Review) and "Scenarios Applied" (Thomas, 1997)

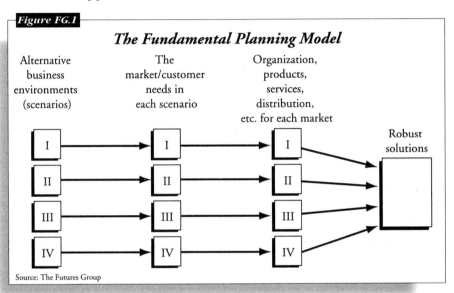

Figure FG.1

The Fundamental Planning Model

Alternative business environments (scenarios)	The market/customer needs in each scenario	Organization, products, services, distribution, etc. for each market	

I → I → I

II → II → II   → Robust solutions

III → III → III

IV → IV → IV

Source: The Futures Group

Method
The Futures Group, a Glastonbury, Connecticut-based international strategy and policy research firm, has developed an approach to scenario planning that is based on trend-impact analysis. Their fundamental planning model is shown in Figure FG.1.

It sees a typical project as having three stages: preparation, development of the scenarios, and reporting and utilization.

1. Preparation
A. Define the focus.
Several questions need to be answered initially to define the boundaries of the scenario effort. What is the planning or decisions issue you are trying to address? What possible future

development need to be probed - for example, new technology, emerging socio-economic trends, resource requirements? How far into the future do you need to look? What "indicator variables" need to be forecast to aid your decision-making - such as rate of market growth, financials, strength of key competitors?

B. Chart the driving forces.
What are the essential drivers of the system/environment that concern you? What forces and developments have the greatest ability to shape its future characteristics?

2. Development
A. Construct a "scenario space".
Systematically arraying the various future states that the drivers could jointly produce yields a comprehensive set of alternative world scenarios. Occasionally, a few need to be excluded as illogical or insufficiently plausible over the planning horizon.

B. Select the alternative worlds to be detailed.
Exploring all of the alternative worlds in detail is often neither necessary nor practical. A smaller set - with choices that encompass the range of major challenges and opportunities - usually suffices.

C. Prepare scenario-contingent forecasts
List the essential trends and events needed to bring each of the selected alternative worlds to pass. Then, depending on the driving assumptions of each alternative world, project the time trend (quantitative or qualitative, as appropriate) for each of the indicator variables the scenario builders have identified.

3. Reporting and utilization
A. Document.
In most cases the best documentation is a simple series of charts and narratives describing the future history represented by each scenario. To promote utilization of the scenarios by planners and managers, it is critical to communicate effectively the assumptions and outcomes of each alternative world.

B. *Contrast the implications of the alternative worlds.*

How different are the business decisions and planning goals you would pursue as you consider each alternative world? What actions and commitments offer your organization the most resilience in the face of these uncertainties?

EXAMPLE: Defining the Future in the Defence Industry

In the early 1990s The Futures Group was asked by a number of US defence companies to create scenarios which would help them examine the shape of the industry in the light of the ending of the Cold War and the tilting of economic power towards the Pacific Rim and the concomitant impact on demand. Having faced a market characterized by steady growth for a number of years, the industry wanted to explore and question the future global demand for a number of defence products and services. One of the critical areas that needed analysis was the proposition that the US might cease to be the primary customer for the defence industry.

A list of key issues was drawn up, including the geographic incidence of political tensions, the nature of alliances and diplomacy, the ease of arms and technology transfer around the world and so on. Eventually, this was reduced to four key areas:

- The extent of US diplomatic, economic and military involvement in the world.

- The character of countervailing military power.

- The vitality of the US economy

- The level of global instability.

A total of 13 scenarios were originally developed, based on different combinations of the variables. Three were eliminated because of illogicality or implausibility. To see how the industry would fare under each of the scenarios, the working group prepared detailed forecasts for six of the alternative worlds, because they represented a diverse and likely group of business settings against which current planning assumptions could be compared.

SIX DIVERSE WORLDS

1. ***The US Driven Market:*** *a strong and relatively traditional planning environment. There is a clear consensus that military forces should be ready to respond to instability.*

2. ***Dangerous Poverty:*** *a very cost-conscious but security-minded world. Instability is high, with much animosity directed at the US.*

3. ***Regional Markets:*** *a non-traditional but active defence market for US suppliers. With instability high, there is a strong global market for arms.*

4. ***Peace and Prosperity:*** *a world of low military priorities. National security is focused on economic vitality. Military conflicts are principally regional. The defence industry is depressed.*

5. ***Confused Priorities:*** *a future in which the defence market is driven by a very poorly performing economy in tandem with an unfocused set of defence priorities for maintaining regional stability. With no definitive issue or enemy, US government defence spending vacillates widely.*

6. ***The Isolationist's Dream:*** *a future with a political mandate to "avoid entangling alliances". Low instability, diffuse global threats and a strong economy brings about a market where the US government can afford what it wants - which is not a lot.*

Charting the US defence expenditures in each scenario showed that while there were sharp differences, the fact that because each scenario contained plausible elements, there were some serious implications to address.

THE GLOBAL BUSINESS NETWORK

Background

When Peter Schwartz left Shell in 1987, he decided that the time was ripe to set up a new type of organization to do the sort of imaginative thinking for other companies using Pierre Wack's work at Shell as a model. As he relates in "The Art of the Long View" (Schwartz, 1991), he joined forces with Jay Ogilvy, then director of research of the SRI Values and Lifestyles Program and formed the Global Business Network (GBN). According to Schwartz, they wanted to help plug clients into a network of "remarkable people", which would include giving them access to a highly focused and filtered information flow, and reorganize their perceptions about alternative futures through the scenario method.

GBN, based in California, was soon developing strategic scenarios for clients such as the International Stock Exchange, AT&T and BellSouth. But it wanted to evolve further beyond acting as a group of conventional consultants working on individual projects, and create a network through which members could share ideas and widen their perceptions and understanding about their environments. This was inspired by the work done by Arie de Geus at Shell, who, with Schwartz, had run a series of "learning" conferences with Volvo and AT&T on the nature of learning and to which people from a wide variety of backgrounds and disciplines had been invited to contribute. GBN wanted to follow that approach, creating itself almost as a form of a club, which worked for clients but was not modelled on traditional consulting firms.

Schwartz and Ogilvy were joined by other partners including Stewart Brand, who had founded the Whole Earth Catalog and CoEvolution Quarterly (now the Whole Earth Review) and who had helped de Geus set up the learning conferences, Napier Collyns who had been a Shell planner, and Lawrence Wilkinson, an Oxford/Harvard Business school alumnus who was president of a film-making/animation studio in San Francisco.

The first corporate members included AT&T, Volvo, Inland Steel, UNOCAL, Shell, BP, Pacific Gas and Electric, the International Stock Exchange, Statoil, ABB and BellSouth.

GBN now has a staff of researchers and consultants located in Emeryville, California, in London and in the Netherlands, and has corporate members from all continents.

Activities

Scenario generation is a major part of its activity, such as scenarios for the world economy. (See as an example, Scenarios for the 21st Century Organization in Part IV.) It holds meetings around the world on key issues, while it also acts as an information filter for clients. Members are linked electronically and converse concurrently on dozens of topics and in focused on-line conferences. Members also receive and contribute to GBN's proprietary research and scenario publications and the GBN Book Club, and have access to GBN's consulting, scenario development and customized learning opportunities.

Its Network comprises strategists and thinkers from a range of disciplines - from anthropology through chemistry and biology to music - as well as from more obvious "business" organizations. It brings these members together in varied ways to explore driving forces and uncertainties and to integrate these insights into alternative stories about the future.

Method

CHECKLIST FROM "THE ART OF THE LONG VIEW"

In "The Art of the Long View", Peter Schwartz offers a useful checklist to use as the basis for developing scenarios. This forms the basis of the GBN approach.

Step One: Identify Focal Issue or Decision
When developing scenarios, it's a good idea to begin "from the inside out" rather than "from the outside in". That is, begin with a specific decision or issue, then build out towards the environment. What will decisions-makers in your company be thinking hard about in the near future? What are the decisions that have to be made that will have a long-term influence on the fortunes of the company?

Scenarios that are developed on the basis of differences in the macro-economy - high growth versus low growth, say - may not highlight differences that make a difference to a particular company. To a movie studio different paths for the diffusion of new distribution technology would generate more useful scenarios than simple variations on economic growth. An automobile company will want to see scenarios built around variations in energy prices. A forest products company might want to look at scenarios that differ around the number of housing starts. Like them, a person buying a home will want to think about interest rates and the housing market.

How can you be sure that the differences that distinguish your scenarios will really make a difference to your business or your life? The best way is to begin with important decisions that have to be made and the mind-set of the management making them:

"Shall we build the major capital facility now on the drawing boards?"
"Shall we launch a major new direction for R&D?"
"Shall we make an acquisition in a new industry?"
"Shall I change careers?"

Step Two: Key Forces in the Local Environment
If the identification of a focal issue or decision is the first step, then listing the key factors influencing the success or failure of that decision is the second step - facts about customers, suppliers, competitors etc. What will decisions-makers want to know when making key choices? What will be seen as success or failure? What are the considerations that will shape those outcomes?

Step Three: Driving Forces
Once the key factors have been listed, the third step involves listing driving forces in the macro-environment that influence the key factors identified earlier. In addition to a checklist of social, economic, political, environmental, and technological forces, another route to the relevant aspects of the macro-environment is the question: What are the forces behind the micro-environment

forces identified in Step two? Some of these forces are predetermined) (e.g. often demographics) and some are highly uncertain (e.g. public opinion). It is very useful to know what is inevitable and necessary and what is unpredictable and still a matter of choice.

It can be useful to imagine oneself in the future saying, "If only I had known that" inflation would fall, or that a new competitor would emerge from another country, or that regulations would change drastically. It is not too hard to remember such comments in the past. What guidance do they provide for the future?

This is the most research-intensive step in the process. In order to adequately define the driving forces research is usually required. Research may cover markets, new technology, political factors, economic forces and so on. One is searching for the major trends and the trend breaks. The latter are most difficult to find: novelty is difficult to anticipate.

Step Four: Rank by Importance and Uncertainty
Next comes the ranking of key factors and driving forces on the basis of two criteria: first, the degree of importance for the success of the focal issue or decision identified in step one: second, the degree of uncertainty surrounding those factors and trends. The point is to identify the two or three factors or trends that are most important and most uncertain.

Scenarios cannot differ over predetermined elements like the inevitable ageing of the baby boomers because predetermined elements are bound to be the same in all scenarios.

Step Five: Selecting the Scenario Logics
The results of this ranking exercise are, in effect, the axes along which the eventual scenarios will differ. Determining these axes is among the most important steps in the entire scenario-generating process. The goal is to end up with just a few scenarios whose differences make a difference to decision-makers. If the scenarios are to function as useful learning tools, the lessons they teach must be based on issues basic to the success of the focal decision. And those fundamental differences - or "scenario drivers" - must be few in number in order to avoid

a proliferation of different scenarios around every possible uncertainty. Many things can happen, but only a few scenarios can be developed in detail, or the process dissipates.

While in the end one may boil the logic down to the directions of a very few variables the process for getting there is not at all simple or mechanical. It is more like playing with a set of issues until you have reshaped and regrouped them in such a way that a logic emerges and a story can be told.

Once the fundamental axes of crucial uncertainties have been identified, it is sometimes useful to present them as a spectrum (along one axis), or a matrix (with two axes), or a volume (with three axes) in which different scenarios can be identified and their details filled in.

The logic of a given scenario will be characterized by its location in the matrix of most significant scenario drivers. For example, if an automobile company determines that fuel prices are two of the most important scenario drivers, there will be four basic scenario logics: (1) High fuel prices in a protectionist environment - where domestic suppliers of small cars will have an advantage; (2) High fuel prices in a global economy - where fuel-efficient imports may capture the low end of the market; (3) Low fuel prices in a protectionist environment - where American gas guzzlers will have a good market at home but not abroad; (4) Low fuel prices in a global economy - where there will be intense competition for fuel-efficient models, but large cars may enjoy strong foreign markets.

The scenario will usually want to be extended beyond such simple logics to encompass, for example, more subtle issues like the evolution of consumer markets or automotive regulation. Thus the resulting scenarios may find their core of logic less in the variations of the cells in a matrix and more in the themes and plots of a story.

The challenge here is identifying the plot that (1) best captures the dynamics of the situation and (2) communicates the point effectively. For example, one of the auto scenarios above for a US automaker might be built around the logic of challenge and response: the challenge of foreign competition and high gas prices.

Step Six: Fleshing Out the Scenarios.

While the most important forces determine the logics that distinguish the scenarios, fleshing out the skeletal scenarios can be accomplished by returning to the lists of key factors and trends identified in steps two and three.

Each key factor and trend should be given some attention in each scenario. Sometimes it is immediately apparent which side of an uncertainty should be located in which scenario, sometimes not. If two scenarios differ over protectionist or non-protectionist policies, then it probably make sense to put a higher inflation rate in the protectionist scenario and a lower inflation rate in the non-protectionist scenario. It is just such connections and mutual implications that scenarios are designed to reveal.

Then weave the pieces together in the form of a narrative. How would the world get from here to there? What events might be necessary to make the end point of the scenario plausible? Are there known individuals whose ascendancy in the public eye might facilitate or help to characterize a given scenario, such as Russian Premier Boris Yeltsin or US Senator William Bradley?

Step Seven: Implications

Once the scenarios have been developed in some detail, then it is time to return to the focal issue or decision identified in step one to rehearse the future. How does the decision look in each scenario? What vulnerabilities have been revealed? Is the decision or strategy robust across all scenarios, or does it look good across only one or two of the scenarios? If a decision looks good in only one of several scenarios, then it qualifies as a high-risk gamble - a bet-the-company strategy - especially if the company has little control over the likelihood of the required scenario coming to pass. How could that strategy be adapted to make it more robust if the desired scenario shows signs of not happening?

Step Eight: Selection of Leading Indicators and Signposts

It is important to know as soon as possible which of the several scenarios is closest to the course of history as it actually unfolds. Sometimes that direction is obvious, especially with regard to factors like the health of the overall economy, but sometimes the leading indicators for a given scenario can be subtle. How, for example, should one calibrate the speed of economic restructuring from a smokestack economy towards an information-intensive economy? - by help-wanted advertising according to different SIC codes? - by union memberships? - by subscriptions to indicative periodicals?

Once the different scenarios have been fleshed out and their implications for the focal issue determined, then it's worth spending time and imagination on identifying a few indicators to monitor in an ongoing way. If those indicators are selected carefully and imaginatively, the company will gain a jump on its competition in knowing what the future holds for a given industry and how that future is likely to affect strategies and decisions in the industry

If the scenarios have been built according to the previous steps, then the scenarios will be able to translate movements of a few key indicators into an orderly set of industry-specific implications. The logical coherence that was built into the scenarios will allow logical implications of leading indicators to be drawn out of the scenarios.

EXAMPLE: Power demand at PG&E

At the end of the 1980s Pacific Gas and Electric (PG&E), a northern Californian utility, asked GBN to write scenarios which would help it deal with the challenge facing it of whether to invest in more power plants or pour resources instead into promoting energy-efficiency. The utility had acquired notoriety in the early 1980s when, having faced huge overrun costs from a nuclear power plant installation, it had tried to push the costs onto rate payers. The company was stopped from doing that, and in 1985 it agreed to recover costs only from selling power from the plant.

GBN considered a number of driving forces. One of the major ones was the strong environmental movement against nuclear power in California. There was also the impact of immigration: the company would have to learn to communicate with many non-English speakers if it wanted to promote energy efficiency among those communities. Economic volatility was another driving force, since huge capital projects are very sensitive to inflation and interest rates. Finally, the company's own realization of the greenhouse effect meant it could see the virtue of pushing energy efficiency, both to stabilize the state's energy demands but also in terms of public relations.

The scenarios highlighted that the company had worked through an unspoken set of goals about how the future would unfold, with people demanding ever more energy. However, the GBN work showed that the future would include aspects of "green 1990s", where citizens demanded more energy savings and less pollution. But there could also be elements of a "Decade of Disorder" with clashes between haves and have-nots. PG&E chose to push energy efficiency as the only profitable route to follow under all possible futures.

As Schwartz points out, the scenarios were typical challenge and response plots. While PG&E had always viewed their world as one of winners and losers, in which they were limited by politics and the supply of energy and where they had to fight to build more power plants. But the better way was to look at challenges as a way to learn and grow. One of the results of this new mindset was the very effective response to the earthquake in San Francisco in 1989.

This example is based on "Why Pacific Gas & Electric Isn't Building Any More Nuclear Power Plants", by Art Kleiner (Kleiner, 1992).

NCRI

Background

Another approach was developed at Northeast Consulting Resources Inc. (NCRI), founded in 1984 in Boston, Massachusetts by David Mason. Its was based on a scenario technique called Future Mapping. The idea of Future Mapping stems from the work of Martin Ernst, a former vice president at Arthur D Little Inc. in the early 1970s. It was developed as a reaction against what Mason felt was the complex and laborious process scenario planning had become compared to the more simplistic and robust approach of the 1970s. This section is based on Mason and Wilson, (1994) (reproducd by permission of The Planning Review), together with commentary and notes from later work.

The Future Mapping Method

Future Mapping is based on two assumptions:

- The future is contingent upon and shaped by the actions of various participants.

- In most industries, efforts in pursuit of competitive advantage will cause structural change.

It uses two sets of tools:

1. Endstates.

These are snapshots of an industry at a particular point in time some number of years into the future and are typically written in sets of four or five. They are high level and holistic, but only one page long. Together they capture the different schools of thought about the future direction of an industry or company. They may describe incomplete or polarized viewpoints that require integration with each other. They are typically set 3-5 years out. They are created from the intuitions of NCRI analysts and the client. The set of endstates may not be mutually exclusive: for example, different technology endstates can coexist with different business model endstates.

2. *Events.*

An event is a specific, concrete, observable manifestation of a key trend or issue. The most important attribute of an event is that you must be able to tell whether or not it has happened. The deconstruction of trends and issues into recognizable events - such as the fact that 10% of credit card payments are for purchases via the Internet with a date associated with each one - e.g., 1999 (+/- 1 year). Also, a second important characteristic of an event is that there are industry people who must actually make it occur. Events are normally written in sets of 150-200, organized by topic and cover the full array of relevant issues confronting an industry. They are printed on cards for easy manipulation, and each one has a title, a description and a date. Future Mapping focuses on specific events that become the basis of actions to be taken by managers.

Method

A series of endstates and related events can address issues on entirely different scales: geopolitical, industry, company, new product design or even functions.

The process begins by creating 4 to 5 endstates and 150-200 events. At a working meeting, if the goal is to help managers think differently, than the first task is to build a conventional wisdom scenario to make the management's existing decision-making context explicit, visible and tangible. It involves identifying events that the management believes to be highly likely or highly unlikely. These events are posted chronologically on a wall and organized by theme in clusters. This can often produce uncomfortable results, particularly if the mental model revealed is not popular. Also, conflicts between group members about the likelihood or not of events are explored to see if they are genuine disagreements or the result of misinterpreted information.

In the second phase of the Future Mapping process, teams are assigned to each endstate, with the brief to assume that the endstate has happened and to construct a logical explanation of how this came about. This puts managers in a position to discover the logical relationships between events and how they develop into the outcome described in the endstate.

The selected events are then clustered into themes that, spread over time, create a series of logical pathways that need to be developed if the endstate is to unfold as written. Several themes are usually required to explain fully how an endstate develops. Because these are logical threads of the endstates' development, the team can use them to explain to colleagues how it came about. The teams must then discover an industry and a business definition that they can build into a compelling success story in the context of the scenario.

As the task of building scenarios comes to a close, there are two ways the team can go.

1. Common features approach. This focuses on the common features of the scenarios, with investments targeted to events occurring in all the scenarios. A monitoring system using events as leading indicators can be set up. They can also be awareness-building tools for training management on how to react if various upheavals confront the industry.

2. Aggressive change approach. This allows companies to be much more aggressive agents of change. Individuals can rank the endstates on two scales: attainability and desirability, which form the basis for a structured discussion about the direction of the industry and the organization's participation in it.

EXAMPLE: Digital Equipment Corp - Searching for New Business Models

This section is based on the article in Planning Review (November/December 1994), by Lucia Luce Quinn, Vice President, Corporate Strategy and Alliance Group of Digital Equipment Corporation and David H Mason, Vice President of Northeast Consulting Resources Inc. (Quinn and Mason, 1994) and is reproduced by permission of The Planning Review.

Digital Equipment Corporation, the US-based information technology company, decided to adopt a scenario-planning technique to consider different strategies in the face of enormous change. This was crucial in the light of industry changes: while Digital had pioneered and won the minicomputer business in the 1980s, in the 1990s the company faced the arrival of low-priced, powerful personal computers and advances in network technology that changed the minicomputer market segment dramatically.

The approach used was based on the Future Mapping methodology, in which scenarios were defined as the stream of events that leads to a particular endstate or outcome, with different teams charged with defining the series of events that would lead to each endstate.

According to Lucia Luce Quinn, *"We discovered that unlearning - previous market realities, behaviors, and mental models - is far more difficult than learning new ones. The unlearning process must be aggressively pursued. For the best chance of success, keep in mind that it is much easier to push on a group of people than to push on any one individual. We have had much more impact inside the company as a result of 17 senior people pushing on each other. You can be far more controversial, even confrontational, in a group environment."*

There were a number of stages in the scenario process. First, Quinn, who had joined Digital three months previously to manage the corporate strategy function, ran a meeting in which teams were given four internally written scenarios and a deck of 50 cards that described the tangible and intangible assets of the corporation. The teams were asked to choose the ten assets the company needed to invest in to become successful in their scenarios and five assets to divest to start them thinking about choices in terms of investment. Each teams then had to list the critical success factors and write a vision statement for its scenario.

What Quinn found was that, although the idea of scenario development appealed to the management group, the scenarios themselves were set too far into the future to be as relevant as they might. So the next step in the process was become more business-focused by carrying out interviews with the managers of the business units to gather relevant information to write more endstates and events. The questions that need to be addressed before writing the endstates included:

- Are the scenarios about the industry or are they about Digital?

- Or are they about both?

- Are they about industry structure or technology - or both - and to what extent?

- Are they supposed to establish a vision for the company as a whole?

- Are they supposed to be a framework for current strategy decisions?

As Quinn noted, *"The interviews help you to determine where management is stuck. Find the problem they can't see past and do scenario work around that issue. If you jump years ahead of that point, you are not really helping management."*

The resulting five endstates were differing perceptions of current realities, and were perceived not as long-term visions but actual business models, related to different types of businesses:

- Model A concerned a commodity business.

- Model B concerned an architectural franchise or technology-driven business.

- Model C was a networking and utilities business at a time beyond the initial stage of convergence.

- Model D was the systems-integration business, which provided value-added solutions mainly through people skills.

- Model E could be characterized as a "legacy" business.

The scenarios, in fact, began to be used as a shorthand and the basis for a common language. According to Quinn, the most valuable discussions dealt with knowing when to shift from operating in one business model to another. The process continued with an analysis of competitors to see what their portfolio of business models would look like if all their business activities were diagrammed.

The next task for Digital was to link the scenarios into the decision-making framework through portfolio analysis. The matrix had models A through E positioned along the top and the competitive position along the side, based at first on information from the business units, and then digging down deeper into the business segments within the units. Other methods were used to "cut" the data, including market valuation and examining interdependencies among the businesses to provide a fresh context for thinking about the future.

Quinn writes that scenario planning spread to other parts of the organization, including human resources, manufacturing and engineering, helped by the creation of a "tool book", while the business units extended and rewrote their scenarios using their set of crucial events. In addition, once the board of directors listened to a presentation of the scenario planning project, they decided to take part in a three-day scenario workshop so they could ask better questions.

EXAMPLE: the Information Industry in 2010

Although we in ICL had built our own scenarios the previous year, in 1996 we decided to get a completely new view in case we had been too blinkered in our approach. We embarked on a project with NCRI because it had worked with IT companies, publishing and telecoms, which seemed the right sort of triangulation to start thinking about the Information Industry beyond the confusion of the present.

NCRI found that we were asking questions that it had not been asked before, in that most people were interested in the following year, whereas we were looking 15 years ahead. When it was decided that the Future Mapping methodology could not be used for the first stage, NCRI's Art Hutchison began to work on the assignment from the perspective of: who will be using this technology 15 years out, in 2010?

NCRI concluded that five different sorts of users could be identified, all with different requirements, which meant that different sorts of industries might be expected to serve those needs. The scenarios looked at who would be buying, what they would buy, and what factors would affect success in each market.

The five markets are:

1. The automated blue-grey collar workplace.

Here job functions centred around conveying, re-packaging, or repetitive processing of information have been heavily automated, or eliminated, by advanced systems that incorporate pattern recognition, dynamic workflow, rule-based reasoning and other information technologies that can "learn" and adapt, as well as interfacing with and interpreting stimuli from their physical environment. In many industries, "smart" robots are used to accomplish a wider and wider array of physical tasks, reducing the need for rote manual labour.

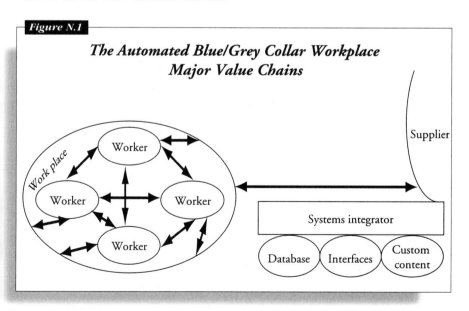

Figure N.1

The Automated Blue/Grey Collar Workplace Major Value Chains

Opportunities: the services of sophisticated, consultative system integrators are in high demand. These firms design, build, maintain and improve complex systems to intimately reflect key business processes.

2. The empowered knowledge worker.

A distinct class of relatively affluent and highly mobile knowledge workers has evolved a set of similar information access requirements and information consumption behaviours around the world. More and more operate as independent or loosely affiliated freelancers, although a significant fraction are still traditionally employed.

Opportunities: network-based services are critical, connecting to large clearinghouses for areas such as financial transactions and rights management while search engines, software agents and brokers enable access to vast stores of information.

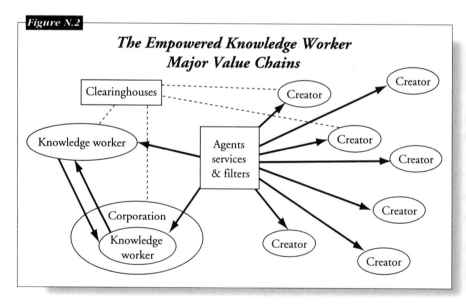

Figure N.2

The Empowered Knowledge Worker Major Value Chains

3. Social impact and community.

The Internet has turned out to be as much a global social revolution as anything else, though this has taken different forms in different parts of the world. Community-based organizations, non-profit institutions, professional associations, affinity groups and governments at many levels have played a major role in influencing how information infrastructure has developed and how it is used, broadening its scope and stimulating very high levels of access and participation. Networked information commerce is growing, although a large proportion of the content on the NET is still free, developed by and for the members of the various groups.

Opportunities: Affinity marketing organizations put together deals and packages that can be placed globally and enable advertising business models, while providers of educational services also have a major opportunity in this world.

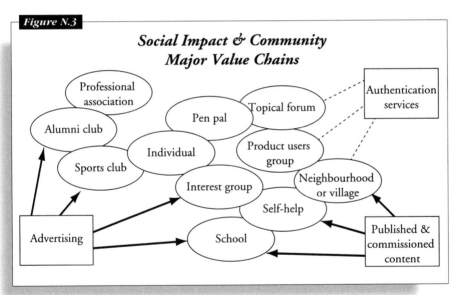

Figure N.3

Social Impact & Community Major Value Chains

4. The active/affluent consumer.

A relatively affluent sector of the industrialized world (representing about 15% of the population in G7 nations), spends a significant and growing share of their household budget on electronic information and entertainment. This group consistently leads their peers in the adoption of cutting-edge information technologies and high-end consumer electronics. Many have found their work and home lives blurring and, as a result, readily purchase content which helps them to manage their time, inform their work or provide relaxation, often at the same time.

Opportunities: designing, building and managing highly complex information transaction processing infrastructures such as clearinghouses and billing systems, integrating "smart-house" technologies such as personal LANs, and low-cost, easy to use multi-media publishing and production tools and services.

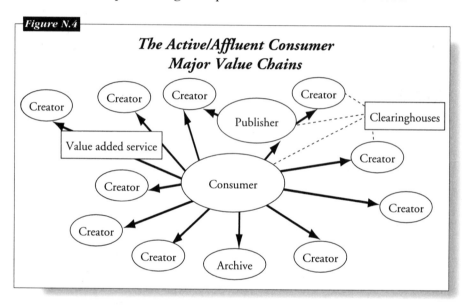

Figure N.4

The Active/Affluent Consumer Major Value Chains

5. The average consumer.
The average information consumer in the developed world is content with programmed broadcast media similar to the television, satellite, radio and cable TV fare of 1996, but provided through a much wider variety of channels (500 to 700 is typical in most homes). Though many homes have multiple broadcast conduits available to them, few subscribe to more than one comprehensive package. These service packages are often bundled with other attractive deals on credit cards, information appliance hardware and frequent buyer clubs.

Opportunities: Standardization and globalization of local industries through superior information delivery and convenience such as groceries and education, leapfrogging infrastructure and content development in "second world" emerging markets, and domination of the info-appliance manufacturing business (risky, but potentially rewarding for the final survivors).

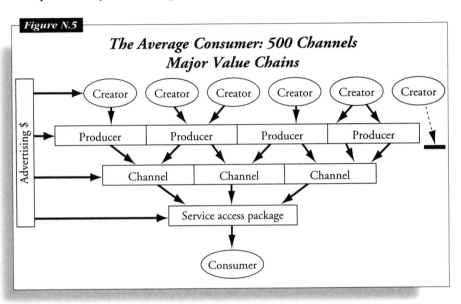

Figure N.5

The Average Consumer: 500 Channels Major Value Chains

SRI

This section is based on "Scenario Based Strategy Development" (Ralston, 1997), and private communications.

SRI International, along with Royal Dutch Shell, General Electric and others, began developing scenario-based planning techniques for studying the future in the mid-1960s. In the late 1970s, SRI revised its scenario methodology to meet the needs of US and international businesses for strategic analyses of future trends and uncertainties that had direct implications for strategic plans, investments, and other decisions being made in the present. This new methodology was developed in parallel with the Royal Dutch/Shell Group's well-known scenario process and has a number of features in common with it. SRIC's methodology is considered the paramount example of "intuitive-logic" approaches to scenario development and application.

SRI's methodology has been adapted over the years to the needs of the joint (consultant-client), highly interactive planning workshop which is key in any strategy development process. Because the methodology is relatively simple and completely transparent, it is easy for participants to follow and put into practice, under the guidance of a workshop leader, in real time. Other advantages include:

- *The process is highly flexible.* It can easily be adapted to the needs of the individual situation, and indeed uses a specific management decision as the focus and starting point for the whole process. This it can do more easily because it is not dependent on the needs and structure of a computer model.

- *A premium is placed on the identification and clarification of issues.* The "logics" and structure of the scenarios are, essentially, a construct of the mind (more exactly, the "collective mind" of the scenario team). This fact imposes on the team a disciplined need to examine, carefully and critically, every key issue and uncertainty in order to clarify the reasons for differing future possibilities.

- *There is a high degree of "ownership" in the final product.* The scenarios have, quite literally, been created by the team, and the resulting sense of ownership (particularly among the corporate members) is absolutely essential for effective use of the scenarios in strategy planning.

By and large, then, SRI's particular approach can be said to have all the strengths and all the limitations of a "model" that depends on the working of the human brain (or a collections of brains). While it may be, for instance, not focused on detailed quantification, it has the inestimable strength of capturing the power of both logic and imagination to create "pictures" of the future. And it has the further advantage of an ability to shape both the formal and informal aspects of the planning system simultaneously.

Over the years, many of SRI's projects have included the use of scenarios to help create and shape an organization's strategy. These projects did not start and end with scenarios. Rather, scenarios were an integral part of the overall process. The overriding objective of the projects was to develop a strategy and an action plan. Because the strategies and action plans were conceived from scenarios, they were flexible approaches, capable of dealing with most eventualities rapidly and effectively.

Now SRI's development focus in scenario planning is on refining the methodologies for scenarios-based strategy development and using scenarios to stimulate discussion about how an organization's actions can help influence the future. Given the scope and scale of this effort, scenarios will continue to be a critical element of SRI's consulting capabilities.

Method

Its scenario methodology is a six-step process (Figure S.1) that a multi-disciplinary team performs in a series of analyses and workshops. The process is decision-focused in that its starting point (Steps 1 and 2) is not the macro-environment, but rather clarification of the strategic decision the scenarios aim to address and of key decision factors - that is, what management would like to know about the future to make a better decision. This start ensures that the resulting scenarios focus sharply on the trends, events, and uncertainties that are strategically relevant to the decision-making process.

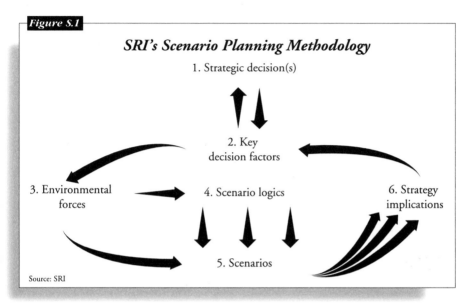

Figure S.1

SRI's Scenario Planning Methodology

1. Strategic decision(s)

2. Key decision factors

3. Environmental forces

4. Scenario logics

6. Strategy implications

5. Scenarios

Source: SRI

This decision-focus has reinforcement at the end of the process (Step 6), when participants analyse and interpret the scenarios to identify their implications for the prospective decision. These implications include the key opportunities and threats that these alternative futures are likely to present and may extend to the identification of strategic issues and strategy options that executives should consider in making the decision.

The intervening steps in this scenario-development process are as follows:

Step 3: Analysis of environmental forces. Participants analyse key decision factors by carefully mapping the full range of environmental forces that will shape the future business environment confronting decisions makers. Analysis of these environmental forces usually focuses on two categories - those at the industry and market (micro) level that most directly affect the key decision factors: and those at the broad social, economic, political, and technological (macro) level that set the overall (often global) context for the business environment. The environmental analysis concludes with a detailed assessment of each force's degree of impact (on the decision factors) and level of uncertainty. This sorts out what is relatively predictable from what is truly uncertain.

Step 4: Development of scenario logics. This step is the heart of the process and establishes the basic structure for the scenarios. Essentially, participants identify a limited number of scenario "logics" - differing view or theories of the way the world might work in the future - that encompass the critical environmental drivers and major uncertainties each logic presents. For example: Will the world move towards further free trade or protectionism? Will the energy market return to a seller's market or continue as a buyer's market?

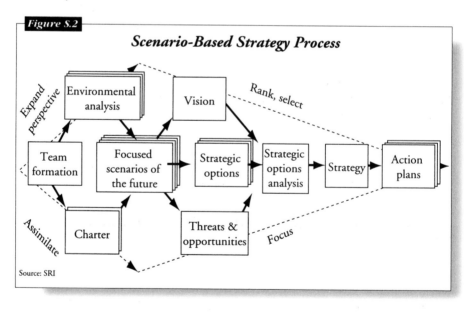

Figure S.2

Scenario-Based Strategy Process

Source: SRI

Step 5: Description of scenarios. Using the logical structure that has emerged in Step 4, participants describe scenarios in sufficient detail to identify decision implications and to help develop and assess strategy options (in a form of risk-reward assessment). Normally, these scenario descriptions include an extended storyline of two to three pages, a tabular description of scenario differences, and selective quantification of key factors.

SRI represent their process flow from scenarios to strategy as shown in Figure S.2.

EXAMPLE: The Introduction of Scenario-based Planning into Statoil (see Stokke et al, 1991)

In 1987 SRI International began to work with the largest Norwegian oil and gas company, Statoil, which was owned by the Norwegian government. Statoil had already been experimenting with the use of scenarios in developing overall corporate strategy. 1987 had been a year characterized by volatile oil prices and Black Monday on 19 October, when the international financial markets seemed on the verge of collapse. The project with SRI was a trial run aimed at exploring the utility of scenarios in developing a long term research and development strategy for Statoil's Exploration and Production (E&P) Division.

While scenario planning was not the only element in the project, it was considered important to help the R&D managers to deal with the inevitable uncertainties they faced in thinking through that strategy. Much of that uncertainty stemmed from high-impact social, political, economic and technological forces and the consequences they would have for the business and thus its technological needs. Factors such as oil and gas prices, as well as the strength of the Norwegian economy and the availability of technical skills had to be considered, along with other issues such as the importance of the oil industry to the country's future, the role of technology, particularly in terms of the new technologies the E&P department would have to master.

All told, the scenario team identified more than 60 forces that had a direct or indirect bearing on R&D planning including:

• Micro forces. These were the principal market and industry forces that would be key determinants of R&D decision making, such as oil and gas demand, oil and gas prices, the market structure for competitive fuels, oil and gas supplies, E&P costs, the Norwegian economy and oil and gas technology.

- Macro drivers. These were the broad economic, technological and social forces that would shape the global and national context for Statoil's operations, such as economic growth and development, energy strategies for OPEC, the US and what was then Comecon; government policies, technology and social forces.

Having carried out a "what-if" exercise to ascertain the full extent and significance of the uncertainties inherent in these forces, the group found that the high-impact, high-uncertainty factors could be clustered into three areas of uncertainty:

1. The structure of the energy market (supply and demand): would there be a return to a seller's market or would the current buyer's market continue?

2. The Norwegian economy: would the economy continue to be heavily energy-dependent or would it successfully restructure into a more diversified form?

3. Technology: would technology evolve, in the general economy and in energy industries, in a fragmented and somewhat incremental manner or would a more integrated and accelerated evolution take place?

These three "axes of uncertainty" enabled the team to structure its thinking and channel the imagination, while providing a useful framework for developing the scenarios. By their diversity, they could also serve as the prism through which to combine the multiple elements of the future into internally consistent "what-if" pictures. Four scenarios were developed:

Scenario A:

The nation's future is dominated by the oil and gas economy. Traditional patterns of industrial and technological development result in continuing high energy dependence; consequently, oil prices rebound and OPEC regains dominance about 1995. The nation debates restructuring its economy, but the actions proposed and taken are not sufficient to divert the strong push towards further development of national oil and gas resources.

Scenario B:

Oil and gas benefits lead to a restructured national economy. A more rapid diffusion of new technology (materials, computers, communications) and the gradual resolution of budget and trade deficits result in higher levels of growth world-wide and closer political and economic relationships among nations. The OECD countries continue to maintain a high level of energy dependence, thus ensuring the return of a seller's market. Norway uses technology and national oil and gas revenues for energy resource development and the diversification of the economy.

Scenario C:

The country struggles in a depressed world. Structural problems in both developed and developing countries reach a crisis and, lacking resolution, result in a prolonged world-wide recession. Commodity and energy prices plunge, and the politics of protectionism and national self-sufficiency help to generate a "siege mentality" in many countries. Under these pressures, Norway seeks to leverage her energy resource advantage into a strategy for national economic survival.

Scenario D:

The country is driven from oil dependence by global restructuring. This scenario represents the furthest evolution of the globalized economy and the "Information Society". High-tech breakthroughs (in such areas as information technology, biotechnology, materials) radically change the structure, mix and location of global economic activity. Material and energy intensity declines dramatically, and information-based value increases correspondingly. In this high-tech but highly competitive world, Norway has no choice but to restructure her economy.

These four scenarios covered the various combinations of energy market outcomes (seller's market-buyer's market) and possible Norwegian economic futures (energy dependence-restructuring) and associated each with a technology future that was both plausible (consistent with the other scenario drivers) and challenging.

Visioning the Future

These "capsule narratives" were written so that they would be brief enough to memorize, while conveying the essence of each scenario. They proved to be very useful as a form of shorthand in the later planning stages. Once they had been written, the next stage was to enlarge them into a detailed tabulation of "key descriptors" (see Figure S.3), which was a selection of the most significant micro forces and macro drivers that had been earlier incorporated into the model of the external environment. However, rather than take all 60 key descriptors, which could have cluttered rather than clarified the mental maps of the participants, a more selective approach was taken, and which resulted in 30 of them being used.

To help further envision the future, one scenario was chosen for extended elaboration, Scenario D, not because it was deemed the most probable, but because it was the most challenging for Statoil and its R&D planning and thus a worthy target for more "what-if" speculation. However, that by no way precluded the need to think through the implications of all the scenarios.

Preparing for the Future

The project team then met for an intensive week long workshop. During the first four days, the team discussed the implications of the scenarios, taking a different one each day. That gave the participants the ability to immerse themselves in the details of each one. On the fifth day, the team reviewed the results to identify the commonalities and differences across the implications.

Figure S.3

Tabular Description of Scenarios

Descriptions	A. Norway's future dominated by the oil & gas economy	B. Oil & gas benefits lead to restructured Norwegian economy	C. Norway struggles in a depressed world	D. Norway driven out of oil dependence by global restructuring
Global economic development	• Persistent economic structural problems • OECD growth: about 2% • Inflation higher: volatile exchange rates	• Moderate growth, some progress toward restructuring • OECD growth: 2.5% • Cyclical swings in inflation, exchange rates	• Severe economic structural problems, protectionism • OECD growth: 1.5% • Volatile inflation (some deflation) & exchange rates	• Strong growth, following restructuring adjustments • OECD growth: 3-3.5% • Relatively stable inflation & exchange rates
Geopolitical relations	• Increasing protectionism • Slowdown/reversal of privatization policies • US-W.Europe tensions exploited by USSR	• Growing international trade & cooperation • Privatization gains in OECD • Relaxation of east-west tensions; increased trade	• Volatile, tension-filled world; protectionism, nationalism grow • Emphasis on govt. controls • East-west relations & trade deteriorate	• Stable political relations lead to economic agreements • Market-oriented policies flourish • COMECON drawn more into global mainstream
Energy market structure	• Oil demand growth: 1% • Gas demand growth: 2% • OPEC regains dominance • N.sea, Barents sea pushed • COMECON gas available • Oil = $30-$35/bbl; Gas = $3-$5/MBtu	• Oil demand growth: 1% • Gas demand growth: 2% • OPEC power increases • N.sea, Barents sea pushed • COMECON gas expands • Oil = $25-$30/bbl; Gas = $3-$4/MBtu	• Oil demand growth: 0% • Gas demand growth: 1% • OPEC struggles to survive • Barents sea devel. delayed • COMECON gas reduced • Oil = $15-$20/bbl; Gas = $2-$3/MBtu	• Oil demand growth: 1% • Gas demand growth: 3% • OPEC loses power & cohesion • N. sea, Barents sea slowed • COMECON gas reduced/more former OPEC • Oil = $10-$15/bbl; Gas = $1-$3/MBtu

Oil & gas industry structure	• Only modest restructuring
	  – Strong upstream operations post 1990
		• Moderate restructuring
		  – More strategic alliances
		  – Greater push downstream
			• Substantial restructuring
			  – Mergers/ consolidations multiply
			  – State-owned companies favoured by national policies
				• Substantial restructuring
				  – Strategic shift from oil to gas
				  – Privatization of some state owned operations

Norwegian situation	• National will: unsure, drifting
	• Economic restructuring
	  – Few initiatives successful
	  – Petroleum sector dominant
	• GNP growth: about 2.5%
		• Moderately dynamic national will
		• Economic restructuring:
		  – Balance between petroleum & non-petroleum sectors
		• GNP growth: 2.5%
			• Malaise: Discouraged, divided
			• Economic restructuring
			  – All sectors struggling
			  – Govt. supports energy sector
			• GNP growth: 1-1.5%
				• Strong dynamic national will
				• Economic restructuring
				  – Most initiatives successful
				  – Gas replaces oil in importance
				• GNP growth: 2.5-3%

Technological change	• Incremental development: disciplines remain fragmented • Norwegian R&D spending: 1.5% of GNP with oil & gas as No.1 priority • Oil & gas technology: Focus on E&P improvement & new reserves	• Accelerated progress: integration of disciplines • Norwegian R&D grows to 2% of GNP, with new priorities • Oil & gas technology: Focus on new reserves access	• Stalled development: Restrictive, protectionist policies • Norwegian R&D spending declines, but oil & gas spending is constant • Oil & gas technology: Focus on productivity/ cost-control	• Rapid progress: Integration, global diffusion of technologies • Norwegian R&D grows to 2-2.5% focus on high-tech restructuring • Oil & gas technology: Focus on gas conversion, AI/Imaging

Source: SRI

Rather than allow that review to become an unfocused and random exercise, a structure was put in place based on the key decision factors. These were defined as those elements of the future about which knowledge, or at least some information, would be most useful in the decision-making process.

Figure S.4

Two Options for Scenario D: Norway Driven Out of Oil Dependency by Global Restructuring

	Option 1	Option 2
Strategy	Becomes an integrated gas company	Pursue high-tech, low-cost solutions. Be strong in applications of new technology
R & D priorities	• Invest in gas technology • Team with existing gas players to gain access to technology • Go after higher-value added gas products	• Monitor technology developments worldwide • Don't lead in technology development
Key R & D programmes	• Basin analysis • Geo data technology • Shallow gas safety	• Production technology • Exploration and production drilling • Technology management systems

Source: SRI

The thinking at this stage was in five discrete steps:

1. Review scenario description. Involving both intellect and emotion, this was more than a review. It was an attempt to get close enough into the scenarios to believe each one was the future.

2. Assess implications of the scenario. The effect of each scenario on the key decision factors was discussed, helped by a more extensive list of questions to answer.

3. Identify the best strategy, opportunities and threats. The focus here was to answer three questions. What seems the best strategy/decision for dealing with the conditions of this scenario? What are the major opportunities and threats inherent in the scenario? What should Statoil do - and not do? The following phrase was used as a lead-in: "If we could forecast the future with certainty, and knew that this scenario would develop as it has been described, then Statoil should ..."

4. Evaluate the scenario's impact on company goals. Earlier in

the project, the team had assessed the linkage between the R&D programmes and company goals, and to what extent those programmes contributed to the goals. Now the team wanted to review that in light of the external conditions represented by the scenarios.

5. Develop a portfolio of priority R&D programmes. R&D priorities could now be re-ordered and a portfolio developed most attuned to the conditions of each scenario.

This was not the end of the project: further steps moved the process from the scenario-specific R&D portfolios towards the selection of an R&D strategy sufficiently resilient to be viable in a variety of possible futures.

What was perhaps the most important outcome was the process itself.

PART III:

Case Studies

The case studies included in this section are intended to provide a feeling for the application of scenarios to strategic planning.

The case studies are in alphabetic order:

British Airways
built scenarios to help highlight a number of issues within the company, to provide a forum in which the various divisions which needed to be aligned could discuss the market changes.

Cable & Wireless
wanted to find a way of transferring thinking about the market effects of new technologies - like the Internet - between business units in its federal structure.

ECRC
used Godet's tool sets and advice to build scenarios for the future of the IT industry in Europe, in order to focus their research programme.

Electrolux
A scenario thinking project developed three scenarios for Europe in relation to global warming, use of toxins, and re-use and reprocessing: with a major strategic change in the commercial cleaning business.

KRONE

used PA Consultants to generate four scenarios based on different technologies being adopted. It then, within each scenario, examined product opportunities using brainstorms and visualizations done by PA designers: over 200 product ideas resulted.

The National Health Service

developed the Hemingford scenarios to help this large (£35 billion) organization, which has many facets, think strategically - about the nature of the organization, relationships between the parts and their customers, and the way forward.

Shell

who have integrated Shell scenarios with the development of strategy, which involves the Shell Group managers worldwide.

United Distillers

started scenario planning in early 1995. Three scenario exercises had been worthwhile since then, each looking at a wide range of cultural lessons in relation to UD's business of spirits sales.

BRITISH AIRWAYS

This is an edited extract, reprinted with permission, from "Scenario Planning at British Airways - A Case Study" by Kathy Moyer, *Long Range Planning,* Vol. 29, No. 2, pp. 172 to 181, 1996, Elsevier Science Ltd, Oxford, England.

Background
Over the past decade or so, British Airways has evolved from a loss making, state-owned national carrier into a customer focused, publicly listed and consistently profitable airline. This transformation, a testament to a clear vision and a strong management team, has been achieved against a turbulent operating environment.

The air travel business is highly sensitive to economic cycles. British Airways reacted quickly and effectively to the last major recession which was precipitated by the Gulf War. So, while the airline industry as a whole lost £10 billion during the period, which is more than its total combined profits since commercial aviation began in 1947, British Airways remained profitable.

The airline industry is a global business. British Airways is the world's largest international passenger carrier, flying 36 million people to 194 scheduled destinations in 82 countries in 1994. But cross-border ownership and landing rights are tightly controlled and in order to expand its global presence, British Airways has developed partnerships through airline investments in America, Australia, France and Germany and through non-equity franchise links in the UK.

While recognizing that British Airways has been successful in the past, it is dangerous to assume that current strategies will remain valid in an increasingly complex and changing business environment. British Airways is capital intensive, operating a fleet of 293 jets with long-term commitments to some 53,000 staff. Management must be able to recognize and interpret external events so that any major shifts in the environment which make current strategies vulnerable are anticipated and possible responses formulated. The airline cannot rely solely on quick reactions.

Given the immediacy of the airline business, however, it is difficult for managers to tear themselves away from the day-to-day running of the operation to take a longer-term view. The existing planning processes, the budget and the business plan look at the coming year and the next three years respectively. They tend to reinforce the assumption that the future will not vary significantly from the present, and plans tend to focus on operational improvements. A process for developing and testing strategies in light of future uncertainty was missing.

Making it Happen

British Airways' Chief Economist, DeAnne Julius, proposed the use of scenarios to the Chairman's Committee in February 1994. Because the expected benefits were somewhat intangible, the decision was made to treat the exercise as an "experiment" to see if the process was suitable for use within the company.

The exercise was divided into two phases: scenario development and scenario workshops. Each phase was led by a senior member from the Corporate Strategy department. The aim was to link the scenario workshops to the business plan from April 1995.

Phase 1: Scenario Development

The first phase of the project was led by the Chief Economist. The development team included eight staff from the Corporate Strategy, Government Affairs and Marketing departments and an external consultant. Work began in mid-March 1994 and was completed by the end of October 1994. Individuals' time spent on the project varied, with no-one working full time. An equivalent of 2 man years was expended.

In an effort to gain top level support and guidance for the project, a "Halo Group" was established. This group of 14 directors and senior managers represented the major departments in the company. Their advice was solicited following the completion of each of the main tasks in the project.

The first task was to determine the significant external issues which are facing the airline. Over 40 individual interviews with managers throughout British Airways were conducted, each lasting between 1 and 2 hours. Five group interviews were held with staff specialists covering topics such as information technology and air transport regulation. Several interviews with academics, government officials and aircraft manufacturers were also completed. Most interviews were conducted by two development team members from a standard set of questions which had been designed in advance. Detailed notes were taken on the condition that the anonymity of participants would be maintained.

From the interview notes the development team were able to compose a story of the "Official Future" which summarized the working assumptions British Airways managers were making about the future environment and highlighted potential blind spots. The important external issues were identified and classified into three categories: predetermined elements (such as population growth), key uncertainties (issues of high importance and high uncertainty such as airline deregulation) and driving forces (such as changes in information technology which could fundamentally affect the airline business).

The development team spent a day debating the issues and 11 were selected for further research. It was not obvious from the interviews what the organizing issue, around which the scenarios would be built, should be and so this was left until further research was completed. These findings were presented to the Halo Group who confirmed that the Official Future was an accurate reflection of thinking within the company and approved the preliminary research agenda.

The second task was to develop challenging yet plausible outcomes for each of the issues. This required an in-depth understanding of each issue and the identification of the critical events which would bring about each outcome. The issues were allocated among the development team who carried out desk-based research and consulted with experts to develop the arguments. The research was condensed into a briefing pack for each issue.

In mid-June 1994, the development team spent two days sharing their findings and exploring inter-connections between the issues. A decision was made to focus on the relationship between growth and governance as the organizing issue and to develop two stories, each covering a 10-year time horizon. Outputs from the 2 days, together with the briefing packs, formed the basis from which the stories were written.

Story writing began in July 1994. A full outline was drawn up by three members of the development team. Draft scenario stories and presentation slides, which showed the main points pictorially rather than as text, were produced. These went through several refinements as they were tested on fellow team members and other experts, and included a presentation to the Chairman's Committee to secure their approval. To ensure a consistent style, the final version of the stories were drafted by the external consultant and finalized by the Chief Economist. Writing was completed by mid-September 1994 and approved by the Halo Group.

Whilst the stories were being written, the numerical data on economic growth, passenger traffic and aircraft supply data was produced. Historical data was retrieved, and models were built to determine how the data would be affected by the events in each story. It was decided that at the end of the 10-year period overall world economic growth levels would be similar in both scenarios. This was to avoid a high case-low case dichotomy which the team felt would not stretch thinking. However, the "boom and bust" economic cycles in one scenario would lead to much higher passenger traffic demand than the slow, steady economic growth and increased product substitution of the second scenario.

A booklet of the stories was produced. The development team was responsible for the text and pictures and a professional designer assisted with the layout and cover design. The cost was just under £10,000 for the design and printing of 2000 copies. A fireworks party for the development team commemorated the completion of the first phase of the project.

The Scenarios
The scenarios took as their starting point the fact that enormous changes have occurred in technology, education, world trade and finance over the past 50 years, and that the pace of change has increased as these four elements reinforce each other (Figure

BA.1). The emergence of a new generation of leaders who lack the personal experience of the World Wars and their search for new models of external growth and governance structures was taken as the organizing issue or "fork" between the two scenarios (see Figure BA.2).

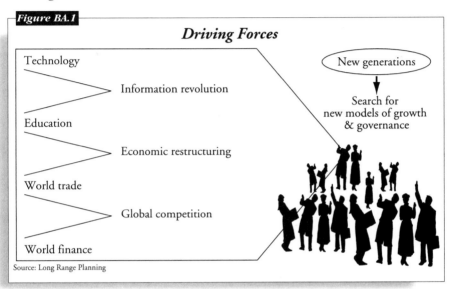

Figure BA.1

Driving Forces

Technology

Information revolution

Education

Economic restructuring

World trade

Global competition

World finance

New generations

Search for
new models of growth
& governance

Source: Long Range Planning

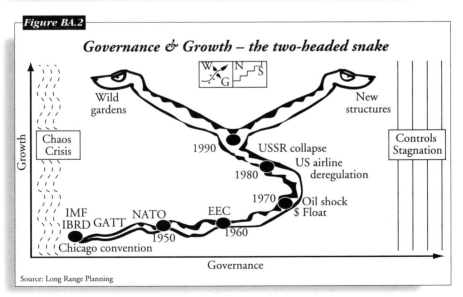

Figure BA.2

Governance & Growth – the two-headed snake

Growth

Wild
gardens

New
structures

Chaos
Crisis

Controls
Stagnation

1990

USSR collapse

US airline
deregulation

1980

1970

Oil shock
$ Float

IMF
IBRD GATT NATO

EEC

1950

1960

Chicago convention

Governance

Source: Long Range Planning

In "Wild Gardens" global integration goes so far that it is impossible to build lasting new structures of governance to replace the old, crumbling structures. In this world it is the Darwinian battle of winners and losers which shapes the future (see Figure BA.3). In "New Structures", however, shared values and new ways of organizing are found which enable growth to continue in a manageable, rather than in a socially disruptive, way (see Figure BA.4).

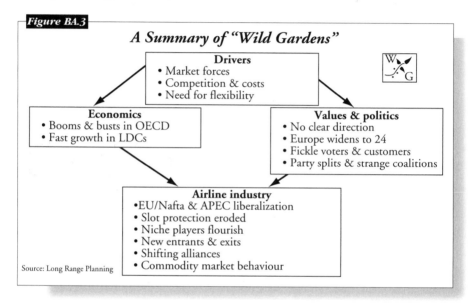

Figure BA.3

A Summary of "Wild Gardens"

Drivers
• Market forces
• Competition & costs
• Need for flexibility

Economics
• Booms & busts in OECD
• Fast growth in LDCs

Values & politics
• No clear direction
• Europe widens to 24
• Fickle voters & customers
• Party splits & strange coalitions

Airline industry
•EU/Nafta & APEC liberalization
• Slot protection eroded
• Niche players flourish
• New entrants & exits
• Shifting alliances
• Commodity market behaviour

Source: Long Range Planning

Phase 2: Scenario Workshops

The scenario workshop phase was led by Rod Muddle, Head of Planning, who represented Corporate Strategy in the company's business planning process. A team of five facilitators was responsible for designing and managing the workshop phase. Work began on the design and marketing of the workshops in June 1994. Training took place during August and September 1994, followed by four trial workshops in October 1994. The equivalent of 2 man months was spent on design, marketing and training.

The purpose of the workshops was to provide an opportunity for participants to hear and discuss the scenarios, and to provide

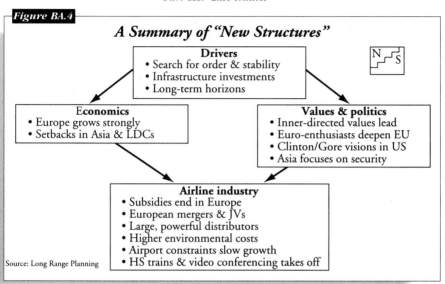

Figure BA.4

A Summary of "New Structures"

Drivers
- Search for order & stability
- Infrastructure investments
- Long-term horizons

Economics
- Europe grows strongly
- Setbacks in Asia & LDCs

Values & politics
- Inner-directed values lead
- Euro-enthusiasts deepen EU
- Clinton/Gore visions in US
- Asia focuses on security

Airline industry
- Subsidies end in Europe
- European mergers & JVs
- Large, powerful distributors
- Higher environmental costs
- Airport constraints slow growth
- HS trains & video conferencing takes off

Source: Long Range Planning

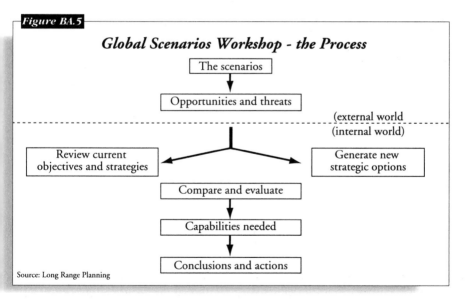

Figure BA.5

Global Scenarios Workshop - the Process

The scenarios

Opportunities and threats

(external world)
(internal world)

Review current objectives and strategies

Generate new strategic options

Compare and evaluate

Capabilities needed

Conclusions and actions

Source: Long Range Planning

a structured framework for developing new strategies and test existing ones (see Figure BA.5). After hearing presentations of the scenarios, brainstorming and creativity techniques were used to generate new strategic ideas for each scenario. The most valuable ideas were then developed and summarized into strategic statements. In order to test robustness, new strategies developed in one scenario were evaluated in the other scenario and existing strategies were evaluated against both scenarios and represented visually using a 2 X 2 matrix (see Figure BA.6). This was followed by a discussion about whether any of the strategies could be modified to improve their robustness. The final states of the process focused on making the strategy work: what capabilities were required; what actions needed to take place; and who, within the client group, was responsible for ensuring actions were taken. Feedback was gathered at the end of each workshop. This was used to improve the process and provide information about how the workshops were progressing.

Figure BA.6

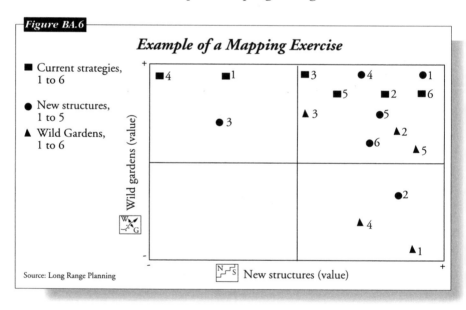

Example of a Mapping Exercise

■ Current strategies, 1 to 6

● New structures, 1 to 5

▲ Wild Gardens, 1 to 6

Source: Long Range Planning

Directors and senior managers with responsibilities for the major components of the business plan were targeted as potential workshop clients. The facilitation team met with these individuals, described the process, explained the benefits and offered to organize a workshop. The facilitation team's policy was that workshops were available to anyone in the airline, on request, with the only proviso that target customers had priority over others. The client was involved in planning the objectives. They selected the participants, paid for the event (room hire, lunch etc.) and had ownership of the content (i.e. the strategies and actions).

A facilitator took responsibility for managing all aspects of a client's workshop. This included meeting the client to plan and agree the objectives; assisting the client to articulate his/her current strategy; sending invitations, organizing the venue, co-ordinating the other scenario team members; co-facilitating the workshop (time management, challenging existing thinking, encouraging open discussion, recording ideas etc.) and, about one month after the workshop, meeting with the client to obtain further feedback and discuss whether any actions had occurred.

The stories were presented by the scenario development team who had the detailed background knowledge. They were responsible for adjusting the core presentation to match the client's focus and responsibility. A presentation for the Americas Region, for example, would provide more detail on geopolitical events in that region, while a presentation to the Purchasing department might go into more detail on aircraft supply. If possible, a different presenter told each story as it helped participants to distinguish between the two. The interview notes and briefing packs put together in the development phase were used by both the presenters and facilitators in preparing for individual workshops.

The output of the workshops was confidential to the participants. All notes were typed up and sent out within 1 week of the workshop. As the workshops progressed, the facilitators drew out common themes of corporate importance. These were presented, discussed, prioritized and actioned at the Group Managing Director's quarterly strategy meetings. This process ensured the corporate strategic initiatives were co-ordinated and linked into the business planning process.

The Halo Group continued to play an important role in the workshop phase of the project. They agreed the workshop process and the list of target clients, received feedback about how the workshops were progressing and acted as champions of the exercise. Indeed, many of the Halo Group members were early clients, sponsoring a workshop in their area and recommending it to colleagues.

Each workshop took a required 4 to 5 man days of effort, including preparation and writing up, from the workshop team.

Successes

The stories themselves were substantive and challenging. They captured the attention of even the more cynical audiences, and there was enough depth of analysis to draw upon when questions were asked. The workshop team ran 28 workshops and over 20 presentations with only two clients from the target list of 20 not sponsoring a workshop. There were several factors from the development and design processes which contributed to delivering this high-quality product.

The Chief Economist and the external consultant had extensive experience in developing and implementing scenarios. Together they provided a clear definition of the project, assigned responsibilities, set deadlines and held progress meetings every two weeks to ensure that the project plan was being followed faithfully. Their expertise gave credibility to the project within the company, and the presence of an experienced team member meant the Chief Economist was able to manage other responsibilities and maintain high level support for the project.

The team members worked well together. All had volunteered for the project and by getting together as a group to agree the key decisions, they became a highly motivated and enthusiastic team. A continuity existed between the scenario development and workshop phases. The team responsible for the design and implementation of the workshops were all involved, in varying degrees, in the scenario development phase which gave them a clear understanding of the objectives of the scenarios and of the stories themselves.

The scenario development phase of the project was extended beyond the scenario development team. For example, members of the Pacific Region helped identify and develop issues relating to Asia. This consultative style ensured the right issues were covered and the stories were robust.

The positioning of the Scenario Planning exercise as an "experiment" and the consultative style engaged people's interest without them feeling that a new structure was being imposed on them. This meant people tended to be predisposed to being involved in the exercise.

Pilot workshops allowed the workshop team to test the process and experiment with different facilitation techniques. The Halo Group members and colleagues from Corporate Strategy who participated in these pilots provided valuable feedback and early practical examples of the scenarios prompting new strategic thinking, which were used by the facilitators when speaking with potential workshop clients.

Scenario workshops were successfully used to develop and link strategies between levels within a department.

The scenarios proved to be relevant for areas at lower levels in the organization than the workshop team had originally envisaged. For example, Customer Relations used the scenarios to develop new ways of linking British Airways to its customers.

Scenario workshops were also successfully used as a tool to inform groups such as the Trade Unions and the management at Qantas Airlines what external issues influenced the British Airways business plan and to stimulate a dialogue between British Airways managers and these groups.

Lessons

In addition to the successes, several lessons were learned. We underestimated the amount of work involved in developing plausible but challenging scenario stories and, because the project deadline was fixed, there was no slack in the timetable for the delays that inevitably occurred.

The most frustrating aspect, which caused the biggest delay, was the development of the numerical database including the passenger traffic model, the balance between business and leisure travel, and the interpretation of the social trends data. Historical data proved illusive and, when finally obtained, the modelling was more complex than anticipated. Data gathering could have begun earlier and the team would have benefited from having a full-time analyst working on the problem.

Most of the development team were new to the scenario concept and research time was broken up by other commitments. In addition, team members tended to be rusty in either interview, presentation, facilitation or research techniques. While these factors were not significant issues in themselves, they did result in progress being slower than anticipated and this affected both the level of detail and the number of issues covered in the research phase. This was partially offset by commissioning work from external bodies but more contact by the team with external experts would have been useful.

The development phase overran by one month, and this reduced the time available for presenters to practise and to become conversant with all the story details prior to the start of the workshop programme. In addition, the booklet was not available until mid-November, after the workshop programme had started.

The project plan anticipated that workshops would be spread over a seven-month period in order to allow clients to choose when it was appropriate for them to think about strategic issues. There was a downside to this approach. Some scenario team members moved to new projects and were not replaced. As a result, by the end of the April facilitators were doubling as presenters and vice versa.

Presenters had to spend a significant amount of time prior to each workshop reacquainting themselves with the background material and ensuring the stories and slides were current. Some tailoring of the core presentation was necessary as the focus of the workshops varied considerably - from Europe Region to Flight Operations, for example. Some areas, e.g. Southern Region, had not been fully covered in the scenario development phase due to the time constraints mentioned above and so required more preparation work than others. Where the presenters were unable to provide this additional focus, the strategy development was less satisfactory. The ongoing commitment required by presenters had not been fully appreciated at the beginning of the process. This could have been overcome if the presenters had been included more in the planning and running of each workshop. Rather than having two facilitators and one or two presenters, a facilitator/presenter team might have been more appropriate.

A benefit of departmental workshops was that participants were already used to working together and could focus on ideas and actions which were in their direct control. However, this group cohesion also made it harder to challenge the implicit assumptions held by the group and get them thinking in new ways. As a result, facilitators recommended to clients that they invite a few participants from outside their area.

The issue-based workshops worked well as long as the participants had clear responsibilities for taking action as a result of the discussions. Early in the programme a couple of workshops were commissioned without clear client ownership, and these proved to be ineffective.

The optimum workshop size was 7 to 10 participants in order for all participants to have an opportunity to contribute. Groups larger than this tended to become unwieldy. A few workshops for 20 participants were run successfully. However, this was achieved by splitting groups into syndicates for the idea generation and development stages, and required extra facilitation, particularly to bring the syndicates together to share their thinking and to keep everyone involved.

Some people found the scenarios too complex to grasp fully all the implications in the time allocated. The presenters tried to overcome this by linking current stories from the press into the scenarios, by encouraging questions and discussion and by providing the numerical data such as passenger demand. However, if time had permitted, more experimentation with the presentation style could have been introduced. In addition, more could have been done to introduce the issues to British Airways management during the scenario development phase. For example, the interviews might have been more of a two-way dialogue rather than just eliciting opinions if reading material had been sent out to interviewees beforehand. In addition, sessions could have been arranged with external experts presenting an issue followed by a group discussion.

In general, one day was not long enough to cover all stages of the process in sufficient detail. The facilitation team's involvement with the Pacific Region's three-day workshop (with Scenario Planning covered on the first day, followed by two days looking at specific strategic issues) led the group to believe that two days was probably optimal if that much management time could be secured.

On a more mundane level, one of the biggest irritants was finding a suitable location to run the workshops. In-house venues were generally preferred as low-cost, but most proved to be inappropriate in terms of lighting, ventilation and the fact that participants tended to get drawn back into the day-to-day business. There were the inevitable fire alarms and lunches that failed to arrive. From an organizational standpoint, it would have been easier if an appropriate venue was selected with workshops offered on specific dates only.

Conclusions
A much better understanding of Scenario Planning exists as a result of the exercise and the management community in British Airways is receptive to using this approach again. Both the development and the workshop phases of the exercise highlighted the fact that developing strategy is a complex and iterative process, and that there are significant benefits to be gained by using structured processes combined with facilitation and creative problem solving techniques.

From the experience of applying Scenario Planning at British Airways, the most important criteria for success in introducing Scenario Planning are:

- Gain support from the top level in the company and build it into existing planning processes from the start.

- It is a major exercise - plan it well, take the time to do the design and research properly and show progress along the way.

- Treat the exercise as a learning process. Consult as many people as possible in the development process so they feel ownership with the final product.

CABLE & WIRELESS EXPERIENCE

Finding a New Approach

The search for a more effective way to decide what information senior management at the £5.5 billion telecommunications group Cable & Wireless needed for decision-making had begun in the early 1990s. It was accelerated in late 1994 with the establishment of a new unit at headquarters called group development.

The purpose of the group was twofold. First, it wanted to try to address the fact that since the company operated through a federal structure, different technologies, both in terms of delivering products and supporting the company, were being developed in autonomous subsidiaries across the group. There was thus very little work being done in terms of standardization or towards achieving group-wide benefit from any of the best technologies that had been deployed by any of the subsidiaries.

The chief executive of group development also wanted to take a slightly different approach to the adoption of technology. Rather than just looking at the technical merits, which do not always guarantee success in the market, he wanted a method by which to examine why some technologies prosper and how factors like consumer demand and price pressures affect the introduction of a technology. That could then be used as a basis for choosing which technologies to opt for, which was crucial given the long lead times and the scale of investment required.

While the term scenario planning was not then used, an examination of ad hoc reports from around the organization showed that there had been attempts to look at different futures, although not in any sort of systematic way. So Adrian Kamellard, former project manager, scenario planning, began to construct a framework for scenario planning. His focus was to create an approach that the business units would use and which would ensure that all of the thinking was done in a fashion that was of good quality, complete, and importantly, plugged into the annual planning process so that decisions resulting from scenario planning affected the allocation of resources. That was to be the litmus test of success.

He decided that the key to making scenario planning effective was common sense and a grounding in business issues: *"One element of scenario planning has to be common sense. The other is taking a particular perspective on the business and having the rigour and the process to complete the work from that perspective. Typically senior managers are involved in line roles that take up all their time so if there is a market going through significant and rapid restructuring very few senior managers can articulate well the current business environment, much less the one that may exist by the time any strategic decisions actually have an effect on the business. They are also working on data about customers and competition which can be at least several months old."*

"The other effect is that when managers do think about the future, it is too easy to become a victim of tunnel vision because even if someone has a fairly broad view of the future it becomes relatively fixed. There is little flexibility or capacity to identify the early warning signs that those views are no longer valid. So what scenario planning comes down to is looking at the world from a particular perspective which examines the industry and the company, through the eyes of suppliers, customers, appropriate governments and others for 5-10 years in the future. Once you have that in your mind, the rest becomes much easier. The critical point at that stage is to take each problem as it is posed and adopt an approach appropriate to the problem."

Choosing the Right Method
In some cases, therefore, he used a highly quantitative approach, with a detailed model to understand the issue. This would take months of work and lots of research. In others, there would be one or two days' worth of brainstorming to come up with an answer. But with both, there was still a series of steps to ensure that the right perspective was being adopted and that all the ideas were being captured and that, whatever the outcome, it would connect with the planning process (see the section on Strat*X in Part II).

For example, he wanted to try to model the impact of the Internet in the UK telecoms market. At that point, in the mid 1990s, there was little hard understanding about the Internet, although there was a lot of noise in the company surrounding it. So a quantitative approach was taken to introduce some rigour into the debate because once people were pressed to give their thought on its actual impact, it made them think much harder about the issues. The process of building the quantitative model and understanding the relationship between the variables brought a clearer view and stood the company in much better stead when the output was used to build some decent stories about what would happen. Forcing rigour into scenario construction kept the thinking on target.

In other cases, he found that where the market was relatively well-understood and comparatively stable, the knowledge of the senior management could be relied on more for scenario construction because of their good understanding of the dynamics and behaviour of the market.

Aiming at the Business Units

Kamellard would run workshops with the senior management of the business units, not at group level, because he wanted to make sure that scenarios were derived from the particular business drivers the units faced. He would facilitate sessions around a particular project of interest to them to help them learn the process and leave one or two people in the business unit behind who could carry on.

Before running workshops, Kamellard would try and find out what the current state of knowledge was, whether through interviews, papers or telephone calls, depending on the issue. That would help him set the scene so he would know how to pitch the two-day workshops. He found that it was useful not in the sense of immersing himself in the topic but to understand current thinking. Also, he did an appropriate level of research so that he could introduce support, ideas or whatever into the sessions. For example, if the scenarios were being developed on an aspect of technology, there would need to be an understanding of how the technology worked, the current players, suppliers, customers etc. to stimulate the debate. Also, he would have in his own mind an early cut of what the key drivers were. While this was not to be prescriptive, if the research was done well he would have a reasonable chance of picking the right driving forces.

Sessions would be held with between 8 and 10 people with Kamellard as facilitator. The first step would be to identify a series of events that were possible under several headings: politics, economics, sociology, technology, customers, suppliers, regulation and competition. Usually the workshops would be separated by time, so that once all the possibilities had been identified under the headings, there would be a filtering process to identify the bullet points which were likely to have any material effect and to get rid of some of the noise.

Validating the Results

There could be an early attempt to construct scenarios at the first session, depending on the participants' level of understanding of their industry. But irrespective of that, he still found it important to break off after the first session and do research on the key areas that had been identified, whether technologies, or pricing regimes, or regulatory issues or whatever. He would go away and either model particular areas, or do research, so he could return with good quality knowledge about the state of play in each of the areas. He found that even in a stable market it was essential to break between the first and second session to do research and reflect on what had been identified. Sometimes there could be a third session as well.

The three-session process thus worked like this: in the first session do brainstorming, research in-between, construct scenarios at the second workshop, of which there could be two, three of four, do further validation, and then hold a third session to convert the information to decisions and actions that could go into the planning process.

The scenarios themselves had to tell a coherent story and be internally consistent, whether written in narrative, bullet points or even pictures, depending on the audience. Often it was found that there were inconsistencies, with one proposition mutually exclusive to another, although for fairly subtle reasons. That was why it was important after constructing the scenarios to validate them.

He found it crucial that the head of the unit be involved. Otherwise, if the chief executive delegated participation because of the time pressures, when the other managers returned with strategies based on the scenario work, these would very likely be changed or over-written. While holding workshops with lower level executives was useful to stimulate thinking about areas like the Internet, to have the scenario process make a material difference the chief executive would have to be involved.

Weaving the Scenarios into Strategy

The objective was to select one of the scenarios or to extract a combination of them to arrive at a base case to use for key strategic and tactical decisions. What Kamellard found happened in practice was that if there were three scenarios, the strategy would be devised geared to the base scenario and perhaps a second. But a contingency plan would be developed in case the third scenario began to emerge.

What proved more difficult was to get the units to create a process that would alert them to trigger points that indicate that a perceived uncertainty was becoming more likely. Nevertheless, the scenarios have become an integral part of strategic planning at the business units where they have been done. For example, the annual plan submitted by one of the biggest units three months after doing scenario planning took almost word for word the two key scenarios that had emerged from the workshops.

ECRC

ECRC was a Research Centre owned in partnership by, and staffed mostly by people from, three IT companies: Bull, ICL and Siemens. The Centre decided that it needed a better understanding of the European IT Industry in the next decade., to ensure that research was concentrated in areas relevant to the partners.

Facilitated by Michel Godet, the group used his MICMAC toolset. to carry out structural analysis under 5 groupings:

Group 1:   Geopolitical and economic constraints

Group 2:   Autonomous/determinant technological factors

Group 3:   Market trends ($ volume of annual sales)

Group 4:   Information/communication technology
infrastructure investment

Group 5:   The strategy/game of the actors

The first stage was to establish the list of factors for the IT industry. Once 69 variables were identified with the help of more than 50 international experts they were grouped and within each group identified as either: internal factor, external factor, actors or markets. The structural analysis matrix was then used to determine the relationships between the factors identified. Finally the MICMAC method established the key variables as a prelude to building the probable scenarios.

Group 1: *Geopolitical and economic constraints.* The participants thought that at the extremes it was possible to distinguish a black scenario, in which all the factors were negative, correlated with a recession (see Figure E.1), and a rosy scenario linked to high growth. In between they saw scenarios with low, fluctuating growth and the EC breaking up; and growth of about 2.5% and integration only of markets in Europe.

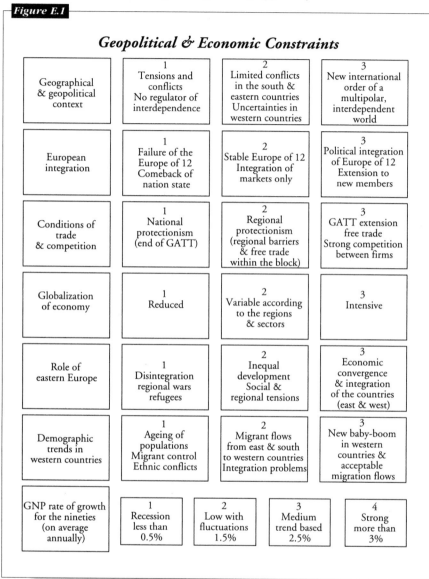

Figure E.1

Geopolitical & Economic Constraints

	1	2	3	
Geographical & geopolitical context	Tensions and conflicts No regulator of interdependence	Limited conflicts in the south & eastern countries Uncertainties in western countries	New international order of a multipolar, interdependent world	
	1	2	3	
European integration	Failure of the Europe of 12 Comeback of nation state	Stable Europe of 12 Integration of markets only	Political integration of Europe of 12 Extension to new members	
	1	2	3	
Conditions of trade & competition	National protectionism (end of GATT)	Regional protectionism (regional barriers & free trade within the block)	GATT extension free trade Strong competition between firms	
	1	2	3	
Globalization of economy	Reduced	Variable according to the regions & sectors	Intensive	
	1	2	3	
Role of eastern Europe	Disintegration regional wars refugees	Inequal development Social & regional tensions	Economic convergence & integration of the countries (east & west)	
	1	2	3	
Demographic trends in western countries	Ageing of populations Migrant control Ethnic conflicts	Migrant flows from east & south to western countries Integration problems	New baby-boom in western countries & acceptable migration flows	
	1	2	3	4
GNP rate of growth for the nineties (on average annually)	Recession less than 0.5%	Low with fluctuations 1.5%	Medium trend based 2.5%	Strong more than 3%

Group 2: *Autonomous/determinant technological factors.* Under this heading they distinguished a Frustration scenario linked to a micro-electronics slow-down, a Breakthrough scenario linked to

a breakthrough in micro-electronics, and the possibility, if the current improvement trend of micro-electronics continued, of seeing radical change. Their conservative scenario was that development would remain specialist, software users would not be able to configure software, and the current trend in MIMD architecture would continue (see Figure E.2).

Figure E.2	**Technological Factors**		
S/W development Technology	A1 Development done by computer experts only	A2 Development predominantly done by interdisciplinary teams	A3 Development done only by end-user domain experts
S/W user Technology	B1 non-configurable non-personalizable	B2 Limited configurability Today's packages, plug-ins, user preference files	B3 Support for new user-added functionalities
Microelectronics	C1 Slowdown	C2 Current improvement trend continues	C3 Breakthrough
Computer architecture	D1 Continuation of current trend in MIMD		D2 Radical change

Group 3: *Market trends.* These were related to the size of the market for the various sectors that the IT industry covers: computer hardware, software, and services.

The participants saw a Shrink scenario in which all the market sectors (see Figure E.3) either shrank or stood still, and a Blue Skies scenario in which personal systems and embedded systems revenues both grew at more than 10% pa. They could see a Leisure scenario with high growth of embedded software (as in computer games, instrumentation) and in personal computers, and in this scenario and their business support scenario they saw reduced corporate information resources. Their Continuity scenario showed growths in systems for groups of workers (Groupware).

Figure E.3				

Market Trends

Personal use systems	[1] Shrinked CAGR	[2] Standstill CAGR	[3] Average CAGR	[4] High CAGR
Systems for working groups use	[1] Standstill CAGR	[2] Average CAGR	[3] High CAGR	
Systems for professional use	[1] Standstill CAGR	[2] Average CAGR	[3] High CAGR	
Enterprise infrastructure systems	[1] Shrinked CAGR	[2] Standstill CAGR	[3] Average CAGR	
Corporate information resources	[1] Shrinked CAGR	[2] Standstill CAGR	[3] Average CAGR	
Inter-enterprise communication systems	[1] Standstill CAGR	[2] Average CAGR	[3] High CAGR	
Embedded systems	[1] Shrinked CAGR	[2] Standstill CAGR	[3] Average CAGR	[4] High CAGR
	<0	<2%	>2%	>10%

Group 4: *Information/communication technology infrastructure investment.* The participants saw failure to ratify standards as leading to a pessimistic scenario, with adoption of standards at the other extreme linking to a world in which users would drive for new technologies and broadband access could become prevalent. They identified the trends then (in 1993) as being towards a proliferation of products not conforming to standards, but enthusiastic adoption of technology based on the existing telephone network (see Figure E.4).

Group 5: *The strategy/game of the actors.* One of the scenarios the group saw was of European IT Industry decline, linked to a protectionist world. In the Virtual Firm scenario of a world network of specialized firms, they could see European firms developing a niche or exclusive business policy. A common

Figure E.4

Investment

Standards (non-telecommunications standards)	ODP not ratified	Plenty of products (not dominant) comply with ODP	Majority of systems bought adopt the ISO ODP standard	
Resistance of users to change	Strong resistance (which is today's situation)	"Fatalistic" acceptance of change	Enthusiastic adoption	Users pushing for new technologies
Integration with telecommunications infrastructures	Second-hand access to IT; no ubiquitous access at all	Direct interaction restricted to professionals; ubiquitous access to high bandwidth for companies	Existing telephone network; full networked services; ubiquitous access to high bandwidth for firms & homes	Ubiquitous access to high bandwidths; firms & home; full networked services; sophisticated interaction modes

European IT Industry would be based in a protectionist world, be a follower, with a mixture of businesses. The last scenario they drew, without a homogeneous structure, good price/ performance, R&D focused on systems integration, and no manufacturing, has been the route taken by ICL, though not so far by the other partners in ECRC (see Figure E.5).

Figure E.5

The strategy/game of the actors

Structure of IT industry	Protectionist world, government involvement, regional focus	No homogeneous structure, business structure as today	World network of specialized firms, "virtual firm"
Company structure & strategy	Regional view, complex company structure, mature technologies, broad product spectrum	Follower strategy generalist frequent alliances, economy of scale	Focused, lean management, dynamic, good price/performance
R&D policy	Reduced R&D budget, cooperation due to budget constraints, public funding	Use of existing technologies, R&D for systems integration	Sustained R&D active cooperation policy, key technologies available
Business policy	Mixture of businesses	No manufacturing, systems integration, supply of professional services	Exclusive product or systems business

ELECTROLUX'S EXPERIENCE

This case study was contributed by Jan Agri of Electrolux.

A key concern for the Electrolux Group is environmental issues and working with environmental issues is all about dealing with short term uncertainties and understanding long term trends. The management team wanted the group staff Environmental Affairs to develop an awareness of those trends and strategies for dealing with environmental issues integrated with the business process throughout the company.

Environmental issues needed to form part of the thinking process of the businesses. The scenario process was key in developing a picture of what was happening in the broader market and business environment that affected the product groups.

The framework

Electrolux surveyed the literature available on scenario planning, internal experience from change programmes, and received advice from Graham Galer, former Strategic Planning Manger at Shell, about Shell's experience of using scenario planning.

The scenario methodology, called the Environmental Change Programme, ECP, was developed using internal expertise and the services of the academic partner Gothenburg Research Institute, and a management consultancy.

Two pilots were run, one with a group from the consumer side and one with a group from the commercial side, commercial cleaning appliances. On the consumer side, the group had already experienced pressure from environmental issues.

The first step of the ECP was to undertake a strategic investigation of the business environment with a special focus on environmental issues and demands. The second step was to look at the impact on the current strategy, of the current and possible future conditions. The process and the results were used as a way of broadening management thinking. However the key was to integrate the concern and awareness of the environmental issues with the business strategy and to set up action plans.

The scenario process worked as an eye opener. The group

started with the product line managers and then rolled it out to other management teams on lower levels.

The scenarios

The process of building the fact base for the scenarios took around three months. During this period there was an extensive data collection process. Interviews were undertaken with suppliers, customers, environmental organizations. The scenarios were developed by a core team of 4 to 5 people from Environmental Affairs. The process was finalized by a brainstorming based on a presentation of the fat base. The resulting skeleton scenarios were then fleshed out by obtaining additional information from experts.

Three scenarios were developed: see Box.

SCENARIOS AT ELECTROLUX

Summer Time:
Focused on Global Warming.
Global Warming had become a reality. Strict legislation in place to restrict use of fossil fuels. Energy prices rising.

Cocktails:
Focusing around the use and abuse of toxins, both real and perceived.

Evergreen:
Focusing on material use, reuse and recycling.

The use of the scenarios

The process of introducing the scenarios with the businesses was started with a slide presentation of the driving forces behind environmental problems and demands. This was, during the first pilots, followed by a set of slides highlighting the most important aspects of each scenario. This was presented to the full product line management team and other key managers, about 15 people. This group was then split to work in three groups looking at the different scenarios. Each group was asked to consider what they would do if they were working in Electrolux and this scenario turned about to be a reality in 10 years' time. For their assistance, they were provided with five pages explaining each scenario in detail.

After presenting their ideas to the other groups, each group was asked to consider what strategies could or should be put in place anyway. The management teams recognized that most of the strategies would be good to implement even if the scenarios did not come true. The actions they had identified made sense in terms of current environmental and business pressures.

The results

There were several impacts of the change in thinking. One was a major strategic change in the commercial cleaning business. As a result triggered by one of the scenarios, the division became more service oriented. Electrolux became more aware that there was value in its products even beyond the economic use for the customers. As a supplier, the materials or parts of the product could be reused. The idea was then to sell the customer a service and not a product. This can be compared with a successful scheme developed by Rank Xerox of renting copiers with full service, guaranteed function, and charging based on the number of copies made, instead of only selling a copier machine.

The scenario process at Electrolux is ongoing. Less effort is now put into data collection and more effort is put into rolling the scenarios out to the businesses. The objective is to pass it on to all the product lines. Currently around 25% of product lines have used the techniques.

THE NATIONAL HEALTH SERVICE

The UK's National Health Service (NHS) is a complex, large £35 billion organization which employs 1 million staff. In 1994 a small group formed to try and replicate the success of commercial organizations with scenario planning to help change planning in the NHS and aid strategic thinking and learning. Traditional approaches to planning for the future were not proving effective for the uncertain and multi-faceted NHS environment.

In 1994 a scenario planning exercise took place to try and overcome these challenges (Hadridge and McIvor, 1996 and following discussions). First, more than 30 people provided expert opinion on the range of future possibilities in relation to a range of issues, including:

- clinical practice
- public values
- the socio-political context of healthcare
- demography
- disease trends

Then a group of 12 people drawn from backgrounds as diverse as a Christian ministry and the oil industry, as well as the NHS, gathered together for a two-day workshop. Participants used the expert database already built up and their own perceptions to build various futures for health and healthcare.

The resulting four scenarios, called the **Hemingford Scenarios** after the village where the work took place, were as follows:

THE HEMINGFORD SCENARIOS

Renewed Welfare Order.
This is essentially a personally satisfying experience for the tax payer. The NHS is delivering quality service and is able to show objectively that it is getting results. It is decidedly state centralized, though with wider democratic processes built in. It is nationally-focused.

Health is Wealth.

The view of health care taken is that it becomes even more international, not just on the supply side (such as pharmaceuticals) but in the patient care side as in managed healthcare organizations. New kinds of multi-national commercial organizations develop (some pharmaceutical companies are already heading that way). The orientation is both to objective science and towards subjective well-being in that both have consumer validity. The system is greatly decentralized but regulated for standards (like provision of food through restaurants).

Science Makes the Big Push.

This leans strongly towards the objective science side but paradoxically has a high element of personal healing and therapy since it is very focused on the informed consumer as patient. In its operation it is pretty state-centralized because of the high cost implications of advanced scientific research. Research links the system in very strongly to the leading edge of international biosciences. The patient/consumer tends to be more inwardly focused on the service mix in their locality.

Well-Being As You Like It.

This has a strong subjective orientation in that individuals each tend to go for some definition and mix of services which feel right to them. There is a myriad of competing authorities as to what works best. The main focus is national but with connections to the international networks that focus on the well-being approach. The diversity has been made possible by the regional devolution of power enabling choices to be made closer to the population.

The scenarios were constructed around three key polarities.

- Between national and international. Although the scenarios are about the UK's NHS, the field of healthcare and medicine has an international dimension. This is through the international nature of medical science itself. Through the multi-national nature of many health product corporations and through a variety of non-governmental organizations.

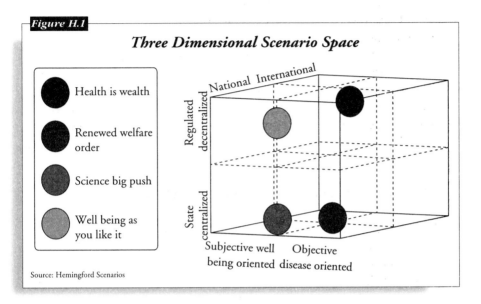

Figure H.1

Three Dimensional Scenario Space

- Health is wealth
- Renewed welfare order
- Science big push
- Well being as you like it

Regulated decentralized / State centralized

National International

Subjective well being oriented / Objective disease oriented

Source: Hemingford Scenarios

- Between state centralized and regulated/decentralized. The historical NHS is a direct state institution with strong central control over standards and resources. This has enabled the health service side of the Welfare State to be realized. However, there are other possibilities emerging which include a health service which is delegated to regional or even commercial organizations that carry out the work subject to a framework of regulations.

- Between objective disease-oriented and subjective well-being oriented. Is health about people? Or is it about biochemical behaviour? This dimension looks at the contrasts between viewing disease as a breakdown or invasion of an organism that can be scientifically studied, and viewing illness as the opposite of well being, a condition that is personally experienced and goes well beyond anything that science would define.

Since building the Hemingford scenarios, scenario planning has continued to be used in the NHS, including at the Department of Health, according to one of the key people involved in the original work, Philip Hadridge, service development manager, NHS Executive (Anglia Oxford Regional Officer). However, the focus is more on using scenarios as a learning experience and as a springboard to strategic thinking and planning by different teams and groups. He and the network of colleagues in other parts of the NHS and the Department of Health who are also involved have found that the technique has proved itself far beyond their original perceptions. For example, it has given them confidence and facilitation tools for running planning events and meetings.

NORTH WEST ANGLIAN HEALTH AUTHORITY

The North West Anglian Health Authority (NWAHA) is the National Health Service (NHS) purchasing authority with responsibility for purchasing healthcare services for over 400,000 people in its area. The budget of between £160 and £180 million is spent in the Primary, Acute and Community Care sectors.

The Authority had been investigating better ways of planning for the NHS. Having examined the Shell approach, it decided that scenario planning had the twin attractions of being values-based but also relatively robust and could help those who take spending decisions do so having considered a multiplicity of variables which could lead to different futures.

The first step was to carry out a process that John McIvor, then deputy chief executive (now chief executive of Doncaster Health Authority) calls "Healthy Horizons", a multi-stakeholder, values-based consensus planning process, in order to develop a vision for mental health services in the future. That included consultations with groups such as carers, voluntary organizations, general practitioners, public health physicians and consultants. The result was a set of shared values against which to assess proposals for better services requested from providers. These were to be the parameters within which to make resource decisions in the light of different health futures.

This process also began to help decide what the key "strategic intents" were. It was backed up by one-to-one interviews carried out by McIvor, Anthony Hodgson of IDON, and another NWAHA manager. They carried out about 30 interviews with people such as directors of social services, top managers at the Authority and in the NHS Trusts and community health councils, using the IDON model of clustering issues to find out what issues North West Anglian would need to address over the next five years.

The three clusters to explore further in the scenario matrix were found to be (see Figure H.2).

- Primary care-led NHS
- Heath and healthcare
- Public involvement

Figure H.2

Applying the Hemingford Scenarios

Strategic intent	1 New welfare order	2 Health is wealth	3 Science big push	4 Well-being as you like it	Robust
24 1 Primary care led NHS	5 Better care closer to home (closer to customer)	6 Managing diversity to minimize inequality	7 High capacity primary care gateway to specialists	8 Extend & regulate	17 Strengthen close to comm resource & knowledge mgmnt
25 2 Health & health care	9 Investing together in health & health care	10 Make sure wealth is for health	11 Developing individual responsibility & social values	12 Be a catalyst for the health continuum	18 Form alliances for prevention priorities for real benefits
26 3 Public involvement	13 Continuously engaging public in a health debate	14 Information ensures no hiding place	15 Choose information technology together	16 Hold the ring	19 Two way info through appropriate technology
	20 National local politics for transferring of resources	21 Monitoring regulating marketing for health & health care	22 Access & sell evidence applied ethics & logic	23 Holistic facilitation tolerance & evaluation skills	

What new learning and development?

Source: Hemingford Scenarios

Two workshops were then run with 20 of the Authority's top team, including executive and non-executive directors, which brought together people from different areas, not just the NHS. The first was one day to "localize" the Hemingford scenarios. That was followed by a two and a half day session to run the cross impact matrix to examine possibilities and probabilities, key actions and skills requirements. McIvor believes that it was about the right size for a successful outcome. Even more important was the participation of senior management who would be making decisions about resource allocations in the future. Understanding alternative futures would make their decisions more robust. The session also fostered board development and team building.

What McIvor has found significant is that, once having done the exercise, the scenarios have stayed in people's minds so when they do have to make decisions they look at the possibilities against the four scenarios. He feels, in fact, that getting people to internalize the scenarios was more valuable than getting them formally to run them against the strategic intents. One of the reasons he feels the scenarios have survived so well is that although holes could be picked in them there was a certain plausibility about each of them for different groups to relate to. Also, they are sufficiently different and stretching to be interesting.

The scenarios were then discussed throughout the Authority with lectures and talks, while tapes of the scenarios were also handed out to give as many people as possible an understanding of the different worlds in which the board makes decisions.

The main objective was to use scenarios to make better planning decisions, not to be seen to be doing "war gaming" in North West Anglia, according to McIvor. On reflection, McIvor believes that perhaps less intention should have been paid to the strategic intents and more to the scenarios themselves. *"The scenarios themselves are useful for months and years to come if they are properly internalized by those who should be considering alternative futures when they are making resource allocations and decisions: whereas for our organization, at least, strategic intents can change quite rapidly."* He feels that some of the decisions taken since about the primary care-led issue of the NHS have been helped by the process they went through. In time, he foresees the organizations doing more scenario planning and creating scenarios more localized in primary care issues, as well as looking at potential models for primary care in the future.

KRONE: SCANNING THE HORIZON

KRONE (UK) Technique Ltd is the British subsidiary of a £300 million German company. The core business is largely based on copper wiring, so that a lot of the activity is involved with telecommunications infrastructure, or the hardware for telecommunications. For example, the company is a major supplier to BT, making products such as telephone socket boxes.

The company decided to examine the future of phone networks, in the light both of new technologies and potential competition. It needed to assess things such as the potential impact of optical fibre, and to what extent the use of cable and mobile telephones, for example, would affect the business. The company also wanted to look for new product opportunities.

KRONE approached PA Consulting Group to assess the business impact of technology and market change on copper wiring to 2005. PA suggested that, because of the pace of change in the market, and because it can be very difficult to predict exactly what might happen with the technologies, that scenario planning would be the most appropriate technique.

Finding the Drivers of Change

According to Dr Stephen Black of PA's Technology Consulting Practice, at that stage there was little understanding of just what the driving forces were, or what was really causing change to happen in those markets.

"That was the first hard bit: to go far enough away from just looking at the market for connectors and find out what drives change. We had to look at questions such as why people want different types of connectors, why people want optical fibre, or why people want different types of wiring in the office."

"So we spent a lot of time doing research both on current technologies and what was driving change. We looked at things like video on demand technologies and at the market for local areas networks in offices to see what the drivers were in terms of the desire for more bandwidth, such as video conferencing and multi-media. The point is, if you're selling wiring to offices, or

connectors and wires to BT, understanding that matters because these factors drive future demand."

In-Depth Research

Three people from PA first spent a number of weeks on research, including interviewing people in the market, reading reports, doing desk research, and collecting other people's projections. The team also found some useful information on the Internet, including some scenarios from Andersen Consulting about the future of multi-media. At the same time, the process included what PA calls stakeholder analysis, which involved one-to-one interviews with KRONE board members, business managers and change consultants. KRONE's business aspirations and capabilities were evaluated, while interviews with customers and competitors provided views about the company, its products and market trends affecting existing or future business.

PA considered the interviews with company managers a crucial part of the project, says Dr Black: *"We had to interview all the key people and really get a feel for their current thinking and what their visions for the company were, and what they thought the future looked like. That is crucial because if you don't understand the politics and you don't understand where the individuals are coming from, you can't get them to buy into the scenarios later on. So they have to be involved in the process. That gives you a good start before you do the scenario workshops. Before the interviews we had also produced a document floating some ideas about the future we though relevant, some of which were relatively provocative ideas to stimulate thinking."*

Creating the Scenarios

Armed with all this data and information, two two-day workshops were done with senior people from within the company. The first day of the first workshop was spent brainstorming to decide what the key drivers were, which were then filtered down according to their impact on the business. The consulting team then spent some time trying to identify the key critical uncertainties from results of the brainstorming. The next day the team presented the group with three key critical certainties for the business, which were agreed after a discussion.

The scenarios were generated during the second day of the workshop and subsequently fleshed out by PA. They were based on the following, well known premises, plus some others that are commercially sensitive:

- Demand for bandwidth-creating services such as video-on-demand or multi-media is driven by the demand for services, not the demand for technologies.

- Technology interacts with services by enabling new types of service that have never before been possible.

- It is the interaction of demand for new services and enabling technologies that drives changes in the network which, in turn, affects KRONE.

The team managed to keep the total number of scenarios to three, though a fourth was developed later to account for another issue significant in all the other worlds.

The scenarios were surprising and challenging. Neither PA nor KRONE expected the pictures of the future that actually emerged, though broad agreement was reached that the possible worlds were credible and consistent portrayals of what might happen. They broadened the firm's horizon beyond its traditional customer base and allowed them to see the major forces driving change in their marketplace. Many of the changes in the hardware of communications networks are driven not by hardware or equipment manufacturers or installers, but by the end users of the information they transmit. The process sensitized KRONE to the risks of "business as usual" and also created an awareness of new opportunities for the firm's existing skill base.

Exploring the Impact of the Scenarios
By the end of the workshop the group were beginning to see the value of the process, including coming to terms with some unexpected implications, particularly in terms of timing.

A second workshop was held to get agreement on the story lines and to assess the impact of the scenarios on the business. First the team examined how the existing business and the skill base would fare in each scenario world. Then the team continued by detailed examining new product opportunities using brainstorms and visualizations of the scenario worlds produced by PA designers. Over 200 product ideas resulted, which were then filtered according to viability and the match with KRONE's existing skills. A further analysis showed what new skills might be required in each world of the future.

The team did a final presentation of the whole project, with KRONE managers describing the scenarios to the senior UK board. The conclusion was that the project really had begun to change the way the company saw the future. The significance of the work to KRONE's future business strategy was such that they are reluctant to allow the content of the scenarios to be used in this case study.

Learning points

A number of important lessons were learned from applying scenario planning in this firm, according to PA.

- Scenario planning is often regarded as a technique dealing only with the abstract "big issues" affecting large multinationals. In this case, however, the technique worked well for a medium-sized firm. With supporting tools, KRONE was able to reach concrete conclusions about business strategy and to generate new ideas for products.

- It is only possible to achieve significant results with scenario planning if it is an integral part of the firm's decision-making process. Stand-alone scenario stories (with no links to the decision-making process about strategy, products or future skill needs) will not create change.

- It is essential that the process of building scenarios involves the key decision makers in the firm. The real focus of scenarios is their mental models of how their business works.

It is the process of building the scenarios that changes those mental models, not the storylines themselves.

- Scenario planning is not a universal tool but, when integrated into a business's other decision-making processes, it can lead to great results.

SHELL'S EXPERIENCE

Shell operated a planning system essentially similar to that described by Schoemaker and van der Heijden through the early 1990s. The description below is from Schoemaker and van der Heijden, *Planning Review,* Vol 20, 1992 reproduced by permission of the Planning Review. It is summarised in Figure SH.1, which reflects the organisational structure of Shell at that time.

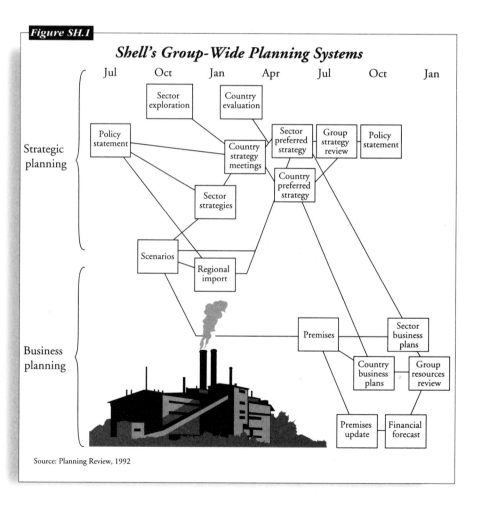

Figure SH.1

Shell's Group-Wide Planning Systems

Source: Planning Review, 1992

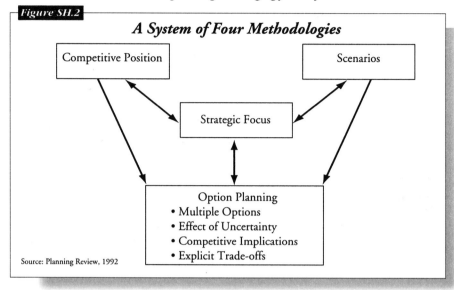

Figure SH.2

A System of Four Methodologies

Source: Planning Review, 1992

A System of Four Methodologies
There were four main elements in the strategic planning process to help managers move from the theoretical to the actual, as represented in Figure SH.2.

A. Scenarios.
Improve decision-making by developing multiple scenarios against a background of possible future environments. Areas to focus on include:

• Issues and information that greatly concern Shell's decision-makers.

• Elements in the environment that are determinable and somewhat predictable.

• Trendbreakers - elements that will affect a system in unpredictable ways, but with understandable dynamics.

• Potential surprises of major significance.

There are four steps in this process:

Step 1. Select the issues. Some appear in most Shell scenarios, such as economic growth, product demand and energy prices. Others will reflect changing events or particular concerns. A big challenge is to find those issues that will be of greatest value by the time the scenarios are being used.

Step 2. Analyse the areas of concern. This will help determine the driving forces, predetermined elements, critical uncertainties, possible discontinuities and linkages with other areas of the business. That can include a range of factors, such as energy, social change and the environment.

Step 3. Organize the scenario around a logical concept. This helps define a scenario and makes sure all the elements are consistent. It also helps establish a basic message such as growing environmentalism.

Step 4. Focusing the scenario. Establish defined boundaries for the scenarios in terms of time frames, geographic regions, industries, business sectors or major project to bring them into sharper focus. While decision-makers should see their concerns reflected in the scenarios, the scenarios should also enable them to further new understanding.

B. Competitive position

Competitive positioning focuses on the business unit's competitive situation, and then devises ways to improve that. That includes defining the business segments, and analysing what can be an extensive range of competitors whether suppliers, customers, other producers and those offering substitute products or services. It considers barriers to entry such as patents, and brings in other factors such as economies of scale, technological know how, customer loyalty, organizational capability and product excellence. The competitive positioning process, based on both hard and soft data, is about learning systematically as much as possible about the competitive issues between each Shell business and its rivals.

C. Strategic focus

The next step is to refine the strategic vision. Done on a systematic basis, it allows the operating company or sector to define its vision of the future and how to reach it. This requires conviction, creative foresight and a practical sense of what is feasible. Once the vision is accepted, the managers can then return to the scenarios and the competitive analysis, which helps the decision makers focus on events, trends and competitive behaviour. It gives the managers a cleared idea of what they need to reach a leadership position, although at this stage the process is not detailed financially since that could detract from innovative strategic thinking.

D. Options planning

This begins the formal process of defining major strategic options and their consequences. It converts everything learned from the previous steps into a unified system that has a major impact on decision-making at the company. It consist of four stages:

Stage 1: Multiple options are generated. Current business assumptions are reviewed which can uncover new options, or ones previously discarded or associated with past failures.

Stage 2: Estimating the consequences. Techniques ranging from the intuitive-best guesses to the mathematically-simulation models based on complex probability distributions are carried out to look at the financial, competitive and strategic consequences of choosing a promising option. At this stage the effect of uncertainty, competitive implications and explicit trade-offs are considered.

Stage 3: Selecting options. Various quantitative techniques are used to make decisions, such as decisions analysis, which is a rigorous means of making systematic trade-offs among competing objectives in an uncertain situation, and options theory which makes it possible for managers to assess the value of avoiding commitments or delaying decisions that are expensive to change.

Stage 4: Option management. Techniques like game theory assess competitor reaction to adopting strategic options. These decisions are ultimately based on judgement, however, and at Shell the emphasis is on team decision-making and consensus, using the experience and expertise of all team members.

Figure SH.3 summarizes the stages leading to implementation.

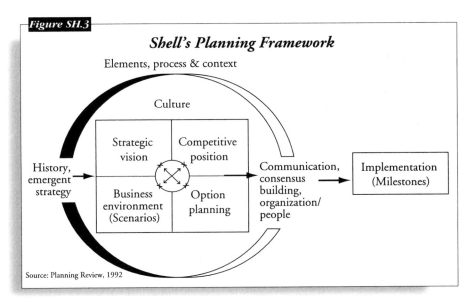

Figure SH.3

Shell's Planning Framework

Elements, process & context

Source: Planning Review, 1992

The 1992 to 2010 scenarios

Some of the more recent experience at Shell has been described in The International Journal of Futures Studies, in two papers by Robbie Davis-Floyd (Davis-Floyd, 1995)

In the first, he discusses with the author of the scenarios, Betty Sue Flowers, the nature of myth, and the ways in which Shell, in its scenarios, is trying to avoid being trapped into narrow ways of thinking. She is a writer who was specifically assigned to the scenario team. The rest of the team was mostly from Shell, both headquarters staff and secondees from the line operations, though a new Director of Scenarios was brought in to head up the three year process.

He describes the writing of the scenarios, which were subject to detailed rework and discussion of nuance. The outputs included videos, a short booklet, the summary book and the full report which was the basis of internal strategic decisions.

Anticipating changed rules

The effect on Shell of both the Brent Spar incident and events in Nigeria highlight the fact that even those companies which try to envision different futures can be caught on the hop. John Elkington and Alex Trisoglio (Elkington and Trisoglio, 1996) argue that Shell may have a self-perpetuating blind spot.

They analyse four different sets of scenarios done by Shell or, in the case of Peter Schwartz, ex-Shell scenario planners, and conclude that Shell missed out on what they call the "egalitarian" view, which characterizes those who form strong group links but reject the values of the outside world. If Shell had worked this view into its scenarios, the authors believe, it might have had a better understanding of how groups like Greenpeace could so quickly influence public opinion against the company. In the case of Brent Spar, for example, this happened despite Shell having looked for the best environmental outcome for disposing of the oil platform.

Changes since 1996

At the beginning of 1996, the Shell Group reorganized. Essentially, the regional tier disappeared and a new business focused structure was implemented. The Group has not yet finalized a replacement planning system reflecting the new structure.

The scenarios used in 1996 as part of the evolving planning process are described in Part IV.

UNITED DISTILLERS' EXPERIENCE - INVESTIGATING MARKET POTENTIAL

Created in 1987 as the spirits company of Guinness PLC, United Distillers (UD) has some of the world's leading drinks brands in its portfolio, including Scotch whiskies such as Johnnie Walker, Bell's and Dewar's, as well as Gordon and Tanqueray gins. Its 1996 sales contributed £2.5 billion to the overall Guinness revenues of £4.7 billion. The other main subsidiary is Guinness Brewing.

UD started scenario planning in early 1995, championed by now-chief economist John Ormerod. He had been in the Far East from 1987 to the end of 1994 latterly as Business Development Director. When he moved back to the London headquarters, he continued to have responsibility for India. His interest in scenario planning had been sparked by reading both Peter Schwartz's "The Art of the Long View" and the Harvard Business Review articles by Pierre Wack. He also attended a scenario planning course at the UK Strategic Planning Society.

Scenarios for India

India was considered a very tough market for alcoholic beverages, being one of the few markets in the world that was completely closed to imports of Scotch whisky, apart from duty-free. After long negotiations, UD had succeeded in persuading the Indians to allow it to import Scotch in bulk and bottle it there, which it had begun by January 1995. But it needed to explore the idea of really putting down roots in a much more substantive sense as a prelude to a longer term investment strategy, on the basis that liberalization was a question of when, not if. Although a difficult market, India was very attractive because even though it has periodic urges for prohibition, the growing middle class love Scotch. So Ormerod managed to persuade the company to invest in a scenario planning exercise to look at the prospects for alcoholic beverages under different scenarios.

Mr. Ormerod enlisted the help of a team from St. Andrews' Management Institute, Gareth Price and Adrian Davies to work on the scenario development, along with a UD manager in India.

Interviews were done with over 100 people, which Mr. Ormerod now feels was probably too many to assimilate effectively without the opportunity of an interim to take stock and redirect efforts to priority areas. Senior managers in UD and the parent company, Guinness, were also interviewed to understand some of their concerns about India, as were external people in the UK who knew India well.

But the bulk of the work was done in the country itself. *"It rapidly became obvious that if you talked with the elite only, and particularly the business elite, you would get a very narrow view. So we made a strong effort to get the St. Andrews' team to interview a range of other people such as social workers, politicians, bureaucrats and small businessmen,"* explains Mr. Ormerod. The fact that UD's name was not used in connection with the study helped the St. Andrews' team get interviews with people who might have shied away from talking to an alcoholic drinks company, since alcohol is such a sensitive issue in India. The interviews took place over about three months.

The St. Andrews' team took the information and fed it into a standard word processing package to slice it up according to subject matter. A first workshop was then held by Mr. Ormerod and the two from St. Andrews' in Bombay to decide on the key issues, a process helped by bringing in Indians from a number of areas to give their views. That was followed by a two-day workshop at St. Andrews' to develop the scenarios.

SCENARIOS FOR INDIA

1. In the Foothills.
This is a projection of the present situation in India, where ambition for betterment through liberalization is not matched by the decisive action needed to escape from the past. This scenario may not be sustainable over a long period and may either move decisively upwards (to Grasping the Nettle or The Korean Model) or shift downwards into India IS different.

2. Grasping the Nettle.
This scenario depends on firm implementation of the present policy of liberalization, despite strong opposition from vested

interests. The actions needed for this scenario to occur would move India decisively closer to the Western world, both internally and externally, and would gradually improve the lot of most Indians, but without India achieving the performance of an Asian tiger.

3. India IS Different.

This scenario shows an India rationalizing round failure to improve life for all its people, in a uniquely Indian way, with pockets of relative success surrounded by areas of turmoil and under performance. Failure to "grasp the nettle" may weaken central government and further shift power to the states, who are already competing for economic advantage. This scenario may provoke a response through reaction to a crisis.

4. The Korean Model.

This scenario shows the effect of a right-wing, determinedly nationalistic drive to emulate the strategic path followed by many of the Asian tigers. Liberalization continues in principle but its scope is restricted to areas of direct Indian interest. This scenario is susceptible to external, mainly US pressure and may be diverted towards "Grasping the Nettle".

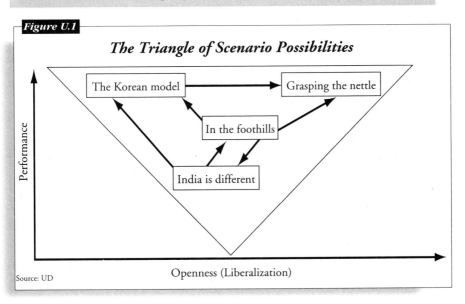

Figure U.1

The Triangle of Scenario Possibilities

Source: UD

311

In Mr. Ormerod's view there was an obvious central scenario, i.e. In the Foothills, which has India muddling along with no one able to take the big decisions necessary for an economic breakthrough. It was felt that for India to break out of this it could "grasp the nettle" and push through deep reforms, which at the time seemed fairly improbable. Alternatively, India could become much more authoritarian, more nationalistic, but more right wing and private-sector oriented that the more socialistically-inclined Congress party. It was felt that in this scenario, over time and under international pressure, the country would migrate to a more acceptable, less nationalistic model.

But there was also a scenario that "India IS Different", which stems from the idea that disillusionment with the unequal results of liberalization could lead to rationalizing around failure, such that India managed to justify a lower rate of growth by reference to its uniqueness and heritage. This scenario could lead to protectionism and a multi-speed India as different states set their own economic and social agendas.

The process lasted from June 1995 to January 1996, with the results written up in a report. Doing the scenarios was a very valuable learning experience, although it did turn out to be very expensive, according to Mr. Ormerod. He reflects that the exercise was probably over-intellectualized, with too much time spent on research and not enough on understanding how to present and use the scenarios. However, the results did heighten awareness of the issues among the middle level management in India in marketing, external affairs and business development who were briefed by Mr. Ormerod.

Scenarios for South Africa

And it also established enough credibility so that the project's sponsor, the managing director of the international region, agreed that scenario planning could be done again as long as it didn't cost as much. The next country chosen was South Africa.

This exercise lasted from April to August 1996. UD realized that despite the feeling among its local management that South Africa was fast going downhill, the company needed to get a better steer on South Africa's potential futures to 2010. Two consultants associated with St. Andrews' Management Institute based in South Africa were used, both of whom were ex-Shell. And this time Mr. Ormerod decided to be more involved: *"One of the problems in selling the India scenarios was that I hadn't been really close enough, although subsequently I became so. But when they were first done I didn't really have them in the blood."*

He took part in about half the interviews, the number of which was trimmed to about 26, with 20 in South Africa and 6 in the UK. *"We were absolutely ruthless in our selection, picking people with a unique, individual perspective. And in India we had used very little published material, particularly published opinion. In South Africa we did a much more extensive literature tour, including reading a number of books to make sure we were on the right track."* It also helped that South Africans knew what scenarios were about, since a number - such as the Mont Fleur scenarios - had been widely publicized.

In addition, an afternoon workshop was held with people from a wide variety of backgrounds both to test the critical issues and to probe them more deeply. There was also a "learning journey" to Zululand. This was followed by the development of the scenarios themselves. This time, milestones were set to be able to monitor the way the world might develop towards the scenarios.

There were three scenarios:

SCENARIOS FOR SOUTH AFRICA

1. Growth First.
In this scenario there are tough economics on IMF principles, the unions are contained, there is a centralized power structure, deregulation and privatization, and an invisible coalition between the African National Congress (ANC) and the opposition.

2. Our Turn.
Here social priorities have the priority over economics. Policy is dogmatic, socialist and populist. There is heavy affirmative action and forced redistribution, while the government becomes more disciplined and authoritarian.

3. Rainbow Compromise.

While social priorities provide the driving force behind this scenario, it is tempered by economic considerations. While socially the aim is to reach what is "fair", this goal remains unreachable because of funding restrictions. There is an alliance among the key players.

These scenarios are based on the critical policy dilemma South Africa faces (see Figure U.2). To enhance understanding, the team drew up a chart (Figure U.3) showing migration paths between the scenarios.

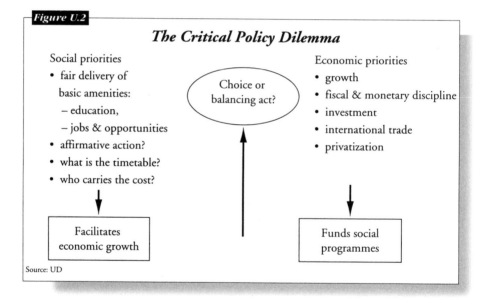

Figure U.2

The Critical Policy Dilemma

Social priorities
• fair delivery of
  basic amenities:
  – education,
  – jobs & opportunities
• affirmative action?
• what is the timetable?
• who carries the cost?

Choice or balancing act?

Economic priorities
• growth
• fiscal & monetary discipline
• investment
• international trade
• privatization

Facilitates economic growth

Funds social programmes

Source: UD

Having again produced a report, Mr. Ormerod then did an audit of the scenarios with influential people. The scenarios have definitely had an impact on the business: *"The three scenarios are now wedged in our strategic planning for South Africa. People know you can't think about South Africa without thinking about the scenarios,"* says Mr. Ormerod.

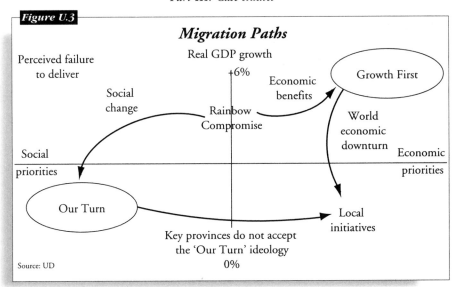

Figure U.3

Migration Paths

Real GDP growth

+6%

Perceived failure to deliver

Social change

Economic benefits

Growth First

Rainbow Compromise

World economic downturn

Social priorities

Economic priorities

Our Turn

Local initiatives

Key provinces do not accept the 'Our Turn' ideology

0%

Source: UD

Further Explorations

The South Africa experience brought more confidence about the technique, in terms of how to use the scenarios and make them relevant to the company, and not be treated as a one-off exercise. The next project was to consider the impact on UD's business in the Middle East of changes in Islamic political, economic, social, cultural and religious thinking. Turkey was chosen as the cornerstone because of the size of the potential market.

It soon became clear to Mr. Ormerod that the issue was not about Islam but about the nature of Turkish politics, particularly the way the country had developed and the tensions between the secular revolution introduced by Ataturk earlier in the century and what he thought the Turks would become, and the creation of Turkey's own interpretation of Islam compared with the traditional Islam of the Middle East. For this project background reading was crucial, as well as interviews. What UD wanted to examine was the forces at work, what the checks and balances were, and whether Islam could become as strong a power as in, say, Iran. The scenarios were being finalized in early 1997.

One of the key benefits of scenario planning Mr. Ormerod has found is that scenarios have helped the people involved in the businesses begin to understand that investment decisions are not just about submitting numbers and justifying budgets, but need to be set in a wider context of what might happen.

PART IV:

Examples of Scenarios

EXAMPLES OF SCENARIOS

The scenarios included in this section are intended to illustrate the range of ways of presenting scenarios, rather than for content per se. Remember that scenarios are stories, not forecasts.

Scenarios Developed by ICL in 1993

are included to illustrate the difficulty of communicating to those outside the initial team through a Table of Factors and terse descriptions.

Scenarios Developed by ICL in 1995

are somewhat easier to read. But we found that we needed to introduce a conceptual brochure (not included) as a scene setter for the detail.

Scenarios for the Internet

are included to show the use of the technique to tackle a fast-changing and confusing topic.

Scenarios for the future of the Telecoms Industry

are included to illustrate the possible migration of an industry between scenarios over time.

The Hemingford Scenarios

were produced by the National Health Service and have been used by a number of constituent parts and associated units to think through the changes - here and to come - in Health Care.

Scenarios for 21st Century Organisations

were produced to help organizations understand the contradictory forces which are gripping them.

Shell Scenarios, 1996

are included as classics, setting the standard.

SCENARIOS DEVELOPED BY ICL IN 1993

The three scenarios can be represented graphically as in Figure
I.1, or as in the following tables.

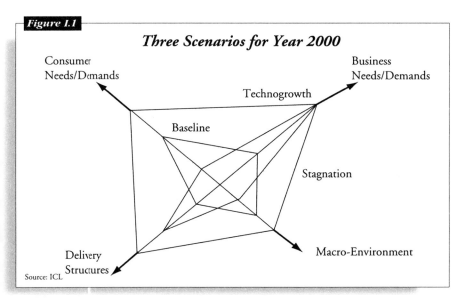

Figure I.1

Three Scenarios for Year 2000

Source: ICL

VARIABLE	ALTERNATIVE "PLUS" TECHNO GROWTH
BASIC DRIVING FORCES	
General geo-economic/political conditions	Free trade, general growth, non-working population not a social problem, market driven, business confidence. Population over 70 increases significantly
World GDP growth	4.0%
Monetary system/Europe	No major fluctuations
Price stability (esp energy)	No oil crisis, stable prices
Armed conflicts (defence spending)	US + Europe defence spending increased
Telecomms harmonization	European rates decrease to US levels
Europe	European area includes EFTA, excludes E. Europe
BUSINESS ENVIRONMENT	
GDP growth/North America	3.5%
GDP growth/West Europe	3.0%
GDP growth/Japan	4.0%
GDP growth/East Europe	4.6%
GDP growth/Far East (S&S-E Asia)	8.0%
GDP growth/China	7.0%
GDP growth/India	6.5%
GDP growth/Latin America	5.0%
Capital for IT Industry	Not limitation to IT
Energy (supply price)	Not problem for IT industry
Physical Environment	Not limiting but "green" is important
Skills availability	IT awareness in business high. IT skills slight constraint
Security of systems	Growing in importance, issues solved, promotes growth
Office Space	Reduction in space needed
Infrastructure (networking)	Bandwidth not a problem. Near universal accessibility in NA/Japan, (home & business), in WE (business) for multi-media video
Technology	Trends in miniaturization and processing power continue, high growth in digital TV
Government/Public sector	Investment in applications of new technologies to infrastructure in WE/NA/Japan, other public sector procurement reduces

BASELINE SCENARIO BUYER DOMINATION	ALTERNATIVE "PLUS" TECHNO GROWTH
Minor limitations in free trade, growth in West, EC trade barriers reduce, unemployment at current rates, business caution. Population over 70 increases significantly	Protectionism, stagnation, national governments interfere, market limitations, unemployment receives major attention at the cost of reduced productivity investments. Population over 70 increases significantly
3.0% Managed exchange rates in Europe No oil crisis, modest increase in prices European defence spending increased	1.5% EMS has collapsed, no replacement One oil crisis: 1998, 1999 European defence spending increased
European rates stay high but harmonized between European countries	European international rates stay high & vary by country
European area includes EFTA, excludes E.Europe	European area includes EFTA, excludes E.Europe
2.5% 2.0% 3.0% 3.6% 7.0% 7.0% 6.0% 4.0%	1.5% 1.0% 1.5% 2.0% 5.5% 6.0% 6.0% 3.5%
Unfriendly toward traditional players, not general limitation to IT	Limitation to IT
Not problem for IT industry	Not problem for IT industry
"Green" is mainstream	"Green" not that important
No constraint in IT skills, skills to exploit IT in business a constraint	IT awareness in business low
Growing importance, issues partly unresolved, some limitation to growth	Issues unresolved, limitation to growth
Reduction in space needed	Reduction in space needed
Some bandwidth limitations, accessibility problems in W Europe for multi-media video	Bandwidth limitations, accessibility limitations in Europe, price tariffs vary considerably between countries
Trends in miniaturization and processing power continue, some digital TV	Trends in miniaturization and processing power continue but shortage of capital and slack demand force slower pace of introduction
Public sector procurement reduces, esp of IT in G7	Public sector procurement reduces, esp of IT in G7

VARIABLE	ALTERNATIVE "PLUS" TECHNO GROWTH
BUYERS	
Buying population: people Decentralization	Increased buying population (LD) Decentralization continues in large organizations, their number does not change significantly
Penetration	Proliferation of small organizations
	High penetration of M/F, Mini, PC (D). Legacy systems significant but lesser problem (D)
Home & business	Home use of IT commonplace Convergence between leisure and business use advanced (D)
Workstation hw useful life Workstation sw useful life Server hw useful life Server sw useful life	4 years 2 years 8 years 8 years
Business processes of organizations (e.g. customers for IT)	Major changes in esp marketing and distribution
Attitude to IT	Significant distributed, mobile workforce with major impact on IT industry
Risk taking	Regards IT as a source of competitive advantage innovative
Entertainment & education markets	Major growth sector. Significant IT based services
Health & Safety markets	Major growth sector. Significant IT based services
Application creation by end-users	End-users increasingly creating own applications Professionals develop & support core applications
SUPPLIERS	
EDI/Networking	Proliferation of EDI/Networked services. Inter-access provided to end users
Telecomms, cable	Telecomms & cable companies will expand IT boundaries
Printing	Printer suppliers increasingly influential
Number of platforms	5-10 significant server, ws, nw, os platforms. Cohabitation partially resolved: tools to distribute and run applications across multiple platforms in widespread use
Number of application shells	Few wp, spreadsheet, email packages

BASELINE SCENARIO BUYER DOMINATION	ALTERNATIVE "PLUS" TECHNO GROWTH
Increased buying population (LD) Decentralization continues in large organizations, their number does not change significantly	Increased buying population (LD) Decentralization continues in large organizations, their number decreases.
Proliferation of small organizations	Proliferation of small organizations
High penetration of M/F, Mini, PC (D). Legacy systems major consideration and limitation to growth (D)	High penetration of M/F, Mini, PC (D). Legacy systems major consideration and limitation to growth (D)
Home use of IT commonplace (>50% households) Convergence between leisure and business use well advanced (D)	Less home use of IT (<50% of households). Convergence between leisure and business use in early phases (D), separate devices
6 years 3 years 10 years 10 years	8 years 4 years 12 years 15 years
Major changes in esp marketing and distribution	Necessity may motivate (different) changes in esp marketing and distribution
Significant distributed, mobile, subcontract workforce with impact on IT industry	Lesser distributed, mobile workforce
Cost conscious Risk averse	Cost conscious Risk averse. Necessity motivates commercial change
Major growth sector. Significant IT based services	Slow growth
Growth sector. Significant IT based services	Slow growth
End-users increasingly creating own applications Professionals develop & support core applications	Less investment
Many EDI/Networked services. Some inter-access problem for users	EDI/Networked services. Inter-access problems especially across national boundaries
Telecomms & cable companies will expand IT boundaries	Telecomms & cable companies will expand IT boundaries
Printer suppliers increasingly influential	Printer suppliers increasingly influential
2-5 significant server, ws, nw, os platforms: Windows, NT, Unix and ANO	Few new servers, ws, nw, os platforms: Windows, NT and Unix survive
Few wp, spreadsheet, email packages	Many wp, spreadsheet, email packages

VARIABLE	ALTERNATIVE "PLUS" TECHNO GROWTH
ENTRIES & EXITS	
Consumer electronics	+ 5-10 consumer electronic companies as suppliers of e.g. peripherals into business IT + 2-5 C.E companies establish strong market share in home computing
Creative & publications rights industries	+ 5-10 companies with publishing rights +>100 (small) companies with games/animator/video skills
Hw & Sw product/component companies	+ Specialist, high volume Hw & Sw product component companies
Telecomms cable	- Strategic alliances reduce no of telecomms & cable companies
Services	+ 5-10 services companies with infrastructure for global play. Proliferation of small, local services. Entry of franchising
Vertically integrated vendors	- Vertically integrated vendors
Business Services	+ IT increasingly delivered as part of a business service
SUBSTITUTIONS	
FM	FM replaces small % of DP departments
Downsizing	Downsizing PCs replace mainframes at fast pace
Mobile	Mobiles & PDAs replace PCs in new systems and in replacement procurement
Multi-media	Multi-media replaces medium proportion of paper
Input	Pen based input main input for some PCs & all PDAs replaces keyboard input.
Other products	Many substitutions
Embedded IT	IT increasingly often embedded in products and services
RIVALRY/COMPETITION Margins	Margins on mainframes continue to decrease, on PDAs & PCs they stabilize, on traditional IT vendor services they decrease. US prices extend to Europe
Role of service companies	Large service organizations wield increasing power
Market leaders - architecture	Fragmentation of architectual standards
Industry structure	More, horizontially organized global players

BASELINE SCENARIO BUYER DOMINATION	ALTERNATIVE "PLUS" TECHNO GROWTH
+ 2-5 consumer electronic companies as suppliers of e.g. peripherals into business IT + 1-2 C.E. companies establish strong market share in home computing	+ 2-5 consumer electronic companies as suppliers of e.g. peripherals into business IT + 1-2 C.E. companies establish strong market share in home computing
+ One or two companies with publishing rights + >100 (small) companies with games/animator/video skills	+ One or two companies with publishing rights + >50 (small) companies with games/animator/video skills
+ Specialist, lower volume Hw & Sw product component companies	+ Fewer specialist Hw & Sw product component companies
+ Telecomms & cable companies	+ Regional/local telecomms & cable companies
+ 5-10 services companies with infrastructure for global play. Proliferation of small, local services	+ Services companies at regional/national level emerge. Proliferation of small, local services
Entry of franchising	
- Some vertically integrated vendors	- Some vertically integrated vendors
+ IT increasingly delivered as part of a business service	+ IT increasingly delivered as part of a business service
FM replaces medium % of DP departments	FM replaces high % of DP departments
Downsizing PCs replace mainframes at medium pace	Downsizing PCs replace mainframes at slower pace
Mobiles & PDAs replace PCs in new systems	Mobiles & PDAs slow to replace PCs
Multi-media replaces some proportion of paper	Less replacement of paper by multi-media Pen based input does not take off
Pen based input used in some PDAs	
Medium substitutions	Few subsitutions, innovations
IT increasingly often embedded in products and services	IT increasingly often embedded in products and services.
Margins on mainframes continue to decrease, on PCs they stabilize, on traditional IT vendor services they decrease. US prices extend to Europe	Margins on mainframes continue to decrease, on PCs they stabilize on higher level. US prices do not extend to Europe
Large service organizations wield increasing power	National/regional service organizations do not wield power
Intel, Microsoft architectures dominate globally	Unix movement strengthens B/O/SN. PCs on desks connected with thin wire, not client/server
Fewer large companies, all global players	Some regional players (Siemens) survive

SCENARIOS DEVELOPED BY ICL IN 1995

Scenarios for Information Markets in 2005

Version 1.0 October 1995

Authors
Paul Clayton
Jane Dowsett
Steve Parker
Gill Ringland

Description of Trends

There are a large number of predictions about the future we can be relatively sure about, for example trends in the population of countries can be fairly accurately predicted by analysis of the present demographics. These trends have been separated out into 'Social Economic Trends' covering the Political, Social and Economic factors that will impact all businesses, and 'Technology Related Trends' which will have a particularly strong impact on the IT market.

Social/Economic Trends

S1 "Increasingly sophisticated and demanding customers"
More and more educated consumers ask for up-to-date, high performance and competitive products.
Mass market will be fragmented into many niches. Competition will be fierce and based on price and quality of services.

S2 "Growth in South East Asia/India/China, with an expanding middle class"
In 2010, the middle class in S.E. Asia (about 700 million) will be larger than that of Europe (about 300 million) and Americas (about 200 million) combined.
This middle class is both a stabilizing factor in the development of S.E Asia/India/China and a tremendous source of buying power.

S3 "2 billion teenagers"
In 2001, there will be 2 billion teenagers world-wide (most of them in Asia and Latin America). That's fifty times the number of teenagers in America in the peak years of the baby boom. Many of them will be in constant contact with each other through technology.

S4 "Increase in the older population in industrial countries"

Medical advances and better life conditions leads to the ageing of the population, mainly in developed countries where birth-rates are low.

The demographic shift to an ageing population will require adjustment in many service industries (health care, leisure, travel). As the costs of the elderly (particularly health) will increase, service industries and governments will look for areas of productivity gains through IT.

S5 "Continuous restructuring of corporations"

The restructuring of corporations will be dominated by the following trends: Globalization of markets, outsourcing of non strategic jobs, and investments directed to the regions which offer the best profit potential.

Increasing number of small companies linked through networks. Competition for customers and financial resources will be intense and delocalized.

S6 "Outsourcing of IT is used by half of all Fortune 500 companies"

This trend will change the structure of the IT industry (large potential growth for outsourcing and technology used as a support of outsourcing businesses).

Development of ICL's outsourcing business. Outsourcing companies become major customers of Fujitsu/ICL systems.

S7 "Increasing environmental concerns"

More environmental concerns force companies on occasion to do business differently (for instance Shell vs Greenpeace).

It has positive implications (more business and some negative ones - possible increase in production cost to conform to environmental pressures...).

Technology Related Trends

T1 "Bandwidth Explosion and development of the Internet"

Large infrastructure investments to increase cable and wireless networks. Both the volume of traffic increases due to price decreases, and the opportunities for exploiting high bandwidth networking. Internet continues to grow.

T2 *"Processing power increases and processing becomes pervasive"*
Moore's law continues to apply for products shipped over the next decade. New generations of more powerful microprocessors (P6...). However, the costs to develop those new chips are high. Processing will be used in more and more mission-critical applications. Increasing use of embedded systems. More IT devices will be available.

T3 *"Ease of use"*
Computers and electronic devices will be more and more friendly (plug and play devices, computers become human literate).

T4 *"Digitalization of content and growth of multi-media"*
Information is held digitally, whether content is text, video or audio. Games, videos, media will be delivered either on electronic storage as an alternative to paper, or increasingly through on-line services.

T5 *"Changes in sources of Value Added in the IT Industry"*
The traditional sources of value added in the IT industry will decrease (mature industry, tough competition, IT increasingly embedded in products...). New sources of Value Added relate to ease of use, access, information security, etc.

T6 *"Litigation in IT increases"*
The risk for IT providers of being sued for misperformance or non performance increases.

T7 *"Semiconductor content of electronics increases"*
The content of electronics devices changes from 7% semiconductor to 27% semiconductor over the 15 years to 2000. This changes the balance of power and added value in the information industry.

Key Uncertainties

Not all events can be predicted with any degree of certainty, some of these can have a huge impact on the business environment. The main uncertainties we have identified can be grouped into the following four factors:

The Role Of Government - the degree of influence/power exerted by governments.

- What will be the balance between government imposed regulation and self-regulation?

- Will governments regulate to protect national cultures?

- Will governments be able to control cross-border information flows and electronic commerce?

Social Values - the strength of community values over individual values.

- How important will be environmental concerns?

- Will individual or community values predominate?

- What will be the level and forms of security threats?

Shape of World Trade - the patterns and degree of global trade.

- What will be the degree of Intra-trading block trade?

- What will be the impact on the west of economic growth in Asia?

Consumer Behaviour - the demand by consumers for innovations.

- How willing will customers be to take on risk themselves?

- How pervasive will outsourcing be?

- What will be the buying points in large organizations?

- Centralized or left to individuals?

- Will consumers become tired of constant change?

- How IT literate will they be?

The Two Scenarios

Introduction

The two scenarios which describe possible ways that our Information Industry world may develop have been called Coral Reef and Deep Sea.

The names were chosen to give an intuitive flavour:
The Coral Reef world is very diverse, with much visible activity and complex food chains. There are many small fish.
The Deep Sea world is less diverse, with fewer species of mainly larger fish. It is a simpler world in many ways.
For people whose reflexes have been formed on land, both the Coral Reef and the Deep Sea can be dangerous places unless the reflexes are retrained.

Applying these analogies to the world in general:
Coral Reef is largely deregulated or self-regulated, Deep Sea is regulated.
Coral Reef exploits energy and innovation, with growth from Asia and new businesses in new areas.
Deep Sea represents Europe and the US reacting somewhat negatively to changes in world balance.

Applying them specifically to the Information Industry:
Under Coral Reef scenario the demanding and sophisticated customer outsources or purchases systems integration because of the potential for IT to change his business, and is interested in new technology.
Under Deep Sea, the demanding and sophisticated customer outsources or purchases systems integration because it is not

his core business. He is interested in a full range supplier taking the risk and reducing cost.

The next sections explore the scenarios in more detail.

Deep Sea Description

What would the world look like in Deep Sea?

DS1   *Impeded world trade due to trade barriers*

DS2   *Low economic growth*

DS3   *Increased economic strength of Asia has limited effects on West due to trade barriers*

DS4   *Governments have effective social policies*

DS5   *Move away from individualism to an approach of community first*

DS6   *Legislation to preserve nation's own cultural identity*

"Very low growth in developed countries and lower than projected growth in developing countries is attributed to hostilities between the US and several of the Asian countries, and a 2 tier Europe"

France, Germany, Holland and Belgium have linked economies and share structural unemployment and low inflation. Much of German manufacturing has moved to Eastern Europe. The EU's activities are focused on tackling the reduction in manufacturing base.

Within the 2nd tier, e.g. in the UK, Scandinavia, and Northern Italy, strong links with the US have led to a number of indigenous companies being bought out by the Americans in the late 1990s. These countries report higher real growth and higher inflation than the 1st tier countries.

Low economic growth has increased the gap between the unemployed and those in Mac jobs, and those in long term employment. Unemployment, especially among the young, who may be third generation unemployed, is increasingly a problem for governments, both as a financial burden and in terms of social unrest.

The US has become isolationist with the exception of links to Mexico for manufacturing. Significant US investment has moved from Asia to Latin America. The US government has several times threatened to block IT exports for strategic reasons but has been overturned by the US IT companies.

The US and China continue trade hostilities over Chinese non-recognition of IPR, and the denial of US markets to China.

"Move away from individualism to an approach of community first"

Communities of like minded people form. For instance, retirement communities providing secure environments and leisure facilities are normal in developed countries. In developing countries, the family is still a strong element of community.

Effective pressure groups of young unemployed graduates in France and Holland have changed government education policy, to make education more stimulating and oriented towards skills needed in the post industrial society.

Family and community pressures are strong in countries with low crime levels.

Business Week carries an annual survey of companies noted for their community activities.

"Pressure on government from ageing populations and pressure groups keep unemployment and immigration under control"

The "2 billion" teenagers, mostly from Asia and Latin America, proves to be a destabilizing force for society. Numbers of them try to emigrate to find work, due to tough social pressures at home. Immigration from North Africa remains a problem in France and Italy.

Germany has introduced a national smart card programme to

control immigration and unrest from the young unemployed. The death penalty has been re-introduced in France. The "3 strikes and you're out" approach applies in most of the US states.

What would the Information Market look like under Deep Sea?

DS7   *Large, mostly US vendors dominate*

DS8   *Many acquisitions have taken place*

DS9   *Business to business marketing style*

DS10   *Limited telecoms network due to lack of deregulation*

DS11   *Government support local content industries*

DS12   *Telecoms companies main interactive content providers*

"Large, mostly US based companies, dominate IT markets and commercial values after many waves of acquisitions. There have been no major discontinuities in silicon based technology or communications which change economies of scale or barriers to entry"

Regulation of telecoms in Europe, North America and Asia causes strategic agreements and cross-ownership to be the basis of interconnect, for instance France Telecom continues to dominate the French market and has agreement with Sprint for non-domestic calls.

The confused regulatory position in North America and Europe leads to increased profits and vertical integration in those markets, plus a drive to invest in cable and telephony services for Asia and developing countries.

High prices from regulated PTTs drive the wireless market to expand and limit the expansion of cable. Cable companies, constrained from supplying telephony, add extra ranges of programmes and interactive entertainment and education services.

Efforts continue to be made to encourage local content creation in order to retain European cultural values.

"Business to business marketing style across the Information Industry"

Long term customer-supplier relationships are cemented through frame agreements and loyalty schemes.

The big full-range vendors dominate the Fortune 1000 and government, using direct and indirect channels. Outsourcing is concentrated in these organizations, and profit margins are vanishingly thin, with the full range vendors taking their profits on hardware and software supply.

Smaller companies are served by small VARs who supply hardware and software primarily based on price criteria.

Individual consumers find that vendors regard them as poor relations.

"Telecoms companies are the major drivers of multi-media services, finding limited market acceptance due to social pressures"

Multi-media applications have not spread into the Fortune 1000 companies, and are limited to education, retail and travel.

In the US, strong government backing has created "universal access" to computers in schools, public libraries, and city (town) halls.

Primary and secondary education in Europe has developed using government initiatives and state networks. US suppliers of tertiary education have sewn up deals with many networks, sometimes based on European content from historic or academic sources. EU initiatives have driven programmes to use networks for remote access to health care and for social regeneration, and for language translation assisted electronic mail services.

Major retailers have linked with network companies to provide home shopping, mostly on national lines. The networks cover most major cities with broadband services: other areas use TV and the telephone.

Since the broadband network suppliers operate in a regulated market it is relatively easy to control the propagation of pornography.

Many European countries see a resurgence of the film and graphics industries.

National legislation applies to IPR and electronic commerce, enforced through intergovernmental bodies and treaties.

Coral Reef Description

What would the world look like in Coral Reef?

CR1   *Strong trade amongst and within trading blocks*

CR2   *High economic growth*

CR3   *Sharp rise in the economic and political power of Asia*

CR4   *Individual values and rights strong*

CR5   *Governments cannot keep up with pace of change and rely more on self-regulation*

CR6   *Increased pace of change causes personal and social stress leading to high crime rate*

"High economic growth and strong trade between NAFTA, ASEAN and the EU, and within blocks, enable the EU to incorporate Eastern Europe. There has been a significant change to work patterns with more flexible working arrangements"

The EU has a single currency for all banking and electronic transactions. The coinage and notes of each country are valid tender in all 24 countries of the EU, and in 3 of the 5 Russian republics.

Speculation in currency movements between blocks is still a problem, and Asia is a net absorber of investment. Much of this comes from Europe and the US through multinationals, and leads to high real interest rates world-wide.

European corporate funding has been the main source of clean-up projects in Eastern Europe, tied to replacement of polluting facilities.

National governments' ability to fund technology investment decreases, but the role of the EU increases particularly as an investor in innovation.

The level of economic growth and pace of change has eventually created a more mobile work force. More people are working but often fewer hours and in more flexible, less secure jobs. In some industries such as retailing and increasingly in financial services the majority of the workforce is made up of contract staff with no guaranteed income. The gap between the haves and have nots has increased. The bottom 10% of the population who are unskilled have found it increasingly difficult to get out of the poverty trap, and the social security safety net is weak.

On the other hand the distinction between countries is blurred, with many sharing similar employment and inflation indicators. Fragmentation of regions along ethnic and cultural boundaries has been a feature.

"Increased pace of change causes personal and social stress leading to a high crime rate"

Stress related withdrawal from work and early retirement reduce the average age of employees in large companies worldwide. A worrying phenomenon in Europe and North America is dropout by failed entrepreneurs or burnout employees, and is linked to family breakdown.

The prime factor of success in both life and business is "knowledge". Individuals take charge of their careers, an important part of which is the acquisition of skills throughout a lifetime. Ability to use IT becomes a key skill.

Leisure activities among the haves are increasingly competitive, and the adoption of technology based games and pursuits is high among males.

Crime rates in cities skyrocket, with the major cause being quoted as drugs.

Brand loyalty is widely used by consumers to reduce the complexity of their choice.

What would the Information Market look like under Coral Reef?

CR7   *Many technological and marketing innovations*

CR8   *IT industry made up of specialized companies, many dominate their niches.*

CR9   *New competition from start-ups and Asia*

CR10   *Many boutique style "people" businesses*

CR11   *Highly competitive markets where the consumer is king*

CR12   *Deregulated and advanced telecoms infrastructure*

"The Information Industry is made up of specialized companies, some dominate their niches. There are many start-ups and Asian competitors"

The telecommunications market is almost totally deregulated in the developed world. The global interconnect market is dominated by three global suppliers, formed from around AT&T, MCI and Sprint. Competing nationwide networks are provided by telcos, utilities and transport companies.

At the consumer and business level, combined cable TV and telecoms companies supply both telephony and TV. The success of wireless voice communications and digital satellite TV is putting serious pressure on the land-line telco/cable TV companies. Wireless and satellite dominates in developing countries.

The European telcos develop businesses outside their geographies, with Telefonica expanding into Latin America, Deutsche Telekom providing world-wide business services, and France Telecom expanding through French-speaking Africa.

There are many niche suppliers of added value services, for entertainment, for special interest groups, and for education.

Competition from content suppliers gives increased choice in the home, with specialist markets supplied by Disney, Dreamworks etc. Asian film and video makers dominate Asian markets and US content dominates European markets.

Software packages are often developed by small (less than £10 million turnover) organizations, some in Asia, and marketed/supported/installed by market specialists for retail, manufacturing, games, etc.

There are very few silicon suppliers sharing the global market because of high process R&D costs and high costs of capital for new plant.

Computing devices are ubiquitous and are embedded in the objects and devices encountered daily, relieving people of the burden of carrying their own computing power. Users trust their personal information to a centralized information store, which can be accessed in various ways through these devices. For example a traveller can use a hotel provided device to check her appointment schedule. The server market is in strong growth driven by the need for central storage and network services.

IBM is a loose federation of companies, each concentrating on their own market segments. EDS has specialized in asset management. CSC has over-run on several public sector projects and gone into loss. Andersen has decided to concentrate on business re-engineering, and sub-contracts all programming to its Asian subsidiary.

"Consumer style marketing techniques dominate, smaller boutique style companies are successful. Added value through innovation and marketing as seen by the customer"

Products and operational services - e.g. help desks, maintenance are marketed to those who will use them. Purchasing decisions will be made by the individual for himself or possibly on behalf of a small group, whether for business or leisure use. This applies for smaller new systems too, driven by cost factors. Only for large infrastructure projects, and complex roll-outs, are business-to-business marketing techniques used.

Innovation in products and marketing are mostly introduced by small companies and quickly copied or bought out by the global players. Innovation in marketing and distribution is as important as innovations in technology. Small boutique style companies specialize - maybe globally - in detailed knowledge of an area, and establish presence through electronic marketing and word of mouth.

Advertising over the network subsidises payment for content.

Outsourcing of information systems is booming as many organizations find that managing information systems is a management distraction. Start-ups using facilities in Asia dominate this market through their front men in North America and Europe.

"Major changes in technologies, high adoption of multi-media and pervasive high bandwidth telecoms, give rise to large numbers of exciting business opportunities"

Added value is created by innovation, with extensive customer comparisons of offers of all sorts, and price breaks following breakthroughs in underlying technology.

Advances in batteries and low power devices free up PCs and mobiles to become 24 hour per day devices without wires. Remote control devices are wireless using infra-red and so are the newer in-building LANs.

Voice recognition and language translation are widely used in travel, retail and legal applications, though the teething problems have made front page news "hohos".

The use of groupware for managing processes and change in business re-engineering is widely recognized as having contributed to the rate of change.

Education - in particular post experience learning - has been revolutionized by multi-media and high bandwidth telecoms. Shopping for specialist courses to increase professional skills is standard, with delivery over the net using video and CBT techniques.

US content for early learning dominates, but is mostly bought by parents and private schools rather than state schools in Europe. The exception is Scandinavia, where national programmes have been instituted.

South Africa has leapfrogged the world in the use of multi-media and high bandwidth in school education, while Singapore and the Tigers continue to develop their systems. Bill Gates has sold up in order to start an educational network in Mexico.

There is universal access in the G7 countries and in the developed city states of Asia to interactive shopping and travel arrangements. Intelligent agent technology is used to find the right offers, based on information stored on personal smart cards. The 2 billion teenagers are a sought after market, with companies taking into account their sense of identity with each other, their cost consciousness and their technological awareness.

"Growth in use of electronic information and electronic cash is not matched by government ability to provide a legislative framework to protect IPR, tax revenue, and national culture. Concern over this has been heightened by a spate of visible and memorable IT disasters"

Global commercial organizations attempt to provide self-regulation of global information and global cash, because of governments' inability to enforce national legislative frameworks - software and films ordered over the net and paid for with cash cannot be traced for tax or royalty payments, or for censorship.

The buoyant Information Industry limits its problems of protecting IPR by central storage and access on demand for business use, and many cinemas use electronically transmitted versions of recent films.

India and China have programmes to provide education over satellite but are concerned that the government receivers are being used to pick up alien entertainment, undermining national values.

The exciting business opportunities have been matched by a number of IT-related disasters. A number of criminal cases come to light involving huge quantities of electronic cash. These include the production of billions of dollars of counterfeit cash, money laundering, and theft by hackers.

Early indicators of Coral Reef

1. Bill deregulating US telecoms markets passed in 1995, European countries meet their deadlines, and Japanese deregulation introduced in 1999.

2. AT&T sells NCR or Siemens sells SNI or Olivetti sells the PC business.

3. Spin-offs increase relative to mergers in the media business.

4. Digital sells its semiconductor business to TI, and TI sells its software business to CA.

5. Semiconductor market share for companies with HQs in Asia Pacific (including Japan) exceeds that of Europe and North America in 1996.

6. Fabrication capacity in Asia (excluding Japan) exceeds that in Japan, Europe and North America combined by 2000.

7. US and China establish a trade treaty in 1996.

8. Microsoft and Intel have been constrained by anti-trust legislation.

Early indicators of Deep Sea
1. The early indicators of Coral Reef are not seen, e.g. the number of mergers increases relative to the number of spin-offs.

2. UK, Spain and Denmark isolated at the 1996 Maastricht conference.

3. US imposes punitive tax on a very visible Japanese export.

4. Successful lobbying of European governments to introduce tough new penalties to combat crime.

5. Windows 95 fails to meet expected shipments in Europe, compared to its take up in the US.

Topics for "Contingency Planning"
These topics were judged to be unlikely, or unrelated to the scenarios, but with enough impact should they occur that it would be prudent for ICL to have contingency plans or at least recognized responsibilities.

Terrorism, militant uprising or regional war
One of our installations could be involved in a terrorist attack, or a regional war or militant uprising could occur in an area where there is an ICL office or ICL employees are located.

Earthquake
One of our installations, or one of our suppliers, could by devastated by earthquake in Japan or California.

IT disaster
A system we developed or operated could be part of a front page "IT disaster".

There is a major breakthrough in underlying technology before 2005
Semiconductor technology, battery technology or transmission technology would have largest effect.

Major staff loss of senior managers
The loss of an entire senior management team for a business - through air disaster, or hiring by companies expanding in the new Information Industry - could cause a major hiatus.

SCENARIOS FOR THE INTERNET: BUILDING SUCCESSFUL WORLD WIDE WEB RELATED BUSINESSES

The following scenarios were created as part of a study conducted by Doug Randall at the Wharton Small Business Development Center at the Wharton School. They are based on over 30 interviews with leading Internet thinkers to find out what perceptions they had of the Internet in the year 2000 (Randall, 1997).

The scenarios were built around the two dimensions of

- how interactive will the Internet be?
- will the Internet be a real-time medium?

The scenarios have been used in a number of workhops to help decision makers understand the relevant drivers of the Internet and so develop more robust business strategies. He describes current business models - advertising, subscription and pay per use - and examines what models could work in the future according to each scenario.

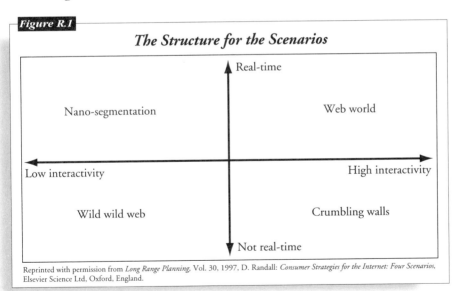

Figure R.1

The Structure for the Scenarios

Reprinted with permission from *Long Range Planning*, Vol. 30, 1997, D. Randall: *Consumer Strategies for the Internet: Four Scenarios*, Elsevier Science Ltd, Oxford, England.

Figure R.2

Four Internet Scenarios

	Web worlds	Nano-segmentation	Crumbling walls	Wild wild web
Markets	Large; mainstream consumers	Medium; information seeking professionals & limited consumers	Large; professionals & consumers	Small; 'Internet culture'
Interactivity	Interactive	Passive	Interactive	Questionable
Primary function	Entertainment destination	Information tool	Access provider & distribution channel	Varies depending on markets
Branding	Aggregators & content providers	Aggregators	Content providers	Questionable

Reprinted with permission from *Long Range Planning*, Vol. 30, 1997, D. Randall: *Consumer Strategies for the Internet: Four Scenarios*, Elsevier Science Ltd, Oxford, England.

Scenario 1. Web World 2000

Here the Internet is an interactive, entertainment-focused community-based medium which has mass-market appeal. The focus is on entertainment, with over 55% of families with Internet access. Communities of users grow, with communities offering a whole array of services. Content providers negotiate with these communities, who bundle and license services. Some are paid on a usage basis, others get a flat fee per community subscriber. Others receive a percentage of the premium charged to users for access to the service. In many cases the community handles advertising, payment and many technical functions.

There are a number of key drivers from today's perspective that need to occur for this scenario to play out:

- Inexpensive high bandwidth to the home.
- The Internet becoming more mainstream.
- Enhanced entertainment services are launched.
- Communities become easy access providers.
- The Internet becomes an experience.

Scenario 2. Nano-segmentation 2000

The Internet is a passive, narrowly-segmented medium which allows users to receive customized information and niche-oriented services. Most major companies make detailed information available about products and services for free. Web navigators emerge to help individual users find what they want. These aggregators are able to target commercial messages at users on a very targeted basis, although some people are worried about privacy violations where so much is known about individuals. As the line between content providers and advertisers becomes more blurred, publishers have to work closely with advertisers in making programming decisions.

Key drivers:

- Internet advertising works.
- Privacy becomes less important to consumers.
- Publishers create alternative "value propositions" and business models.
- Branding shifts from content provider to aggregator.

Scenario 3. Crumbling Walls 2000

The Internet is an interactive, transaction-oriented medium which provides both consumers and professionals with a range of commerce-based activities. Users buy more products through the Internet, going directly to providers or using intelligent agents to find what they want. Many providers of products and services now go directly to customers rather than through intermediaries. Users pay on an ad hoc basis for what they want. The technology becomes sophisticated enough for the rights' holders to contemplate a range of pricing techniques.

Key drivers:

- Consumers become comfortable purchasing products on the Internet.
- An Internet micro-payment system is accepted.
- Intelligent agents and search engines are really smart.
- Publishers sell content on a pay-per-use basis.

Scenario 4. Wild Wild Web 2000

The Internet is mostly an unorganized, unstructured, chaotic frontier which offers questionable value to consumer and professional markets. Too many technological and service users cause annoyance, leaving the main audience Web surfers looking for computer-related information. Other distribution vehicles such as interactive digital television and Intranets are used as alternatives by some companies. A variety of payment methods emerges, including advertising, subscriptions and other methods, although most content companies are not profitable.

Key drivers:
- Bandwidth problem is not solved.
- The Internet is too confusing for the mass market.
- Consumers refuse to pay; the emphasis shifts to the professionals.
- Proprietary systems take off.

What strategy to follow in light of these possible scenarios?

Randall offers the following general guidelines for creating an Internet strategy:

- Follow the people: users are becoming more experienced and developing new wants.

- The old Internet is not the new one: the new one is mainstream.

- Be radical in terms of business model and application.

- Be robust against changes in the market and the business model.

- Focus on niches: the Internet creates communities of interest in a way that hasn't been seen before.

And in particular, for content providers, he suggests the strategies shown in Table R.1.

TABLE R.1 LIKELY STRATEGIES FOR CONTENT PROVIDERS

Content providers	Web worlds	Nano-segmentation	Crumbling walls	Wild wild web
Information aggregators	Form licensing relationships with web worlds	Accumulate information about customer preferences	Adopt a micro-payment transaction technology	Adopt a niche strategy focused on markets which have an Internet presence
	Provide easy access to information (i.e. user friendly interface)	Target focused services at populations which need them	Focus on intelligent agent technology	Offer services which make the Internet easier to use
Video game companies	Offer intense interactivity and multi-player capability	Focus on non-Internet technology	Create a strong brand name	Focus on non-Internet technology
	Create a strong brand name	Launch products which do not require high bandwidth connections and real-time interactivity	Launch products appropriate for professional markets (i.e. training, professional education)	Offer products which engage existing Internet markets
Newspapers	Offer broad content on multiple mediums	Offer focused content	Set up a unique web site, rather than using aggregators to distribute	Develop a cross-medium strategy for both content and advertising
	Provide an experience for customers	Align with re-packagers who distribute information and attract advertisers	Offer high-quality, high-value content	Focus on niches (i.e. regions, special interests)
Specialty journals	Bundle traditional content with additional services such as chat	Maintain focus on defined populations	Develop and promote a brand name	Maintain focus on defined populations
	Form licensing relationships with web worlds	Integrate content with advertising campaigns to maximize effectiveness	Develop a strong presence among markets which might be attracted to your products	Target professional markets who are more likely to pay for Internet services

Reprinted with permission from *Long Range Planning*, Vol. 30, 1997, D. Randall: *Consumer Strategies for the Internet: Four Scenarios*, Elsevier Science Ltd, Oxford, England.

SCENARIOS FOR THE TELECOM SUPPLY INDUSTRY

SRI developed four scenarios for the telecoms industry as part of the BIT3M project (see Chapter 4). It is clear from the research that there is a lot of uncertainty and chaos in the telecom industry, in Asia, Europe and the US. Figure T.1 shows the progress of deregulation and privatization, world wide.

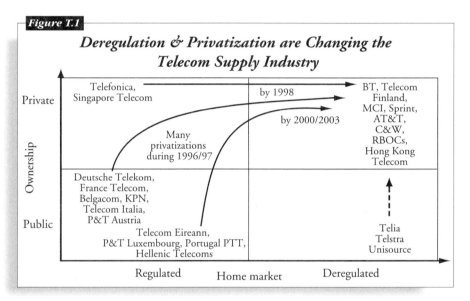

Figure T.1

Deregulation & Privatization are Changing the Telecom Supply Industry

SRI identified three major axes of uncertainty contributing to the confused picture for the future of the telecom industry. (See Figure T.2)

One is in the area of competition because of the effect of deregulation on commoditization of products and services, on the number of competitors, on investment confidence and issues such as pricing, outsourcing and the added value services providers actually provide.

There is also a big question mark on convergence. What technologies will be used: will they be voice, data transmission or fax transmission technologies? What architecture will be used? For instance, the Internet architecture is peer-to-peer, whereas network computing assumes the existence of an intelligent switching mechanism. Mobile technologies, on the other hand, introduce a totally different type of switching which can deal with roaming. With convergence, a number of technologies are intersecting which in many ways are incompatible, but have different advantages. Nor is it clear what will encompass the way we see life, which is that people are mobile and that data is no longer just voice or bits, but to do with pictures and sound, with colours, shape and movement.

There is a whole range of technologies that were not cost-effective 5 to 10 years ago which are now becoming so. The question is how they will shake out in providing a useful level of service for individuals who can start doing things they haven't been able to before.

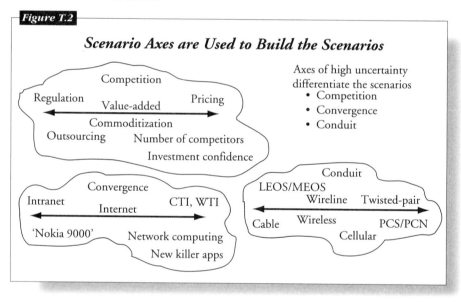

Figure T.2

Scenario Axes are Used to Build the Scenarios

Axes of high uncertainty differentiate the scenarios
- Competition
- Convergence
- Conduit

Conduit is the third aspect. This set of questions, as in the PA work for KRONE, is about how electrical or light signals are transferred from A to B, and whether it is wireless, wireline or whatever. There are both price and ending-device implications for each technology. For instance, it is very cheap to send signals along fibre optic lines to reach the interface of a fibre optic modem. But for the domestic market, the price of these modems has been high while reliability has been low. The hardest part is the "last 500 yards", which is getting to premises from some sort of distribution point.

Figure T.3

Four Plausible Scenarios

Competition	Convergence	Conduit	Impact	Likelihood	Most plausible scenarios
Weak	Fragmented	Wireline/cable	✓✓✓	✓✓✓	Global giants
Weak	Fragmented	Wireless	✓✓	✓	
Weak	Integrated	Wireline/cable	✓✓	✓✓	
Weak	Integrated	Wireless	✓✓	✓	
Strong	Fragmented	Wireline/cable	✓✓✓	✓✓✓	Do-it-yourself
Strong	Fragmented	Wireless	✓✓	✓	
Strong	Integrated	Wireline/cable	✓✓✓	✓✓✓	Blurring boundaries
Strong	Integrated	Wireless	✓✓✓	✓✓✓	Wireless world

SRI then looked at a combination of plausibilities in terms of competition, convergence and conduit, judging impact and likelihood (Figure T.3).

Four plausible scenarios resulted for beyond the year 2000.

1. Global Giants

Here there are a few large, global telecommunications companies. Competition is weak, convergence is fragmented and connections are through wires and cables. The companies work in partnership, encourage long term agreements, and keep voice and data apart.

2. Do-It-Yourself

In this scenario the incumbents are caught off balance, and competition heats up as many small players enter the market offering a number of different solutions.

3. *Blurring Boundaries*

In this scenario voice, data and video merge, with the Internet/Intranet the main driver. Competition is strong, while the main connections are through wireline and cable.

4. *Wireless World*

This is the world of wireless wide networks and local area networks. Everyone has a personal number for life. Wireline connections now serve only as the backbone of the system.

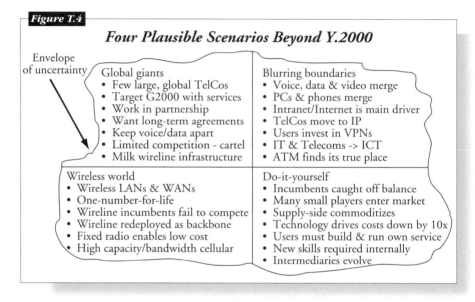

Figure T.4

Four Plausible Scenarios Beyond Y.2000

Envelope of uncertainty

Global giants
- Few large, global TelCos
- Target G2000 with services
- Work in partnership
- Want long-term agreements
- Keep voice/data apart
- Limited competition - cartel
- Milk wireline infrastructure

Blurring boundaries
- Voice, data & video merge
- PCs & phones merge
- Intranet/Internet is main driver
- TelCos move to IP
- Users invest in VPNs
- IT & Telecoms -> ICT
- ATM finds its true place

Wireless world
- Wireless LANs & WANs
- One-number-for-life
- Wireline incumbents fail to compete
- Wireline redeployed as backbone
- Fixed radio enables low cost
- High capacity/bandwidth cellular

Do-it-yourself
- Incumbents caught off balance
- Many small players enter market
- Supply-side commoditizes
- Technology drives costs down by 10x
- Users must build & run own service
- New skills required internally
- Intermediaries evolve

These scenarios represent different global competitive structures; these differences are highlighted in Figure T.5, while Figure T.6 suggests a possible migration path from Do-It-Yourself in 1998, with a lot of competition and a range of ways of supplying services, to Global Giants in 2002, as the shake-out occurs and global giants emerge. As technology advances and price differences smooth out, Blurring Boundaries appears in 2005, leading to Wireless World in 2010 as prices become more competitive with wireline.

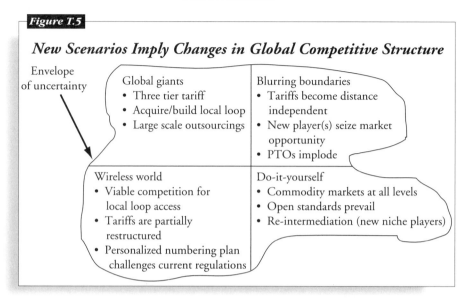

Figure T.5

New Scenarios Imply Changes in Global Competitive Structure

Envelope
of uncertainty

Global giants
- Three tier tariff
- Acquire/build local loop
- Large scale outsourcings

Blurring boundaries
- Tariffs become distance independent
- New player(s) seize market opportunity
- PTOs implode

Wireless world
- Viable competition for local loop access
- Tariffs are partially restructured
- Personalized numbering plan challenges current regulations

Do-it-yourself
- Commodity markets at all levels
- Open standards prevail
- Re-intermediation (new niche players)

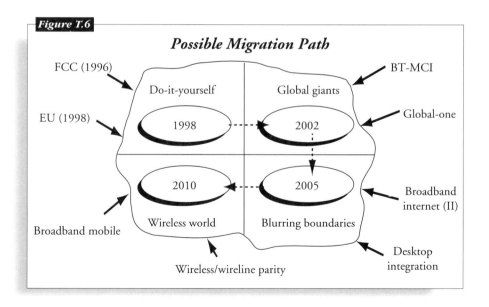

Figure T.6

Possible Migration Path

FCC (1996)

Do-it-yourself

EU (1998)

1998

Global giants

2002

BT-MCI

Global-one

2010

2005

Broadband internet (II)

Broadband mobile

Wireless world

Blurring boundaries

Desktop integration

Wireless/wireline parity

THE HEMINGFORD SCENARIOS

The Hemingford scenarios were developed by the UK's National Health Service in 1994. The case study in Part III describes how they were built and one example of their application.

The renewed welfare order: The NHS delivers

In this future an approach to health and welfare services emerges somewhat similar to the one that has prevailed recently. Many of the fears about the sustainability of the NHS are not realized by 2010. The public health care system continues to have a central place in the social fabric of Britain. There is a rejuvenation of the traditional ideals of welfare support. But what is around the corner?

After all the troubles of the late 1980s and early 1990s the National Health Service is settling down. The public's distrust of managers and politicians is melting away. This is helped by the fact that the NHS Executive funded a proper evaluation of some aspects of the 1991 reforms. As a headline in the *Independent* of October 1995 says "Study confirms reducing waiting lists". There is a steady stream of such reports that begin to build up faith in the system. Indeed in 1997 there is a major assessment of different health systems by the World Health Organization. This is reported in the *Daily Mail* under the headline, "OK to NHS says WHO".

Throughout this period the economy grows slowly. The cheap labour associated with this economic track is tackled by European legislation for a minimum wage within the Health and Safety competence of the EU. The effects of this on the health sector, with its historic low pay, result in fewer job opportunities. This is reported in *The Times* Health Care supplement as "Brussels Euro-wage Slashes Care Possibilities". However, the problem is addressed during the early 2000s through the growth in the WorkFare scheme for the jobless and use of lower paid guest workers from North Africa within the health sector.

Socially, WorkFare and the minimum wage manage to reduce the sense of marginalization and demoralization amongst some groups of disadvantaged people. By early in the next century the ill-health differences associated with deprivation and unemployment start to narrow for the first time in decades.

Against all expectations science comes down on the side of health promotion. Up until now health promotion activities have been based on gut feelings and crossed fingers. A major university has now had long enough, and has studied deeply enough, to demonstrate that a major Scottish health promotion initiative has produced benefits in mortality, morbidity and well being. It is taken up by the Government. The *Daily Express* reports in April 1997, "Scots Health Initiative goes Nation-wide".

As a result the exhortation of individuals to be responsible for their own health is heeded. In particular, many in the mid-age groups start adapting their lifestyles, for example by modifying their diet, to improve their chances of living to a ripe old age. This thrust continues pressure on smoking. The number of smokers dwindles through the 1990s. By 2010 smoking is a rare habit indeed.

By 2005 there have been significant developments in the way that people relate to technology. Society is beginning to discount the rush to high-tech solutions for all health problems. Disenchantment with complex transplantology increases following transplantations for Laura Davies in 1993/4 and the multiple organ transplants at Addenbrooke's in the mid 1990s. One Marplan survey, conducted by *The Times* in 1997, illustrates the public concerns about the costs and results of such treatment: "The Nation Rejects Multiple Transplants". Nonetheless, new technology continues to be introduced on clinical whim as much as due to rigorous evaluation.

Technology, however, is not always a problem and the uptake of gene cures for malignant disease was rapid in the late 1990s. Whilst at first it was inordinately expensive and the results poor, research continued so that it becomes the accepted treatment.

Clinical practice remains largely self-regulated. There were some managerial attempts to tinker with skill mix following acceptance of the EU working time directive in 1996 that reduced the junior doctors' working week to a maximum 48 hours.

The population continues to age, accentuated by the slight net outward migration of skilled workers to mainland Europe and the retirement of some EU citizens in England, where tax funded public services continue to be available. However, the doom merchants of the 1980s who spoke of the "Demographic Timebomb" are proved over-pessimistic.

In general then, the Health Service continues to deliver into the next century. There are some problems, some stresses but through it all the Health Service survives in a way that would be recognizable to people in the early 1990s. All in all the National Health Service is doing what it was set up to do. The public increasingly has faith in the system, but recognizes that it cannot do everything for everybody and that rationing is acceptable.

Health is wealth: Private provision works

This story tells of a future world where economic and social differences persist within the UK population. However, the concept of the NHS proves remarkably resilient in face of health inequalities and increasing consumerist pressure. NHS Trust hospitals and community services become a thing of the past and are replaced by impressive, lower cost private provision. Nonetheless, core health services remain available to all.

This scenario presumes four separate but linked drivers starting with the success of Clinton Health Reforms where the US Government is successful in squeezing the US pharmaceutical industry. Under commercial pressure the UK loses control of drug prices through the normal mechanisms of the NHS control on supply. Combined with the more effective implementation of EU competition rules this prompts a change in Government policy in 1997. This now enhances and develops the UK pharmaceutical industry as a basis for a wider health industry. Tax breaks for investment in the health industry are introduced. The result is that a thriving and vibrant industry begins to develop in the UK with large export potential. Pharmaceutical companies diversify into wider health care service companies.

The second driver is that there is further growth of "two tierism" in the NHS with an expansion and extension of GP fundholding and the introduction of franchising for NHS purchasing authorities. Individuals begin to accept this when they realize they have some choice about whether their health care is in the top tier or not.

The third driver is the continued pressure on local authority funding following local government reorganization. The Government does not fully resolve the vexed question of the health/social purchasing responsibility divide. However, it hints that the NHS is not a social breakdown service. As a result the Government accepts local access controls, for example, minimizing the number of older people admitted to hospital for social breakdown reasons and to reduce the role of Health Visitors in routine child care and abuse issues.

The fourth driver is the continued increase in explicit discussions around rationing and cynicism about the political control of the NHS, in the context of increasing public expectations. This leads to a crescendo of criticism about the NHS - its failure to deal adequately with complaints and its failure to consistently achieve Charter standards, such as waiting times. Private provision, whether individually funded (such as birthing centres) or NHS resourced (for example, cardiac care), is increasingly respected.

Stimulated by the clinical brain drain from public hospitals to the increasing number of private, European and North American based contractors within the NHS market, the Government decides to privatize NHS Trusts in 1998 by selling them to the highest bidder. To some this seems the natural ideological result of increased market testing during the mid 1990s, stimulated by the 1993 EU public services directive and a 1995 legal ruling that judged NHS contracts to be, after all, real in law.

However, the impetus of private management techniques increases the efficiency of the newly privatized hospitals to recover or maintain any competitive edge. Within the health system convalescent motels are widely used and more clinical procedures are performed on a day and out patient basis. As a result lengths of stay fall and hospitals that are not efficient suppliers of effective care close. There is heavy investment in IT to improve billing, clinical accuracy and reduce duplication, for example, of tests. This enables the abolishing of much middle management - a result that pleases clinicians. In particular, managers that seek to increase nurses' levels of responsibility please that profession. The overall effect is to create innovation that increases quality and reduces costs.

The private providers support an initiative promoting accreditation of their hospital processes to minimum standards. An associated move involves developing the Health Service Ombudsman into a national body to arbitrate in cases of patient complaint about the provision of management or clinical care. This pleases those who were concerned by the apparent lack of professional interest that may lead, for example, to unscrupulous clinicians recommending unnecessary procedures. As a result of these initiatives the remnants of public and professional concern about privatization subside by the close of the century.

By 2000 the UK economy is reasonably healthy, despite the continuing structural unemployment with its resultant health and social problems. One important economic engine is the wider health industry. Health care is widely regarded as wealth creating and is becoming a major export, improving the UK balance of payments. However, the widely held expectation of low taxation continues to restrict the funds available to the NHS.

A public debate grows about whether or not the NHS should be reserved only for the poor and not for the whole of the population. A Government Green Paper, written within the prevailing international trend against big government, proposes an income limit above which no one will have access to NHS funded care. This promotes a middle class backlash against the concept of a safety net. These tax contributors are fearful of losing access to what has become much better quality provision since the privatization of NHS Trusts.

The result is the introduction of a rights based voucher system in 2002 which excludes categories of treatment deemed to be "unnecessary" or "inappropriate" (for example, gender reassignment, IVF and non-life threatening elective procedures). Within the NHS's 6% of national income, a basic care package is created covering core requirements such as A&E, cancer services and paediatrics. There is some local flexibility in creating the package. Individuals are then expected to supplement this in one of two ways.

First, there is convergence with the rest of Europe and an increase in co-payments, for example a means tested fee of £10 for every visit to a GP. This successfully regulates demand and for the first time in years GP morale is no longer an issue. Second, a plethora of "top up" private insurance schemes become available. The poor receive means tested access to a further voucher that covers more than the limited list.

A network of not-for-profit Health Agencies (supporting a number of GP practices to manage primary and hospital based care) are established out of Health Commissions where individuals can present their vouchers in return for managed care. However, these organizations are denied the opportunity of offering insurance based top up cover, as a government measure to boost the private health insurance industry. These start to link with similar organizations internationally, such as HMOs in the US. Initially for mutual learning and later, by 2008, as hybrid bodies.

There is a growth of charitable funding for the "deserving poor" who slip through the net, such as those marginally too rich to receive the state "top up" voucher. This philanthropic response is focused on quality of life enhancing care (such as IVF, varicose vein ligation, breast reduction and dermatology) and helping older people who lack informal care support.

The vibrant economy has produced a less equitable distribution of income leading to continued growth in health inequalities. This is accentuated by different demands on the system. The middle classes, who tend to have good access to the new information services (such as help lines and inter-active expert video packages by cable), become even better at getting what they want from the system.

The clinical practice of the now fully self-employed medical profession becomes quite defensive. This is especially so when in 2004 advertising is allowed and some doctors market their skills in a competitive way by pointing to the failures of specific colleagues.

Due to relaxation of UK legislation "medical tourism" increases. We have seen how European health care providers have found the UK fertile ground for their business aspirations. Now the

Health Agencies scour the wider European market for the best deals, in terms of quality and cost.

Having been through some turbulent times health care settles down into its new form in the years leading to 2010. The NHS has surprised many international observers by its resilience in an era of social differences and consumerism.

Science makes the big push: High cost, high gain health services

In this picture of the future, science becomes an increasingly respected part of everyone's life. The British economy makes the transition to one that fully exploits technological innovation, no more so than in the health sector. Within the NHS significant shifts occur. Patients demand more from their clinicians in terms of effective care and personal interaction. Changes in professional boundaries and a proper focus on the evidence base of medicine shifts the pattern of clinical practice within the NHS in a quite remarkable way.

The basic forces driving this scenario are, first, the push of technology and, second, the pull of informed consumerism. This coupled with the information revolution and developments in information technology create a very powerful force for change.

The rising expectations of consumers become increasingly evident during the 1990s. Increased information - via IT, GPs, women's magazines etc. - raises understanding of outcome differences between different treatments and centres. When services do not fulfil Patients Charter standards or clinicians make a mistake litigation and complaints increasingly occur. There is also growth in complementary medicine. This is a reaction to technologically driven scientific medicine of the 1980s and 1990s. While highly effective this ceases to meet the requirements of consumers for interaction with a "healer". The greater professional/client interaction that complementary therapists can bring and the time that they can give to their clients forces traditional practitioners to spend more time with their patients. Increasingly sophisticated individuals are pleased to have more time for quality interaction.

Time is expensive and as a consequence four things happen towards the end of the century that provide funds to permit greater input from clinicians and, hence, better satisfy consumers. First, whilst the costs of the NHS increase, the resources devoted by Government to it also rise. Spending on the NHS is seen as a way of stimulating the newly emerging group of UK owned international health technology companies. Second, there is an increase in some sort of co-payments, such as hotel charges.

Third, certain treatments will no longer be seen as priorities for NHS limited funds. The randomized controlled trial has become the clinical as well as managerial bench mark for deciding what is to be available on the NHS. As well as this evidence based approach certain quality of life treatments - such as sport injury physiotherapy, homoeopathy and dentistry - are restricted. Many people take out supplementary insurance premiums for these minor exclusions by 2002. This shift allows increased investment in new technology; innovation that on the whole increases costs, but with significant gains in effectiveness.

Fourth, throughout this period the increasing acceptance of protocols and expert IT systems allow radical experiments in skill mix. The traditional boundaries are lost and the professional territory redrawn. The re-evaluation of the role of the GP contrasts her or his role as healer with that of the GP as scientific doctor. The boundary between the general practitioner and the specialist diminishes, with the proliferation in protocol based care.

There is also a loss of definition between doctors and other health professionals. For example, many nurses become medical technicians so that doctors are freed to become high-tech healers. Within the ranks of medics some will earn huge sums as internationally tele-communicated superstars. The substitution of non-medics for doctors is enforced by a new cadre of clinical managers who carry the public with them and thus alter traditional loyalties. This is symbolic of the flowering of health service management. The "grey suits" disappear to be replaced, at least in the media's eye, by men and women committed to empowering and helping the clinician deliver high quality care.

The evidence based approach is stimulated by greater State

investment in medical R&D following the 1994 UK Technology Foresight programme run by the Office of Science and Technology. This central input, whilst encouraging private innovation, leads to a more controlled introduction of new technologies, thus avoiding the so called "evaluation bypass".

The benefits of science are clearly evident and welcomed by the new generation of increasingly science literate adults. The hugely expensive artificial pancreas, let alone the drug cures for dementia and the common cold, are felt worth every penny. This is especially so because scientific blunders become rarer due to central control of the transition from research to mainstream application.

Genetic and molecular biology is a key driving force following the successful completion of the Human Genome Project. Gene therapy and transplants revolutionize the treatment of cancers and other disorders which hitherto have defied therapeutic interventions. For example, in 1998 a genetic cure for cystic fibrosis is marketed that takes medical science beyond the half-way technology (of heart and lung transplantation and prophylactic drug therapy). By 2000 screening for certain disease markers, where cost-effective treatments are available, becomes widespread.

Genetics also give rise to the new preventive medicine. By the early 2000s the human genome has been fully mapped. Science is able to determine the risk profiles of individuals and how their genetics react with specific environmental factors. Individuals and employers will pay for genetic CVs. The fear of genetic discrimination leads to individuals going to huge lengths to alter their lifestyles to check any biological predispositions (such as to alcohol dependence) they may have. There is some public concern about the ethical implications of genetic medicine. No one (Government, clinicians or research scientists) wish to be responsible for mistakes.

Bio-technology also helps reduce environmental toxicity, for example, by enabling increased crop yields without the use of pesticides.

Another major advance is in the neurosciences. These will expand into mental illness. New therapies and diagnostic tools will be available for mental ill-health such as schizophrenia and the depressive psychoses. Technology will also enable some of the psychological problems associated with unemployment to be ameliorated and the genes associated with drug and alcohol abuse to be replaced by 2006.

There are also further major advances in imaging and non-invasive techniques. The Information Super Highway becomes routinely used in medicine, starting with imaging in the early 1990s and extending to widespread long distance robotic surgery by the end of the decade. By separating patient and information flows individuals receive the very best support as near to their homes as possible - sometimes even within it (for example, tele-counselling). As the reliance on hospital beds lessens, many general hospitals start closing from the mid 1990s on. There is surprisingly little public hostility. The remaining hospitals become more efficient by capitalizing on the fashion for Business Process Re-engineering. Major out-patient centres develop where investigation and diagnosis is possible for most people on the same day.

However, the interaction of these technological advances with consumer expectation is not entirely easy. The interaction between the public's interest in the high-tech as well as the high-nature result's in significant ethical considerations. Nonetheless, public increasingly appreciates what can and can't be done at the same time.

One result is a society in which euthanasia is acceptable by 2008, with the associated huge downward impact on the cost of health care. This shift is fuelled by an increasingly assertive grey rights movement. Individuals are resentful of the increasing costs they have to bear for their own personal social care, such as nursing home placements and support at home. Many older people also demand appropriate care - such as the longevity gene therapy in 2007 - and the right to say "No more".

Some are worried that this pro-ability movement may negatively influence the social position of younger disabled people, particularly those with an intellectual impairment. Will informal care, in particular, lessen as a consequence of stigma?

This future closes with the NHS internal market in a strong

position. Purchasers, particularly GPs who are increasingly seen as treatment brokers, ensure resources are properly allocated on the basis of current knowledge. The mixed economy of provision has enabled innovation and efficiency.

Well being as you like it: State sponsored feel good services

In this scenario there is the emergence of greater social cohesion. We see the maintenance of a publicly run health service by new regional boards. Health care becomes more responsive to personal differences and preferences. Holistic local services, including new NHS professionals such as chiropractors and aromatherapists, become available from true health centres.

During the mid 1990s health rises up the political agenda, following on from the of finding of the governmental expert group on Disadvantage and Health. Indeed, all political parties make health the key to their election campaigns. Within the context of increased convergence with the rest of Europe, regionalization becomes the preferred way of tackling the "democratic deficit" within the NHS in 1997.

Regional Health and Welfare Boards are established as the forerunner of a wider regional government. Political activists are directly elected to these bodies that integrate the purchasing of health care, social services, housing and education. Whilst these bodies may have providing arms, most accept the value of a separation between strategic and operational responsibilities.

They are responsible for spending a centrally determined budget to certain minimum standards, such as waiting times. Merging all welfare services, particularly health and social services, could easily undermine the "free at the point of use" nature of the NHS and replace it with means tested, locally derived co-payments. However, social care - following the German lead of the early 1990s - becomes funded out of taxation (particularly inheritance tax).

The boards become composed of health activists, rather than people who want to represent a particular political position. Health in its widest sense becomes the context of debate and decision making. There is a continued separation of strategic and operational roles of the regional boards. The independent sector becomes an increasingly important supplier of services.

Also at the institutional level, EU legislation begins to bite. Health in the workplace becomes an increasingly important aspect of EU regulation. This is associated with growing international interest in health. The World Health Organization finally seems to be achieving its aims. Following on from UK initiative, The Health of Union is launched, with stretching health targets, in 1998 in Brussels.

By the turn of the millennium governmental barriers have subsided so that money follows patients within the European health market. This leads to niche marketing by providers in different countries. UK Trusts increasingly seeks to emphazise their specialist reputation.

There is also convergence in the ways health care systems are funded. To enable worker mobility, earmarked taxes become the main funding mechanism for welfare. Within the NHS there are limited co-payments for consultations and accommodation.

However, the new regional structures which are in place by the beginning of the next century are unable to control the expenditure on health to the degree required, despite the increased resources that become available. This leads to a growing public debate about the nature and extent of rationing required.

The result is a much more lively exchange of views, orchestrated at the regional level, about what sort of health needs should legitimately be met by the publicly funded health service. Overall many see health as a right and that rationing care on the basis of individual merit unappealing. The dilemmas around the priority of different sorts of needs - such as children services versus care for older people, and acute versus chronic needs - are never fully sorted. In a sense the regional boards merely muddle through with different solutions in each region.

In a context of increasing social fragmentation this debate would probably lead to heightened hostility towards minority concerns (such as ethnic and some women's issues) and self-inflicted harm (such as drug, alcohol and tobacco abuse). But two things check this. Firstly, despite the rhetoric of the 1980s and early 1990s health care needs are seen as finite in the context of the push to improve health and the increasing practice of living wills and euthanasia.

Secondly, the movement towards full employment is important. Tackling unemployment is seen as the key public health measure by regional, national and European government. High investment in vocationally relevant education during the mid 1990s boosts British competitiveness, breaks the dependency culture and starts to create job opportunities. Further, the long predicted leisure society starts to unfold - our Protestant ethic is tamed and the finite paid work available starts to be shared more evenly as the post-industrial society emerges by 2010.

The legalization of some hard and soft drugs in 1998 and the rise in militant Islam amongst the poor black people emasculates the criminal drug element and the streets of most inner cities become safer again. A corollary is the reduction in drug related ill health, such as HIV and gun shot wounds, and the huge tax revenues from the regulated drugs market. Overall social inequalities lessen in tandem with the emphasis on the responsible citizen. The growth of citizen politics is a sign of the revitalized sense of community. There is a growing tolerance to personal differences and to minority values.

The result of this is a renewed confidence in an accountable public sector and a willingness to engage in debates about how such a health service with financial constraints should meet the needs of all citizens.

There is some opposition to the broadening of what it means to be healthy and how health services can help. In particular the established health professions believe that many of the changes taking place are threatening to orthodox practice (though some see them as a way of checking the technological "medicalization of sadness"). This results in a variety of initiatives including King Charles deciding that alongside the long established Royal Colleges, there should be a variety of new Royal bodies, such as the Royal Colleges of Homoeopathy and Acupuncture, that are chartered in 2001. This creates even more interest from the general public.

Whilst there are some differences between regions, most Health and Welfare Boards want the traditional hospital to focus on emergency and critical care. Managers of hospitals are encouraged by the regional boards to see themselves as enablers rather than controllers of even the hospital based old-school clinicians.

Within hospital settings public concerns force greater use of recyclable products and reduced waste. Single and twin rooms become the standard design feature in new and refurbished buildings.

Outside of these institutions there is greater tolerance of heterogeneity in service support. In the more locally based community health centres there are a variety of facilities including leisure complexes, health food and disability appliance shops and access to voluntary bodies and information agencies as well as primary medical care.

Primary care, while still largely independent of the managed NHS, moves further into the driving seat and manages the allocation of resources to specialist hospital care within guidelines set by the regional boards and constituent sub-committee Area Panels. Individuals will travel for services that have been proved to improve well-being. The independent sector is often the preferred option.

There is a funded growth in talking therapies to help individuals cope better with the stresses of life. There is a fall in the incidence of the common cold and other viral and post-viral infections due to individuals tackling the widely held view of the link between healthy living, including diet and positive attitude, and health.

The growth in the "feel good" professions, including reflexology and aromatherapy, is legitimized by the deliberate broadening of the traditional view of effectiveness by the regional boards. By 2001 the main driving force is not just the amelioration of disease but also the promotion of well-being as defined by the lay public.

Self treatment and use of over the counter pharmaceuticals increases. Consumers become more discerning. A whole variety of different means to support and inform consumers develop during the late 1990s. Components of this network of support include: patients' associations, self-help groups, private health advisers, GP resource brokers, soft-ware to help individuals analyse their computerized hand held medical records and information available on cable in everyone's homes. This enables a confronting and reduction in professional domination. Even the most traditional members of the older professions practise a form of partnership with their clients.

The slight increase in the birth rate (due to new legislation in 2000 introducing 5 year maternity leave breaks to help share out the limited availability of paid work) and the acceptance of voluntary euthanasia (due to the focus on well-being and feeling good) eliminates any anxiety about the greying of the population.

The overall outcome is a publicly funded and largely publicly run health service. Regional accountability is associated with a growth in the vibrancy of citizen power and sense of community. This results in provision of a wide variety of health resources and the continued funding and effectiveness of the new system.

SCENARIOS FOR ORGANIZATIONS IN THE 21ST CENTURY: FOUR VIEWS OF ORGANIZATIONAL DESTINY

These scenarios are reproduced from "Twenty-First Century Organization: Four Plausible Prospects" (GBN, 1996b).

Figure 0.1	
Communities and Families	
Lock-in	Takes place late, accentuating networking
Human values	Take precedence in managerial concern, but only through a free-market structure of benefits and a liberated, non-paternalistic attitude
Global economy	Tolerant and experimental, permitting investment in a variety of forms; but set up so that local money is reinvested more in local venues
Geopolitical stability	The "have-nots" are seen as a prime responsibility of all organizational life. "Colombianization" is self-corrected by the systems
Corporate structure	Extremely; blurred line between corporations and all other forms (nonprofits, even families)
Knowledge work	Part and parcel of everyday life

Communities and Families

It is the year 2010...

A form of organization has emerged, more or less on its own in the last 10 years, that is geared to boosting creativity and local relationships. With the full flowering of networks, people have finally felt free to develop local roots, as they haven't since the beginning of the industrial revolution. Flexible manufacturing has meant that factories can stay close to their customers; "one-on-one" marketing has increased the value of local customs and attitudes, at the same time that people have become more comfortable exchanging thoughts and images with others around the globe. They have found they can stay in one place and work anywhere in the world. Most companies have shrunk to small

373

"core competency" firms, outsourcing most of their work. We have the freedom and fluidity of a world of "small companies and big networks". There is no stability in any job or task. And yet we do not feel adrift.

Communities and families have filled the gap. Everyone grows up in a constantly shifting web of nonprofit organizations, school and church groups, guilds, family based pension plans, trusts, affinity groups, and barter networks. Some are local; some are worldwide. Some take their flavour from a world-wide profession; others are unique to their locale, be it Moradabad, Little Rock, Cape Town, or Limón. All are linked by a vibrant electronic network. Very few large corporations remain. There are brand names still, which have existed for a century or more, maintained by family firms that have shrunk back to the size of the family, all else is outsourced, often to other families and sometimes to free-floating temporary organizations.

It began when governments, in full neo-conservative force, eliminated the tax deductibility of employment benefits. A few pioneer corporations, beginning with Microsoft, began to pay people the value of their benefits in the form of increased salary, letting employees make their own choices. To provide the necessary services, other networks emerged - for health insurance, pensions, and training/education. Government liberalized the rules which formerly restricted these options, and the rules governing liability and risk. Now people have discovered that they can combine many of their investments and life services with their support networks of friends, family members, and communities. Voucher systems have emerged, designed by a team at MIT, that allow people without money or connections to gain admittance to the networks. Basic security has been decoupled from its industrial sources: the dole and the job. It has returned to its preindustrial source: the human relationship, but now with an unprecedented level of network-based support.

Could this world plausibly take place? It might require a reneging on mobility, and a reframing of family ties that seems inconceivable in the 1990s. It might also require an end to the time-honoured industrial principle of economy of scale.

Figure O.2

Corporate Virtual Countries

Lock-in	Takes place early, accentuating "virtual countries"
Human values	Take precedence in managerial concern, through "cradle-to-grave" approach
Global economy	Investment is tied up in keiretsu which seek stable, long-term mutual relationships amidst the turbulence of the marketplace
Geopolitical stability	The "have-nots" are either welcomed into organizational roles, treated as corporate charity, or ignored. Great socio-economic pressure exists as investment circles resist any suggestion that they have social welfare responsibility. Government probably does not intervene
Corporate structure	Vast, interlocked hierarchy-democracies, in which management acts on a day-to-day basis with autonomy, but is elected by the "membership" of the firm
Knowledge work	A key specialization and path to elite success

Corporate Virtual Countries

This future essentially repeats the MIT Virtual Countries seed scenario; but with more detail. It plays out in a severe geopolitical environment. The scenario team described the prevailing organizational ideology in this world as "friendly fascism", meaning that benevolent corporations would take on all the functions of society, including the provision of a geopolitical safety net. These organizations would be oligopolistic, dedicated to controlling competition, "much more mission-driven than profit-driven".

The scenario team saw this future ending on a pessimistic note. They did not seem to believe it was plausible that oligopolistic virtual countries could keep hegemony in a turbulent network-laden world. With the first set of serious economic shocks, the keiretsu would get into difficulties. Authoritarian managements would take over. Benevolence would shrink, "People must go out into the cold; there's no more safety net for those outside the firm". The virtual country becomes, essentially, a corporate version of Ted Newland's "gilded cage". Given this possibility, how can we prepare now for a world of "corporate virtual countries", to prevent the dark side of this scenario from overwhelming all other possibilities?

Figure O.3	
	Tribes
Lock-in	Takes place early, accentuating Virtual Counties
Human values	Take precedence in managerial concern, in ideological froms that span the boundaries of corporation, churches, and nonprofits
Global economy	Dominated by large-scale investment
Geopolitical stability	Most likely, chaos would be held back by last-ditch involvement of large churches, corporation, and governments, which increasingly become detached from the land (but not from their members' identities)
Corporate structure	Like the Mormon Church
Knowledge work	Relegated to serving the "tribal" needs

Tribes

The year is 2010...

Corporations are no longer considered corporations. They are vast meeting grounds, reservoirs within which people spend their lives, buttressed by the fine-grained interactions of dedicated networks. The closest parallels from the 1990S were the growing churches. These churches came to provide everything for their members: employment, belonging, education, and a sense of ideological or spiritual identity. As the churches grew in popularity worldwide, secular-oriented people responded with churches of their own. There is no more Microsoft; long ago, it melded with the Archdiocese of Seattle. There is no more Daewoo; long ago, it melded with the international fraternity-sorority of people of Korean descent. The world is democratic; people participate in their churches, and the churches participate in global political life together.

Back in 1995...

At first glance, this scenario may not seem plausible. It was not fleshed out very far in the WorldView meeting. However, it seems to have a lot to offer people thinking about the organization of the future. It is disturbing and perhaps dangerous, with its subsuming of individual identity to the needs of the hive; yet, it also fulfils a human need which no other scenario in this report begins to address. It fulfils the burning desire to belong to something, to be secure, and to be taken care of by the larger system.

Figure 0.4

Roll Your Own: Networks in a Tough World

Lock-in	Takes place late, accentuating networking
Human values	"Hey - If they matter to you, they matter to you. No skin off my nose. I'll be kept in line by my customers, suppliers, and the law of the network"
Global economy	Tolerant and experimental, permitting investment in a variety of forms, with little restriction on the structure of the market
Geopolitical stability	"Colombianization" is held back by self-correcting economic growth
Corporate structure	Extremely diverse; blurred line between corporations and all other institutional forms (nonprofits, even families)
Knowledge work	The most essential skill is the knowledge of how to learn. Second most essential, how to manage learners

Roll Your Own: Networks in a Tough World

It is the year 2010, and this future is only beginning to emerge.
It has taken 15 years, because of the reactions to the immense wave of downsizing and restructuring of the mid-to-late 1990s. The networks have been in place technologically all along, but the financial structure was weak. Growth expectations were hampered in a global recession. Regionalism dominated political activity. America retracted its power. The European Community

shrank back into itself; so did Japan. Conventional companies were now on a clear downward slope, in which profits kept rising but the structure of the company fell apart. "My stock split so many times that I had to hire a storage locker for the certificates".

This atmosphere has now paved the way for a network-dominated economy growing rapidly now, after a soft, gentle decade. Managers pushed out from big companies, plus young university graduates, have formed an interconnected web of commercial activity, based on joint ventures, alliances, "clusters", and short-term organizations. There are so many corporate forms that pundits speak of having a "roll-your-own" economy. The financial system does not quite keep up with them; everyone is perpetually in debt, at least on a commercial basis. Since there are no assets available on which to borrow money, people's collateral is their relationships: their abilities to guarantee returns based on who they know.

For 10 years, people have been frustrated about the state of the world. The number of "have-nots" continues to rise, and the "haves" are powerless to do anything about it. But this situation is about to change. Finally, enough wealth has been created on a broad scale to make up for the shrinking of the middle class in the 1990s. We look ahead to an optimistic future, in which everyone with a terminal or telephone can count on making a living - as long as they know how to communicate. However, to be plausible, this scenario depends upon a long gestation. What forces could lead a dangerously unstable situation to "flip" into a benign future?

SHELL SCENARIOS IN 1996

(Reproduced from a speech "Charting a course - preparing for the oil and gas business of the 21st century" by Maarten van den Bergh, Group Managing Director Royal Dutch/Shell to the VERAF Conference at the State University of Groningen in November 1996)

In a world of rapid and profound change business people still face the challenge of making decisions that will affect their enterprises for decades. Shell companies have used scenarios to help them think about the future since the early 1970s.

The latest Shell scenarios assume a world which, over the next quarter of a century, will continue to be shaped by liberalization, globalization, and technological innovation. They explore the energy and economic implications of two alternative futures - one emphasizing individualism, flexibility and competition; the other cohesion, relationships and long-term vision.

Longer term scenarios focus on the energy market through to 2060. These explore two possible futures - one in which there is continuing abundant energy supplies at competitive prices, and another in which much greater energy efficiency is achieved.

Key questions to be considered in charting a course for the Royal Dutch/Shell Group into the 21st century include:

- what sort of businesses should we be in,

- what sort of business relationships will they require,

- what sort of organization will we need, and

- what sort of societal pressures will we face?

How the relationship between business and society evolves will have a profound impact on prosperity and progress in the 21st century. However, there is the potential to achieve the wider economic development which will provide better lives for an increasing proportion of the world's people, whilst still safeguarding our environment.

Shell companies take many strengths into the next century - financial, reserves, technological leadership, business portfolios and, particularly, their people.

I have the responsibility of helping to chart the course of a great enterprise - on which many thousands of people depend - into the 21st century. Our business is inherently long-term and the decisions we take today will affect it for decades. In a world of rapid and profound change that is a challenging prospect.

To put this into perspective let me remind you of how the world appeared as I left Groningen University at the end of the 1960s - and how it actually turned out.

The industrialized world was then enjoying a continuing economic boom. Demand for oil and gas was increasing by 8% a year. All this ended with the "oil shocks" of the 1970s. Since then economic growth has been more problematic. OECD oil consumption fell by nearly a fifth in the five years after 1979 - and has never fully recovered.

In 1968, as Russian tanks crushed the "Prague spring" and China endured the Cultural Revolution, the world seemed irreconcilably split into two opposing political and economic camps. Few expected communism to fail so decisively.

The divide between the industrialized rich and the "third world" poor seemed equally stark. This division is now less clear-cut - although many people still live in desperate poverty. In 1968 Gunnar Myrdal's book *Asian Drama* focused on the barriers to Asian development. We now talk of the coming "Asian century".

In 1972, the influential book *Limits to Growth* foresaw the early exhaustion of essential minerals and fuels. Estimated reserves of these have grown - and attention has switched to other perceived environmental threats.

There is no reason to suppose that our current assumptions about the world will be any more durable.

Business people cannot, however, escape having to make decisions about the future. Shell companies invest $10 billion a year - often in very long-term projects.

The giant Troll gas field off Norway was brought into

production this June at a cost of $5 billion - 17 years after Norske Shell discovered it, 10 years after development began, and with a planned life of 50 years.

The Nigerian liquefied natural gas project has taken almost three decades to bring to fruition. The plant will cost some $3.8 billion - probably the largest private investment in Africa. It is expected to operate for 30 years and shareholders are unlikely to receive dividends before 2007.

In such a changeable world how can we hope to make decisions that stand the test of time?

We started using scenarios to help think about the future in the early 1970s. Those first scenarios explored the possibility that OPEC producers would exert their power to raise oil prices - so Shell companies were able to react more quickly when this actually happened.

Scenarios offer questions not answers. They don't seek to describe the future, which is impossible - but to illuminate the major driving forces which may shape it. By challenging our assumptions they awaken us to future possibilities, threats and opportunities - and help us recognize significant changes as they occur.

We believe our scenario process helps us to learn and adapt more quickly than our competitors.

The latest in our regular series of long-range planning scenarios - looking forward to 2020 - assumes the world will continue to be shaped by:

- liberalization,

- globalization, and

- technological innovation.

Countries and companies must respond to the demands of an open economy by adopting the best methods and latest technologies. Those who do not are punished by global financial markets and well-informed customers.

But what sort of societies and business structures will succeed best in such a world? Our scenarios explore two different models.

- One emphasizes speed, flexibility and innovation - the world of individualism, libertarianism and competition exemplified by the United States. We call this Just do it!

- The other emphazises cohesion, relationships and shared vision. This is a world in which there is still an important role for government - as in East Asia and the German Soziale Marktwirtschaft - but which has adapted to globalization. We call this Da Wo (from a Chinese proverb about the individual's place in the community).

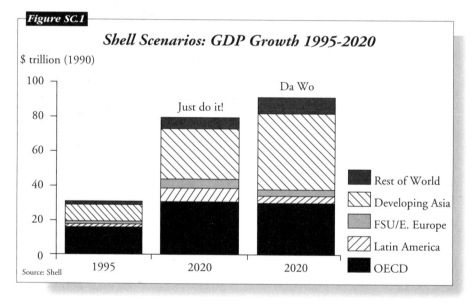

Figure SC.1

Shell Scenarios: GDP Growth 1995-2020

$ trillion (1990)

Da Wo

Just do it!

Rest of World
Developing Asia
FSU/E. Europe
Latin America
OECD

Source: Shell   1995   2020   2020

The first is an intensely competitive, innovative and individualistic world. Companies must be agile and flexible to exploit fleeting opportunities. Many people find the relentless change and uncertainty uncomfortable.

The second is a world which recognizes that - while it is essential to respond to the opportunities and demands of global markets - this is best done by retaining a sense of community and

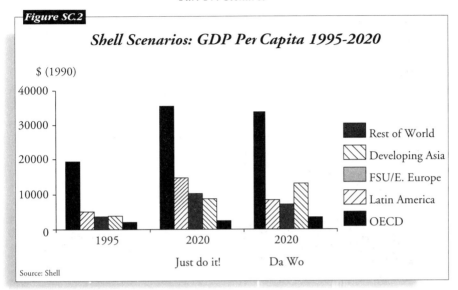

Figure SC.2

Shell Scenarios: GDP Per Capita 1995-2020

Source: Shell

long-term vision. Employers recognize the advantages of stable, experienced and secure workforces. Governments are expected to maintain social infrastructure.

There is no time to share with you the detailed analysis behind these scenarios. But let me touch briefly on economic and energy aspects.

Both scenarios suggest strong economic growth over the next quarter of a century. Growth is faster in Da Wo because of the performance of East Asia which, on a purchasing power parity basis, could account for nearly half world output by 2020. Western Europe also does better under this scenario.

Despite population growth, per capita incomes should rise. By 2020 people in Asian developing countries - over 40% of the world's population - could have average incomes more than two-thirds the level of those in industrialized countries today.

In Da Wo, oil demand grows by 2% a year. World consumption would rise by two-thirds by 2020. However, growth would be much slower in Just do it! Which assumes that environmental concerns and technological advance will drive rapid improvements in energy efficiency. Oil consumption in industrialized countries would decline from early next century.

Because of its efficiency and cleanliness, gas consumption

would continue growing in both scenarios. In Da Wo it would double by 2020.

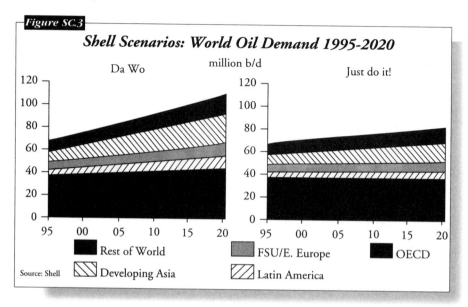

Figure SC.3

Shell Scenarios: World Oil Demand 1995-2020

Da Wo   million b/d   Just do it!

Rest of World   FSU/E. Europe   OECD

Source: Shell   Developing Asia   Latin America

Where would these additional supplies of oil and gas come from?

We have long anticipated the decline of non-OPEC oil production - because we underestimate the international oil and gas industry's continuing ability to reduce costs, increase recovery, and access more difficult reserves. Such production levels may be maintained for some time. Sluggish demand would mean continuing excess capacity, and low prices as producers compete for market share. There would be considerable geo-political strains.

The major challenge for the gas industry is not the availability of the resource but our ability to deliver it to market over increasing distances. This depends on continuing cost reduction, as well as overcoming the political complexities of cross border pipelines.

Increasingly flexible, short-term international gas markets may make it more difficult to fund major long-term infrastructure.

Let me turn to some recent longer term scenarios which explore energy demand and supply through to 2060. These are, naturally, much simpler and less detailed. They assume that population growth will slow, reaching 10 billion by 2060. Economic growth would continue at 3% a year, raising average GDP per capita to current British levels by 2060.

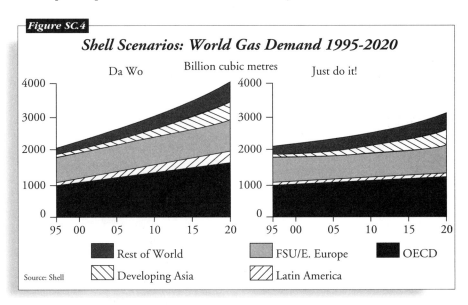

Figure SC.4

Shell Scenarios: World Gas Demand 1995-2020

Da Wo · Billion cubic metres · Just do it!

Rest of World — FSU/E. Europe — OECD — Developing Asia — Latin America

Source: Shell

The two scenarios are called Sustained Growth and Dematerialization.

Sustained growth suggests that productivity improvements would deliver continuing abundant energy supplies at competitive prices. Demand for fossil fuels would increase steadily until 2020 - when renewable sources would begin to gain a growing share of the market. Average annual energy consumption would rise to 25 barrels of oil equivalent per person - Japanese levels today - by 2060.

There are good reasons for thinking that renewable energy sources will become competitive over the next quarter of a century. The real cost of electricity from wind turbines, for example, has fallen by 10% a year over the past 15 years.

However, it is important to understand that this will be achieved by commercial optimization in competitive markets - the normal pattern of technology development. Limited "pump priming" may be useful to stimulate development but should not distort market processes. We lack the prescience to "pick winners".

The Dematerialization scenario assumes that we will achieve much greater energy efficiency. Average annual per capita energy consumption would only rise to 15 barrels of oil equivalent - Italian levels of 25 years ago - by 2060. Continuing advances in information, materials and biotechnologies would allow energy intensity to fall by 2% a year, double the historical rate.

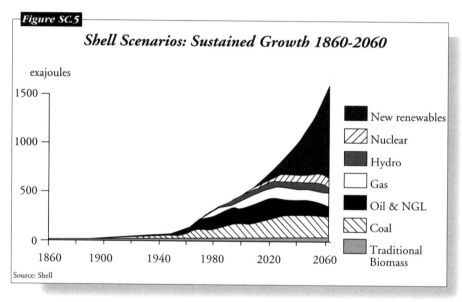

Figure SC.5

Shell Scenarios: Sustained Growth 1860-2060

exajoules

Legend:
- New renewables
- Nuclear
- Hydro
- Gas
- Oil & NGL
- Coal
- Traditional Biomass

Source: Shell

Governments and automobile manufacturers are, for instance, now focusing on improving vehicle fuel efficiency. Cars capable of 3 litres/100 km may soon be available as a result of converging technological advances in such areas as lightweight materials, hybrid combustion/electric engines, and advanced electronic controls.

This is just one of many areas where advancing technology offers striking increases in energy efficiency. Even the humble window is being improved.

The potential of the information revolution to change lifestyles - reducing, for instance, the need to travel - is widely discussed. And we should not forget the greater efficiency that comes from a competitive energy market.

I referred at the beginning to the pessimistic forecast in Limits to Growth that oil reserves would soon be exhausted. This was based on estimated reserves of 550 billion barrels. We have consumed more than this since 1970 but proved reserves have risen to 1,000 billion barrels.

Estimates of remaining recoverable conventional oil resources are considerably higher - 1,800 billion barrels according to the US Geological Survey, over half in the Middle East. Continuing improvements in recovery techniques may increase this. Nevertheless, conventional oil supplies are likely to plateau during the first half of next century.

Substitutes for conventional oil include natural gas liquids, synthetic crudes from heavy oils and tars, and liquids synthesized from gas. The Shell Middle Distillate Synthesis plant in Sarawak produces the ultimate "city diesel" from gas - sulphur free, clean-burning, no particulates. Fuel synthesized from biomass should become increasingly competitive.

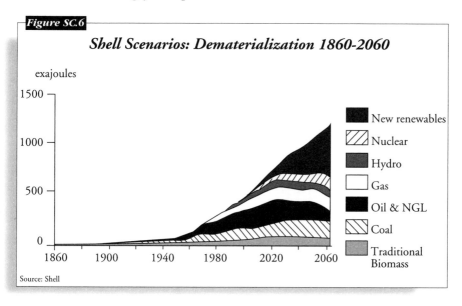

Figure SC.6

Shell Scenarios: Dematerialization 1860-2060

Source: Shell

Fuel prices should be restrained by increasing competition.

One of the most important factors driving efforts to improve energy efficiency is, of course, concern for the impact on global climate of emissions of man-made carbon dioxide - primarily from burning fossil fuels. These act within much larger and very complex natural systems and the scientific evidence is far from clear - but it does seem increasingly possible that they are affecting our climate. The potential consequences - and the extent of our uncertainty requires us to consider precautionary measures.

But these must be based on a proper understanding of the problem. The Intergovernmental Panel on Climate Change "business as usual" scenario (IS92a) presumes that emissions from fossil fuels will continue rising throughout the 21st century. This is very unlikely because of the limitations of economic resources and developments in energy markets. Emissions should decline much earlier. Even under our Sustained Growth scenario, they would peak before mid-century and fall below 1980 levels by 2100.

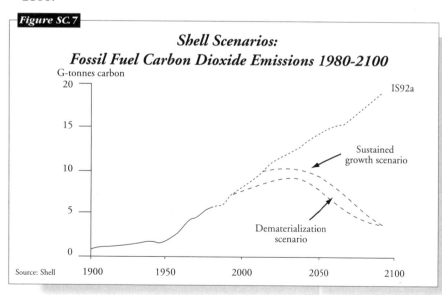

Figure SC. 7

Shell Scenarios:
Fossil Fuel Carbon Dioxide Emissions 1980-2100

Source: Shell

In developing measures to deal with this most complex of problems we must take great care not to inhibit unnecessarily the economic development on which people depend for better living standards - and which is essential for progress towards a sustainable world.

References

Albert, Kenneth J (ed), *"The Strategic Management Handbook"*, McGraw-Hill, 1983

Ansoff, Igor, *"Corporate Strategy"*, New York: McGraw-Hill, 1965

Amara, R, and A J Lipinski, *"Business Planning for an Uncertain Future: Scenarios and Strategies"*, Pergamon, 1983

Barker, Derek, and David J H Smith, *"Technology Foresight Using Road Maps"*, Long Range Planning, **28,** 2, 1995

Boroush, Mark A, and Charles W Thomas, *"Alternative Scenarios for the Defense Industry After 1995"*, Planning Review, May/June 1992

Business Week, *"Strategic Planning"*, 2 September 1996

Buzzell, Robert D, and Bradley T Gale, *"The PIMS Principles"*, Free Press, 1987

Caminer, David (ed), *"User-driven innovation"*, McGraw Hill, 1996

Campbell-Kelly, Martin, *"ICL, a business and technical history"*, OUP, 1989: ISBN 0-19-853918-5

Canarelli, P, *"Scenario Building using the Method of Fuzzy Scenarios - China by the year 2010"*, a study carried out with the Forward Studies Unit by Complex Systems of Paris, October, 1996a

Canarelli, P, *"Fuzzy Scenarios"*, IPTS Report *"Scenario Building"*, European Commission, EUR-17298-EN, 1996b

Carmichael, Hamish, *"An ICL Anthology"*, Laidlaw Hicks, 1996

Chatham House Forum, *"Unsettled Times"*, published by The Royal Institute of International Affairs, 10 St James Square, London, SW1Y 4LE

Cohen, Eliot A, and John Gooch, *"Military Misfortunes: The Anatomy of Failure in War"*, The Free Press, 1990: ISBN 0-02-906060-5

Currie, David, EIU Research report, *"The Pros and Cons of EMU"*, 1997

Davis-Floyd, Robbie, *"Storying Corporate Futures: The Shell Scenarios"*, International Journal of Futures Studies, Volume 1, 1995-1997

DTI/Office of Science and Technology, *"Taking foresight to the Millennium"*, URN 96/1123, 1996

Dyson, R G (ed), Strategic Planning: *"Models and Techniques"*, Wiley, 1990

Elkington, John and Alex Trisoglio, *"Developing realistic scenarios for the Environment: lessons from Brent Spar"*, Long Range Planning, **29,** June 1996

European Commission, *"The Future of North - South Relations, - Towards Sustainable Economic and Social Development"*, Luxembourg, 1997

Farrell, Christopher, *"The Triple Revolution"*, Business Week, 12 December 1994

Faulkner, David, *"International Strategic Alliances"*, McGraw Hill, 1996

Forrester, Jay, *"Industrial Dynamics"*, MIT Press 1961 and republished by the Productivity Press of Portland, Oregon

Galt, Miriam et al, *"IDON Scenario Thinking: How to navigate the Uncertainties of Unknown Futures"* Idon Ltd, Edradour House, Pitlochry, PH16 5JW, Scotland: ISBN 0-9530421-03, 1997

Georgantzas, Nicholas C, and William Acar, *"Scenario-Driven Planning"*, Quorum, 1995: ISBN 0-89930-825-2

Georghiou, Luke, *"The UK Technology Foresight Programme"*, Futures, **28,** May 1996

Gibson, Rowan (ed), *"Rethinking the Future"*, Nicholas Brearley, 1997: ISBN 1-85788-103-6

Godet, Michel, *"Scenarios and Strategic Management"*, Butterworths, 1987

Godet, Michel, *"From Anticipation to Action"*, 2nd edition, Paris, UNESCO, 1993

Godet, M and F Roubelat, *"Creating the Future: the use and misuse of scenarios"*, Long Range Planning, **29,** February 1996

Goffee, Rob et al, *"Case Study - International Computers Ltd"*, London Business School, 1991

References

Goold, Michael, Andrew Campbell and Marcus Alexander, *"Corporate-level Strategy"*, John Wiley, 1994

Goold, Michael, and Andrew Campbell, *"Strategy and Styles"*, OUP, 1987

GBN, *"Scenario Thinking - Concept and Approaches"*, PO Box 8295, Emeryville, California 94662, USA, 1996a

GBN, *"Twenty-First Century Organizations: Four Plausible Prospects"*, PO Box 8295, Emeryville, California 94662, USA, 1996b

Hadridge, Philip, and John McIvor *"Determining the resources required to ensure successful scenario planning"*, in "Implementing and Applying Scenario Planning" IIR Conference, 29 Bressenden Place, London SW1E 5DR, 1996

Handel, Michael I (ed), *"Clausewitz and Modern Strategy"*, Frank Cass & Company, 1989: ISBN 0-7146-4053-0

Helmer, Olaf, *"Looking Forward"*, Gage, 1983

Herodotus, *"The Histories"*, Penguin, 1972

Huntingdon, Samuel P, *"The Clash of Civilzation and the Remaking of the World Order"*, Simon E Schuster, 1989: ISBN 0-684-81164-2

Huss, W R, and E J Honton, *"Scenario Planning, What Style should you use?"* in Long Range Planning, **20,** April 1987

Jacquemin, A, and D Wright, *"The European Challenge Post - 1992"*, Edward Elgar Publishing, 1993

Japanese National Institute for Science and Technology Policy, Int Conf Tech Forecasting, Tokyo 13, 1995

Jensen, Rolf, in *"Future Orientation"*, Copenhagen Institute for Future Studies, Pilestrade 59, DK-1112, Copenhagen K, Denmark, 1996

Kahn, Herman, and Anthony J Weiner, *"The Year 2000: a framework for speculation on the next thirty years"*, Macmillan Publishing, 1967

Kamellard, Adrian, *"Achieving support of long term planning by ensuring shared ownership of the strategic process"*, in *"Implementing and Applying Scenario Planning"*, IIR Conference, 29 Bressenden Place, London SW1E 5DR, 1996

Kay, John, *"Foundations of Corporate Success"*, OUP, 1993

Kleiner, Art, *"The Age of Heretics"*, Doubleday, 1996: ISBN 0-385-41576-1

Kleiner, Art, *"Why Pacific Gas and Electric Isn't Building Any More Nuclear Power Plants"*, Garbage, March/April, 1992

Kotler, Philip, Gary Armstrong, John Saunders and Veronica Wong *"Principles of Marketing"*, Prentice Hall, 1996: ISBN 0-13-165903-0

Lank, Elizabeth, *"Leveraging Invisible Assets; the Human Factor in Knowledge Management"*, Long Range Planning, **30**, 3, 1997

Linneman, R E, and H E Klein, *"The Use of multiple scenarios by US industrial companies: a comparison study, 1977-81"*, Long Range Planning, **16,** June 1983

Mandel, Thomas F, and Ian Wilson, *"How Companies Use Scenarios: Practices and Prescription"*, an SRI Business Intelligence Programme Report, R 822, Spring 1993

Mason, David, and Robert G Wilson, *"Scenario Based Planning: Decision Model for the Learning Organisation"*, Planning Review, **22**, March/April 1994

Mason, David, *"Future Mapping, a new approach to managing strategic uncertainties"*, Planning Review, May/June 1987

Mayo, Andrew, and Elizabeth Lank, *"The Power of Learning, a Guide to Gaining Competitive Advantage"*, IPD, 1994

Meadows, Donella H, Dennis L Meadows and Jorgen Randers, *"Beyond the Limits"*, 1992, an updated version of *"Limits to Growth"*, published by Chelsea Green Publishing Company

Millett, Steven, *"Batelle's Scenario Analysis of a European High Tech Market"*, in Planning Review, **20,** 2, 1992

Minkin, Barry Howard, *"Future In Sight"*, Macmillan, 1995

Mintzberg, Henry, *"Thats not turbulence, Chicken Little"*, Planning Review, **22,** June 1994a

Mintzberg, Henry, *"The Fall and Rise of Strategic Planning"*, Harvard Business Review, January/February 1994b

Moore, P G, and S D Hodges, *"Programming for Optimal Decisions"*, Penguin, 1970

Moyer, Kathy, *"Scenario Planning at British Airways - a Case Study"*, Long Range Planning, **29,** February 1996

Negroponte, Nicholas, *"Being Digital"*, Hodder & Stoughton, 1995

Neill, Ian, Stephanie Bell and Roger Mills, *"A Systems Approach to Value Based*

References

Management", to be published

Pape, W (ed), *"Shaping Facts in East Asia by the Year 2000 and Beyond"*, Institute of Asian Affairs, Hamburg, 1996

Peters, Glen, *"Beyond the Next Wave"*, Pitman Publishing, 1996: ISBN 0-273-62417-2

Petersen, John, *"The Road to 2015"*, Waite Group Press, 1994

Pine II, B Joseph, *"Peter Schwartz offers Two Scenarios for the Future"*, Planning Review, September/October 1995

Porter, Michael, *"Competitive Advantage"*, New York: Free Press, 1985

Prahalad, C K, and Gary Hamel, *"Competing for the Future"*, Harvard Business Press, 1994

Quinn, Lucia Luce, and David H Mason, *"How Digital Uses Scenarios to Rethink the Present"*, Planning Review, November/December 1994

Ralston, William K, *"Scenario Based Strategy Development"*, in *"Implementing and Applying Scenario Planning"*, IIR Inc, 708 Third Avenue, New York 10017-4103, USA, 1997

Randall, Doug, *"Consumer Strategies for the Internet: Four Scenarios"*, Long Range Planning, **30,** 2, April 1997.

Randell, Brian et al (ed), *"Software 2000"*, ICL

Ringland, Gill, *"Communicating Scenarios"* in Implementing and Applying Scenario Planning, IIR Conference, 29 Bressenden Place, London SW1E 5DR, 1996

Rosell, Steven et al, *"Governing in an Information Society"*, Montreal: *"Institute for Research on Public Policy"*, 1992

Rosell, Steven et al, *"Changing Maps"*, Carleton University Press, 1995: ISBN 0-88629-264-6

Schnaars, Steven P, *"Megamistakes"*, Macmillan Inc, 1989: ISBN 0-02-927952-6

Schoemaker, P J H, *"How to Link Strategic Vision to Core Capabilities"*, Sloan Management Review, **34,** 1, 1992

Schoemaker, P J H, and Cornelius van der Heijden, *"Integrating scenarios into strategic planning at Royal Dutch/Shell"* in Planning Review, **20,** 3, May/June 1992

Schwartz, Peter, *"The Art of the Long View"*, Doubleday, 1991: ISBN 0-385-26731-2

Schwartz, Peter, *"Composing a Plot for Your Scenario"*, Planning Review, May/June 1992

Slaughter, Richard A, *"Foresight Beyond Strategy"*, Long Range Planning, **29,** p.156-163, 1996

Stokke, Per R, Thomas A Boyce, William K Ralston and Ian H Wilson, *"Visioning (and Preparing for) the Future"*, Technological Forecasting and Social Change, **40,** 1991

Taylor, Bernard, *"The Return of Strategic Planning - Once More with Feeling"*, Long Range Planning, **30,** March 1997

Taylor, Jim et al, *"The 500-Year Delta"*, Harper Business, 1997: ISBN 0-88730-838-4

Thomas, Charles W, *"Scenarios Applied"*, in *"Implementing and Applying Scenario Planning"*, IIR Inc, 708 Third Avenue, New York 10017-4103, USA, 1997

van der Heijden, Kees, *"Scenarios, The Art of Strategic Conversation"*, Wiley, 1996: ISBN 0-471-96639-8

Vester, Frederic, *"The Biocybernetic Approach as a Basis for Planning Our Environment"*, Systems Practice, **4,** 1988, pp. 399-413

Wack, Pierre, *"Scenarios, uncharted waters ahead"* in Harvard Business Review, September/October 1985, and *"Scenarios, shooting the rapids"*, ibid, Nov/Dec 1995

Wilson, Ian H, *"The State of Strategic Planning: What went wrong? What goes right?"*, in Technological Forecasting and Social Change, 1990, pp. 103-111

Winslow, Charles D, and William L Bramer, *"FutureWork"*, Free Press, 1994: ISBN 0-02-935415-3

A Short History of ICL

Introduction

This note describes some of the events and milestones in ICL's history, and its current mode of operation, to provide a context for describing our experience of scenario planning. It emphasizes that ICL is typical of many companies, in that it has been formed through growing, absorbing and merging with a number of cultures. During that time it has redefined what business it is in, as the world has changed.

ICL's roots as a "computer" company go back to 1951, when the first routine office job - Bakery Valuations for Lyons - was run on a computer (see "User-driven Innovation", by Caminer et al). The LEO Computers Ltd company was formed in 1954, and the company was soon providing systems for payroll, parts and stock jobbing, in the UK and South Africa. It developed a time-sharing system in 1962 - for HM Customs & Excise - and in 1963 LEO Computers merged with the computer department of English Electric.

Another UK computer company had its roots in the punched card machines invented by Herman Hollerith in the 1880s. The British Tabulating Machine Company (BTM) was incorporated in 1907, and its history included the production of components for the cryptography operation undertaken at Bletchley Park, UK, during the Second World War. The Powers-Samas company was set up in 1925, and in an agreement with Remington Rand in 1936 "divided the world" with Powers taking the British Empire, Scandinavia and the Middle East. In 1950, the UK National Research & Development Council invited BTM and Powers-Samas to satisfy themselves that a market for electronic computers existed, in 1955 BTM started to deliver its HEC2 computer, in 1956 Powers-Samas delivered the PCC. In 1959, Powers-Samas merged with BTM to form ICT - International Computers & Tabulators Ltd.

ICT

The ICT strategy was (quoted here from "ICL, a business & technical history", Martin Campbell-Kelly):

1. To become a large scale vertically integrated data-processing equipment manufacturer

2. To supply products for the traditional punched card machine market

3. To become a peripheral manufacturer and OEM supplier.

By 1965, ICT had become focused on computers and was starting to introduce the 1900 series and to develop the "new range" - the 2900 series of mainframes. English Electric had a range of computers - the System4 range - based on IBM mainframe architecture. Both were in the DP (data processing) rather than process control end of the market. And both were candidates for take-over by other players in the electronics industry.

ICL

ICL was formed in 1968 as a government initiated merger of English Electric and ICT, as part of the then Labour government's "white heat of technology" theme; to create a strong British player in the growing computer business.

The company remained UK and commonwealth-centric for several years, and focused on bringing the "new range" to market. During this time the mainframe business matured, and a new industry started to grow - supplying minicomputers and small business systems. In 1976, ICL bought the Singer Business Systems company, which had a base of small business systems and intelligent terminals across the UK, continental Europe and North America, and a headquarters and manufacturing facility in Utica, New York.

Through 1979-81, the company ran into trouble. Ambitious product development programmes with high costs - partially arising from the inheritance of the incompatible product lines in the original merger - and declining sales led to a cash flow crisis. The British Government made extensive use of ICL equipment, and provided bank guarantees for two years. This gave breathing space to reduce the cost base, but survival depended on more than cutting costs. Three factors were crucial: a new management team, including Robb Wilmot and Peter Bonfield from Texas Instruments, and establishing a long term relationship with Fujitsu of Japan to develop the processors for our mainframe range. The third factor was perhaps just as important. It was to reset the strategies.

These were stated as:

- deliver complete solutions not components

- create and work with a network of alliances

- lead the introduction of Open Systems (i.e. the break down of vertical integration) in Europe

- concentrate on a few markets, e.g. Retail, Financial Services, Government

- organize the company into units meeting the needs of markets.

Since then it has become an often-quoted example of UK corporate renewal (e.g. Goffee, Perie and Truss, 1991).

The STC years

As the company recovered, grew and became profitable, it was bought by STC (Standard Telecommunications and Cables of the UK) in 1984. The rationale for the acquisition was the much touted "convergence" of telecoms and computing. However it proved difficult to find extensive synergies, due mainly to the very different cultures of the two industries. The cultures worked to different timescales, different customer profiles, different management skills - the emergence of shared semiconductor technology seemed to be comparatively irrelevant.

During the mid-1980s we were active in a number of European Community sponsored activities - such as Esprit - and in 1984 setting up a joint R&D centre with Siemens of Germany and Bull of France (ECRC), and working with Bull, Siemens, Olivetti and Nixdorf on a number of industry standards (Open Systems) initiatives. In fact a recent count suggested that to date ICL has been party to 43 joint ventures and 146 collaborations.

In 1986 we began a Total Quality Programme, this has now become part of life, and for instance our manufacturing company D2D won the European TQM (Total Quality Management) award in 1994.

In 1988 we bought CCI, an office systems supplier with a North American base. In 1989 we bought Datachecker of the US and combined it with our ICL Retail Business. These reflected our strategic view that the information industry was becoming global, with much of the initiative coming from the US.

Fujitsu as major shareholder

In 1989 STC sold a major stake in ICL to Fujitsu, with whom ICL had enjoyed a strategic technology partnership since 1981. This was followed by Northern Telecom's acquisition of STC. Fujitsu and Northern Telecom are the two shareholders in ICL. Fujitsu also saw the information industry as becoming global, and already had stakes in US based companies such as Amdahl. ICL and Fujitsu now have jointly owned companies in North America and Australia/Pacific, and have in 1996 decided to merge our PC and small computer (Volume Products) organizations.

ICL's relationship with Fujitsu over the years since the early 1980s has been discussed in several books on alliances - for instance David Faulkner "International Strategic Alliances" and C K Prahalad & Gary Hamel's "Competing for the Future".

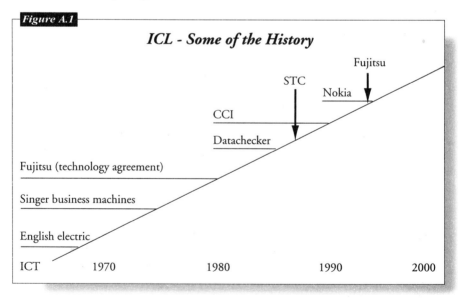

Figure A.1

ICL - Some of the History

In 1991 and 1992 we bought a number of software houses across Europe, as the search for skilled staff and the focus on solutions intensified. And in 1991 we merged with Nokia Telecom's systems business, which brought us factories and R&D facilities in Sweden and

Finland. Nokia in continental Europe was nearly twice the size of ICL's operations there - in terms of revenue, people, sites - and we merged the two by absorbing the ICL business into the Nokia structure which was flatter and less bureaucratic: see for instance Mayo and Lank, (1994)

Anecdotes from ICL's history are to be found in H Carmichael, "An ICL Anthology".

ICL now

As the history suggests, ICL is an amalgam of cultures - from different industries and geographies. We are headquartered in the UK but operate globally. We are also part of a group with Japanese, Canadian and United States links.

Fujitsu is our major shareholder. We actively work together on a number of programmes - for instance global software products, personal computers. In financial terms the relationship is arm's length and the companies trade on explicit terms, since the intention is to re-establish a public share listing of ICL in due course

And we have recently changed our Chief Executive Officer (CEO), with Peter Bonfield moving to run British Telecom and the Finance & Business Strategy Director Keith Todd taking over. Keith Todd originally joined ICL in 1985 as part of the STC team after our purchase by STC.

In 1996 the company was reorganized to focus on systems and services. The award winning manufacturing business, D2D, was divested to Celestica of Canada, and the PC and server platform (hardware) business merged with Fujitsu's hardware division.

Our core business is now as systems and services company, and we operate in the technology sector with Fujitsu. We are based in Europe. We provide computer & networking systems and services for our customers across Europe: and globally with partners.

ICL's philosophy is based on our traditional strength of "we listen to our customers and deliver what we promise", but in many ways the company is unrecognizable from that seen ten years ago. And our motto is "eyes on the future, feet on the ground". We expect that the next ten years will see at least as many changes as the last ten, as the information society evolves.

Index

Scenario Planning